The Emerging Role of Intelligence in the World of the Future

The Emerging Role of Intelligence in the World of the Future

Special Issue Editor

Robert J. Sternberg

MDPI • Basel • Beijing • Wuhan • Barcelona • Belgrade

MDPI

Special Issue Editor
Robert J. Sternberg
Cornell University
USA

Editorial Office
MDPI
St. Alban-Anlage 66
Basel, Switzerland

This is a reprint of articles from the Special Issue published online in the open access journal *Journal of Intelligence* (ISSN 2079-3200) in 2018 (available at: http://www.mdpi.com/journal/jintelligence/special_issues/Intelligence_IQs_Problems)

For citation purposes, cite each article independently as indicated on the article page online and as indicated below:

LastName, A.A.; LastName, B.B.; LastName, C.C. Article Title. *Journal Name* **Year**, *Article Number, Page Range.*

ISBN 978-3-03897-262-4 (Pbk)
ISBN 978-3-03897-263-1 (PDF)

Contents

About the Special Issue Editor

Robert J. Sternberg is Professor of Human Development in the College of Human Ecology at Cornell University and Honorary Professor of Psychology at Heidelberg University, Germany. Sternberg was briefly President and Professor of Psychology and Education at the University of Wyoming. Before that, he was Provost, Senior Vice President, Regents Professor of Psychology and Education, and George Kaiser Family Foundation Chair of Ethical Leadership at Oklahoma State University. Prior to going to Oklahoma State, Sternberg was Dean of Arts and Sciences and Professor of Psychology and Education at Tufts University, and before that, IBM Professor of Psychology and Education, Professor of Management, and Director of the Center for the Psychology of Abilities, Competencies, and Expertise at Yale. Sternberg is a Past President of the American Psychological Association, the Federation of Associations in Behavioral and Brain Sciences, the Eastern Psychological Association, and the International Association for Cognitive Education and Psychology. He also is past-Treasurer of the Association of American Colleges and Universities. Sternberg also has been president of four divisions of the American Psychological Association. Sternberg's BA is from Yale University summa cum laude, Phi Beta Kappa, his PhD is from Stanford University, and he holds 13 honorary doctorates from 11 countries. Sternberg has won more than two dozen awards for his work, including the James McKeen Cattell Award (1999) and the William James Fellow Award (2017) from APS. He has also won the Grawemeyer Award in Psychology. He is the author of over 1700 publications and, as a principal investigator, has received over $20 million in grant funding. Sternberg was cited in an *APA Monitor on Psychology* report as one of the top 100 psychologists of the 20th century (#60) and in a report in *Archives of Scientific Psychology by Diener* and colleagues as one of the top 200 psychologists of the modern era (#60). He was cited by Griggs and Christopher in *Teaching of Psychology* as one of the top-cited scholars in introductory-psychology textbooks (#5). He has been cited by ISI for being one of the most highly cited (top 1/2 of 1) among psychologists and psychiatrists. He has been editor of *Psychological Bulletin, The APA Review of Books: Contemporary Psychology, and Perspectives on Psychological Science*. Sternberg is a member of the National Academy of Education and the American Academy of Arts and Sciences. He is a Fellow of the American Association for the Advancement of Science. Sternberg has written extensively about human intelligence, and his theory of successful intelligence is covered in every introductory-psychology book in the US. He has won many awards specifically for his research on intelligence. He is married to Karin Sternberg, PhD, and has two grown-up children, Seth and Sara, as well as 7-year-old triplets, Samuel, Brittany, and Melody.

Preface to "The Emerging Role of Intelligence in the World of the Future"

During the 20th century, the world experienced an unprecedented rise in people's cognitive abilities. IQs increased 30 points (with the average IQ remaining 100 only because publishers reset the "average" on their tests). Yet, society's ability to confront serious problems in the world seems as challenged as ever. Problems such as air pollution, global climate change, increasing disparity of incomes, disputes that never seem to move toward resolution (such as between the Israelis and Palestinians), and increasing antibiotic resistance—all of these and many other problems seem to defy us, despite our elevated IQs. Why are there so many serious problems still confronting the world? Why is IQ insufficient for solving serious problems in which differences in people's interests are at stake? How can intelligence, broadly defined, help us to create a better world and solve the seemingly intractable problems the world confronts? The essays in this book address these questions and provide some directions for answers.

I decided to edit this symposium, originally published in the *Journal of Intelligence*, because I was concerned that intelligence researchers, in their understandable quest to study biological, cognitive, and behavioral underpinnings of general intelligence (often called "g") were focusing on issues that, while scientifically important, left out the sociocultural role that intelligence should play in helping to resolve issues of world importance. No matter how much we know about the connection of intelligence to the brain, for example, we still will not know why intelligent people cannot resolve issues as basic as global climate change, when massive fires, hurricanes, heating of oceans, and disappearance of polar ice caps are staring us in the face. This book will point to directions where intelligence, broadly defined, can help make the world a better place.

Robert J. Sternberg
Special Issue Editor

Journal of
Intelligence

MDPI

Editorial

Why Real-World Problems Go Unresolved and What We Can Do about It: Inferences from a Limited-Resource Model of Successful Intelligence [†]

Robert J. Sternberg

Department of Human Development, College of Human Ecology, Ithaca, NY 14853, USA;
robert.sternberg@cornell.edu

† Introductory Essay for the Special Issue "If Intelligence Is Truly Important to Real-World Adaptation, and IQs
Have Risen 30+ Points in the Past Century (Flynn Effect), then Why Are There So Many Unresolved and
Dramatic Problems in the World, and What Can Be Done About It?"

Received: 29 August 2018; Accepted: 12 September 2018; Published: 13 September 2018

Abstract: In this article I suggest why a symposium is desirable on the topic of why, despite worldwide increases in IQ since the beginning of the 20th century, there are so many unresolved and dramatic problems in the world. I briefly discuss what some of these problems are, and the paradox of people with higher IQs not only being unable to solve them, but in some cases people being unwilling to address them. I suggest that higher IQ is not always highly relevant to the problems, and in some cases, may displace other skills that better would apply to the solution of the problems. I present a limited-resource model as an adjunct to the augmented theory of successful intelligence. The model suggests that increasing societal emphases on analytical abilities have displaced development and utilization of other skills, especially creative, practical, and wisdom-based ones, that better could be applied to serious world problems. I also discuss the importance of cognitive inoculation against unscrupulous and sometimes malevolent attempts to change belief systems.

Keywords: components; creativity; inoculation; intelligence; limited-resource model; wisdom

---

1. Introduction

The essays in this special section of the *Journal of Intelligence* deal with why intelligence, defined narrowly, is not sufficient for creating a better world and may even lead to a worse world. They also address the more important question: What can we do about it? In this editorial, I present here some of my personal views on why IQ is not sufficient for creating a better world—these views, I believe, are consistent with but also extend beyond conclusions drawn directly from empirical research. Here is the conundrum: IQs rose 30+ points in the 20th century, but serious world problems remain and in some cases are getting worse. For example, air pollution around the world is so bad that it is cutting a year, on average, off people's lives [1]. Income inequality is bad and growing worse [2], leading to populist movements [3] and an increased likelihood of irresponsible governments that cater to whims rather than to reason. Attempts at global denuclearization of weapons largely have failed [4], leaving the world susceptible to the vagaries of deteriorating international relations, especially with regard to North Korea and Iran.

If people are so smart, why can they not solve or often even begin realistically to address the most pressing problems the world is facing? I propose in this article a model to explain why increasing IQs actually may decrease the probability of solving any of these problems. Although the Flynn effect may now be reversing in some locales [5], substantial increases in IQ from the very beginning of the twentieth century remain.

2. A Limited-Resource Model

According to the theory of successful intelligence, intelligence at its base comprises a series of information-processing components acting upon mental representations in a variety of environmental contexts [6]. These components are of three kinds: metacomponents, performance components, and knowledge-acquisition components. Metacomponents are used to plan, monitor, and evaluate reasoning, problem solving, and decision making. Performance components are used to execute these higher order cognitive tasks. Knowledge-acquisition components are used to learn how to do these tasks in the first place (see Note 6).

The three kinds of components, according to the original triarchic theory of intelligence and its later manifestation as the theory of successful intelligence, produce three basic kinds of mental functioning and a subsidiary one. Creative intelligence is involved when the components are applied to tasks and situations that are relatively (but not completely) novel. Analytical intelligence is involved when the components are applied to fairly abstract but nevertheless relatively familiar kinds of problems, such as the ones students encounter in school. And practical intelligence is involved when the components are applied to relatively concrete and familiar kinds of problems, such as the challenges of everyday life [7]. The key point here is that the same information-processing components are involved in creative, analytical, and practical thinking—what differs is how they are applied. A fourth kind of thinking, wise thinking, is involved when the components engage in creative, analytical, and practical thinking to help achieve a common good, over the long as well as the short term [8,9].

The theory as originally proposed did not consider resource constraints. That is, what cognitive limitations are there in the generation of components to accomplish the tasks necessary for one's life? Research would suggest that there are three major sets of constraints, or at least, cognitive ones. The first set comprises working-memory constraints [10,11]. One can do only as many tasks as one can hold in one's working memory. A second set of constraints is attentional [12,13]. To execute a task, one needs to attend to it. And to execute it well, one needs to ensure that one's attention is directed properly to the various elements of the task. A third set of constraints is speed-related [14,15]. The faster one mentally processes information, the more components one can execute in a given amount of time. Of course, speed says nothing about the accuracy with which the components will be executed, and accuracy matters at least as much as speed [16].

These constraints (and doubtless, others) are important because they limit an individual's ability to execute components in intelligent reasoning, decision making, and problem solving. That is, one's ability to solve problems and accomplish life tasks will depend on one's componential skills, on the one hand, and one's cognitive constraints (working memory, attention, mental speed) for applying them.

3. Effects of Societal Context

At different points in the development of a society and the sociocultural context in which it is embedded, rewards for different kinds of thinking and behaving will differ. For example, Renaissance Florence saw an explosion of creative intelligence because of the patron system and because of mutual reinforcement of artists for each other's work. After the Soviet Union's launch of Sputnik, creative work in space engineering exploded because of societal needs. What kind(s) of abilities are most being rewarded today? Let's look at where the rewards are?

I argued as early as 1985 that US society, and perhaps other societies as well, were tipping the reward system very heavily toward analytical uses of components (see Note 6). That trend has accelerated greatly as a result of several societal trends.

3.1. Rising IQs

As IQs rose in the 20th century, the memory and analytical skills contributing to them increased and society saw some gains from these enhanced skills. People became better able to understand and use technology, for example—cell phones, computers, even everyday appliances connected to the

Internet. Just as tall people are more likely to play basketball, or attractive people more likely to model, high-IQ people are more likely to find jobs that match their considerable intellectual skills. As IQs rose, people needed them more, just as when people have grown taller as a result of better nutrition, society took these heights into account in designing furniture, vehicles of conveyance, and the like. Those who did not participate in the growth may have found more and more resources simply physically out of reach. Short people today have trouble reaching many things, but those people may be average or even above average relative to heights just a century ago, in the same way that many of the lower IQ people of today would have been above average a century ago.

3.2. Standardized Testing

Standardized testing as done in the United States and in many other countries very heavily emphasizes memory and analytical skills, largely to the exclusion of creative, practical, and wisdom-based skills [17]. The items used assess accumulated knowledge and the ability to analyze that knowledge, but stop there [18]. Those are useful skills. But the tests do not measure students' abilities to come up with new ideas, to apply those new ideas in practical settings, or to ensure that their ideas help to achieve some kind of common good [19,20]. So students are admitted to private schools, gifted programs, and institutions of higher education largely on the basis of their memory and analytical skills, skills that are useful but inadequate in and of themselves for solving serious world problems.

Once a certain group starts to dominate in an institutional setting, self-fulfilling prophecies tend to take root. People expect more from the people identified as "winners," and they get more. The result is that those people expected to be successful become successful, and the preference for like people passes on from one generation to the next. The next generation, in evaluating people, looks for others more or less like themselves, leading to whatever traits were valuable before to matter even more (see Note 6).

3.3. Instruction in Schools

Because school curricula, at least today, are so heavily geared toward whatever it is that standardized tests measure, instruction in schools has become in its emphases, as it has been for a long time, much like the tests. Instruction emphasizes the same memory and analytical abilities that the tests test. The tests and the schools reinforce each other in an unending loop. Indeed, Alfred Binet created the IQ test to reflect skills needed for success in school, and schools teach to the kinds of skills that his test and others like it measure. This is not in itself a bad thing, of course, but it may crowd out other kinds of skills that also matter, such as creative, practical, and wisdom-based ones.

3.4. Social Media

Social media undoubtedly have served some useful functions in connecting people who otherwise would never have been connected. And they have provided a way for people to reach out with their ideas in the past who never could have had any audience. But social media bypass a crucial part of the creative process—refereeing. The result is that people often pretty much say whatever occurs to them. This is bad for analytical-skill development and utilization and even worse for creative-skill development and utilization. Creativity requires critique of whether a novel idea is good and may serve some positive function. Because negative and even untrue postings spread faster on social media than do positive and true postings [21], the reinforcement system encourages only a low level of the serious analytical scrutiny that is necessary for the entire creative process. And because wisdom requires reflection and careful scrutiny of what one says, social media's emphasis on quick and unreflective responses almost certainly discourage wise thinking.

Even worse, the reinforcement system of social media is oriented toward making money for advertisers, as that is the source of income for the companies that produce social media. Advertising today, as always, works best when it bypasses critical thinking. There is nothing new in all this. Even in the 1950s, skeptics were concerned about how the medium of the moment–television–bypassed critical thinking and allowed advertisers to get a toehold on a person's consciousness [22]. Social media and many Internet applications are designed to free users from cognitive inhibitions—that is what advertising is about–and in the process, they have degraded the thinking even of people with high levels of intelligence [23,24].

People who are intelligent may believe that they are immune to any potential dumbing-down effects of social media. But a number of researchers have argued the opposite—that people's belief that they are immune to foolish or mindless work actually makes them become more susceptible to it [25–29]. They may be intelligent as a "trait," but even people who are more intelligent as a trait may behave foolishly as a state—that is, they can fall for the same tricks as others, maybe more so because they believe they cannot.

3.5. Surveillance

We live, more and more, in surveillance societies [29–31]. In parts of the world, surveillance is so tight that one can be viewed as having little more privacy than in George Orwell's *"1984"* [32]. In some places, it is hard to walk anywhere in a public space without cameras observing one's movements. One's use of the Internet is closely monitored by companies such as Facebook and Google, as well as by advertisers looking to get an edge in sales.

The surveillance is not all from the top-down. People are doing more surveillance on each other. Some of it is probably good, as in the open-science movement, designed to achieve greater transparency in scientific research. But the cost of such a movement is more surveillance of scientists by one another, with increased emphasis, again, on analytical processing at the expense of creative and perhaps wisdom-related information processing. The amount of registration and paperwork increases, leaving potentially less time for creative work [33]. And current emphasis on replication has the same effect, leading researchers to spend time processing information analytically—to be sure of exactly replicating someone else's work—rather than going much beyond what has been done before. Indeed, in a strict replication, the idea is *not* to go beyond what was done before—to replicate methods as exactly as possible [34]. A conceptual replication goes a bit beyond the past, but is a limiting form of creative enterprise [35]. On the positive side, of course, science becomes more open and transparent. But the emphasis on analytical processing, once again, increases, in a limited-resource model, at the possible expense of creative processing in generating novel and useful ideas.

Of course, many other forces operate in society, but the point, I believe, is clear. Many societies in the world, including that in the United States, have come more and more to reward memory and analytical skills. I believe there are exceptions, such as the culture of Silicon Valley, which also emphasizes creative and, to an extent, practical skills. But the isolation of Silicon Valley from much of the rest of the United States bespeaks the cultural difference between it and much of the rest of the country.

If, indeed, resources are limited, then the emphasis placed on memory and analytical skills will tend to crowd out the development of creative and practical skills. The result will be successive generations of students who become increasingly analytical in their focus, in the mode of thinking required for problems on IQ tests and related tests, such as the SAT and ACT. It should be noted that this analytical focus is quite different from the focus of rational thinking. That is, one can have a high IQ and be lacking in rational and critical thinking capacities of the kinds needed for success in everyday life [36–38]. So smart people not only can be foolish (lacking in wisdom for the common good), but also, lacking in rationality.

4. Interaction of Components of Intelligence with Societal Context

To return to the original question that motivated this essay: If intelligence is truly important to real-world adaptation, and IQs have risen 30+ points in the past century, then why are there so many unresolved and dramatic problems in the world today, and what can be done about it?

I have argued that a number of societal forces have conspired with the limited resources of the human brain to emphasize some skills over others, namely, memory and analytical skills at the potential expense of creative, practical (common-sense), and wisdom-based skills. Individuals start with a wide range of potentials for the development of cognitive skills. Their own predispositions plus societal forces then result in the greater development of some and the lesser development of others into competencies. And then, again, their predispositions and societal forces lead some people to become experts of one kind or another [39–41]. In many of our societies, students simply are not developing the creative skills they need for success in solving difficult world problems [42], nor the practical nor the wisdom-based skills either. Like the carpenter who has a hammer and looks for things to be hammered, they look for problems they can solve by memory or analytically, which often means that they will be looking for things, ideas, and people to critique more than they will be looking for things and ideas to create in common-sense ways so that they help to achieve a common good. In essence, we risk becoming a society of replicators and critics (see Note 6).

Fortunately, there are many forces that also encourage creativity—competiveness in most fields (from research to industry), rapid changes in social customs, rapid changes in the technology we can creatively exploit to get our work done, and sometimes even rare work environments that actually encourage creative thinking rather than merely saying they do. But the greatest problem is that that there are few forces that encourage the development of wisdom—using our creative, analytical, and practical skills to seek a common good.

For most of its history, the United States was a country that sought a "common good." Unfortunately, the common good was not quite "common"—it was almost exclusively for white people, mostly for males, and often excluded people of non-Christian religions, and even at times excluded Catholics. The Civil Rights movement of the 1960s and 1970s helped achieve something more nearly approaching equality of various groups, but what recent times have made clear is that it did so at a cost: Many people who before had been in the privileged class—even if they were not economically well off—felt that their rightful place was either being stolen from them, or else, that it was being too widely shared. Partly as a result, the United States is highly polarized today, perhaps as never before since the Civil War. Similar problems have arisen in in Europe and beyond. Those who once felt themselves to be "have's" came to feel like "have-not's," and through populist movements are seeking to become have's again (see Note 3).

The only viable solution to this problem is for people to use their creative, analytic, and practical intelligence wisely—toward a common good. But the forces described above—testing, schooling, social media, surveillance—all lead people away from this goal. And the individualism of many of our societies, combined with cultural clashes within and between those societies, have made it difficult for people to see beyond their own tribal interests [43]. If there is one thing schools are not doing, however, it is teaching for wisdom [44], arguably the most important element in the augmented theory of successful intelligence [45]. Teachers do not know how and because wisdom is not tested, it remains nearly invisible in the schooling process.

On top of this, the intelligence field, after perhaps a brief flirtation with broader theories of intelligence such as those of Gardner [46] and Sternberg [45], seems to be moving back toward its traditional position in favor of narrower psychometrically-based views [47–49] that, while multifaceted, still view intelligence as having general ability, or g at the top of a hierarchy of abilities. Some argue for the psychometric model above other models [50] and others argue that the task of intelligence research is simply to understand the biology of g and related constructs [51].

All of this might not matter if the state of the world were not of such great concern at the moment. Perhaps people always feel that things are precarious. But the return of somewhat mindless populism [52], as existed before World War II, has to be a major concern to a world in which democracy is on the decline [53], where income inequality favoring those with high IQ is feeding resentment producing the very populism that is threatening democracy [54], and where air pollution is not only shortening life spans, but apparently lowering global intelligence [55].

5. Failure of Cognitive Inoculation

Professor William McGuire was a social psychologist and, in particular, a cognitive-consistency theorist. But in retrospect, he might be viewed as well as a distinguished theorist of practical intelligence. He proposed an inoculation theory, according to which people could be helped to maintain sensible and cognitively consistent beliefs if they were "inoculated" against (sometimes malevolent) attempts to change these beliefs [56–58]. The idea was much like physical inoculation: By challenging people's beliefs with weak counterarguments, one could inoculate their cognitive systems against later stronger (and sometimes less than rational) counterarguments.

Of course, sometimes people do need to change their beliefs. McGuire's concern was, however, as is that here, with attempts to change beliefs that people need to maintain clear and cognitively consistent thinking. Demagogues in all domains (not just political—business, religion, science, whatever) attempt to change beliefs by repeating, over and over, powerful and often simplistic belief-changing statements. They recruit allies to assist them in their attempts to overthrow reason. No one is immune to such forces, least of all the "smart" people who may believe they are immune and thus may put up little resistance.

According to McGuire, four elements are necessary for inoculation to occur:

1. *Threat.* The individual must recognize that there is a threat to his or her considered beliefs. In our case, the threat might be to the view that democracy is desirable and that people should have equal rights.
2. *Refutational preemption.* The individual must be able to activate his or her own arguments and strengthen those beliefs through countering threats to the beliefs.
3. *Delay.* As with a biological inoculation, people need some time, in this case after the presentation of the weak counterarguments, for cognitive inoculation to work. Perhaps people use that time to reflect upon their views and why they are solid.
4. *Involvement.* People need to have sufficient involvement in the issue at hand to want to defend their beliefs and to activate them in the face of threat to them. Otherwise, they may not care enough to counter attacks on their beliefs.

Again, some beliefs of course need changing. None of us should view our beliefs as sacrosanct. Nothing said here stands against that basic fact.

Yet, today, fundamental beliefs are under attack. It often is hard to figure out what one or another political party in a given country stands for. How could beliefs change so quickly? There is good reason to believe that cognitive inoculation today is at threat. The main reason is perhaps that people are just not ready to apply cognitive inoculation to new media, such as the Internet and in particular the social media through which so much new information is now presented. People just have not had a chance to adjust. People of course need some time to adjust to any new medium, even newspapers or television. But going back just a decade or two, most media, at least in democracies, made at least some attempt to present balanced news. In the United States, whether one listened on the television of the 1960s to Chet Huntley and David Brinkley (NBC), Walter Cronkite (CBS), or Howard K. Smith (ABC), one received basically the same news. Today that is no longer true. The world as presented by Fox is unrecognizable to viewers of (or listeners to) CNN, and vice versa. The Internet allows people and clever social-media providers to screen out what particular people don't want to hear, with the result that they live in a mini-universe of like-minded people. They find it hard to understand why anyone would disagree [59].

Biologically, people actually have two immune systems, not just one [60]. The older immune system is a general-purpose one, which can protect us against generalized biological (bacterial, viral, parasitic, etc.) threats. The newer immune system specifically targets particular new threats that the body has not previously mobilized specific mechanisms to defend against. The problem is that the new immune system is slower to act, because it needs to recruit new antibodies to guard against and attack the specific threats. In the meantime, while the need for antibodies is being assessed, the antibodies are being created, and when the antibodies are being mobilized, the challenge to the body can defeat it, or render it permanently incapacitated.

I suggest that the cognitive immune system may have the same challenge as the biological one. Some threats to our cognitive system, such as when someone tries to cheat us in an interpersonal interaction, may stimulate our "old" cognitive immune system. That is, we are used to such threats and know how to handle them. People have been dealing with such challenges over the millennia. But the newer threats—such as via social media—invoke much less of a hard-wired response, and that response is probably generalized and weak, as would be our biological response to a new threat. By the time the newer cognitive immune system is recruited, it may or may not be too late. Our minds may already be "infected" with maladaptive "viruses" by the time the new cognitive immune system sets to work, and by then, we may not be able to marshal sufficient cognitive resistance to change what have become maladaptive modes of thought. Thus can we be beguiled by would-be despots and their henchmen.

It is useful that intelligence theorists are studying intelligence in the laboratory using biological, reaction-time, and other related methods. But our ability to direct our intelligence to face the challenges of modern society is under threat. Is it not time for intelligence theorists to take seriously threats that are themselves serious to the well-being of civilization? The essays in this special section of the *Journal of Intelligence* consider current challenges to, and problems in the world, and how intelligence, broadly considered, can help us better to face and perhaps even solve them.

Conflicts of Interest: The author declares no conflicts of interest.

References

1. Daigle, K. Air Pollution Is Shaving A Year Off Our Average Life Expectancy. *Science News*. 22 August 2018. Available online: https://www.sciencenews.org/article/air-pollution-shaving-year-our-average-life-expectancy (accessed on 12 September 2018).
2. Ingraham, C. Massive New Data Set Suggests Income Inequality Is about to Get Even Worse. *Washington Post*. 4 January 2018. Available online: https://www.washingtonpost.com/news/wonk/wp/2018/01/04/massive-new-data-set-suggests-inequality-is-about-to-get-even-worse/?utm_term=.94f32377dbc0 (accessed on 12 September 2018).
3. O'Connor, N. Three connections between rising income inequality and the rise of populism. *Ir. Stud. Int. Aff.* **2017**, *28*, 29–43.
4. Chandran, N. Denuclearization A Pipe Dream? UN Holds Talks to Ban Nukes, and Major Powers don't Show Up. 27 March 2017. Available online: https://www.cnbc.com/2017/03/27/global-reluctance-towards-nuclear-denuclearization-as-un-hold-talks.html (accessed on 12 September 2018).
5. Bratsberg, B.; Rogeberg, O. Flynn effect and its reversal are both environmentally caused. *Proc. Natl. Acad. Sci. USA* **2018**, *115*, 6674–6678. [CrossRef] [PubMed]
6. Sternberg, R.J. *Beyond IQ: A Triarchic Theory of Human Intelligence*; Cambridge University Press: Cambridge, UK, 1985.
7. Sternberg, R.J. *Successful Intelligence*; Plume: New York, NY, USA, 1997.
8. Sternberg, R.J. *Wisdom, Intelligence, and Creativity Synthesized*; Cambridge University Press: New York, NY, USA, 2003.
9. Sternberg, R.J. Teaching for wisdom. In *Oxford Handbook of Happiness*; David, S., Boniwell, I., Ayers, A.C., Eds.; Oxford University Press: Oxford, UK, 2013; pp. 631–643.
10. Engle, R.W. Working memory capacity as executive attention. *Curr. Dir. Psychol. Sci.* **2002**, *11*, 19–23. [CrossRef]
11. Engle, R.W. Working memory and executive attention: A revisit. *Perspect. Psychol. Sci.* **2018**, *13*, 190–193. [CrossRef] [PubMed]
12. Cowan, N.; Fristoe, N.M.; Elliott, E.M.; Brunner, R.P.; Saults, J.S. Scope of attention, control of attention, and intelligence in children and adults. *J. Educ. Psychol.* **2006**, *34*, 1754–1768. [CrossRef]
13. Stankov, L. Attention and intelligence. *J. Educ. Psychol.* **1983**, *75*, 471–490. [CrossRef]

14. Coyle, T.R. A differential-developmental model (DDM): Mental speed, attention lapses, and general intelligence (*g*). *J. Intell.* **2017**, *5*, 25. [CrossRef]
15. Neubauer, A.C. The mental speed approach to the assessment of intelligence. In *Advances in Cognition and Educational Practice: Reflections on the Concept of Intelligence*; Kingma, J., Tomic, W., Eds.; JAI: Greenwich, CT, USA, 1997; Volume 4, pp. 149–173.
16. Sternberg, R.J. Components of human intelligence. *Cognition* **1983**, *15*, 1–48. [CrossRef]
17. Sternberg, R.J. *The Triarchic Mind: A New Theory of Intelligence*; Viking: New York, NY, USA, 1988.
18. Koretz, D. *Measuring Up: What Educational Testing Really Tells Us*; Harvard University Press: Cambridge, MA, USA, 2008.
19. Sternberg, R.J. *College Admissions for the 21st Century*; Harvard University Press: Cambridge, MA, USA, 2010.
20. Sternberg, R.J. *What Universities Can Be*; Cornell University Press: Ithaca, NY, USA, 2016.
21. Vosoughi, S.; Roy, D.; Aral, S. The spread of true and false news online. *Science* **2018**, *359*, 1146–1151. [CrossRef] [PubMed]
22. Packard, V. *The Hidden Persuaders*; Pocket Books: New York, NY, USA, 1959.
23. Carr, N. *The Shallows: What the Internet Is Doing to Our Brains*; WW Norton & Company: New York, NY, USA, 2011.
24. Carr, N. *The Glass Cage: How Our Computers Are Changing Us*; WW Norton & Company: New York, NY, USA, 2011.
25. Aczel, B. Low levels of wisdom—Foolishness. In *Cambridge Handbook of Wisdom*; Sternberg, R.J., Glueck, J., Eds.; Cambridge University Press: New York, NY, USA, 2018; in press.
26. Aczel, B.; Palfi, B.; Kekecs, Z. What is stupid? People's conception of unintelligent behavior. *Intelligence* **2015**, *53*, 51–58. [CrossRef]
27. Sternberg, R.J. Why smart people can be so foolish. *Eur. Psychol.* **2004**, *9*, 145–150. [CrossRef]
28. Sternberg, R.J. Wisdom, foolishness, and toxicity in human development. *Res. Hum. Dev.* **2018**, in press. [CrossRef]
29. Gilliom, J. *SuperVision: An Introduction to The Surveillance Society*; University of Chicago Press: Chicago, IL, USA, 2012.
30. Cohen, E.D. *Mass Surveillance and State Control: The Total Information Awareness Project*; Palgrave Macmillan: New York, NY, USA, 2010.
31. Keller, W.M. *Democracy Betrayed: The Rise of the Surveillance Security State*; Counterpoint: New York, NY, USA, 2017.
32. Orwell, G. *1984*; Signet: New York, NY, USA, 1950.
33. Brainerd, C.J.; Reyna, V.F. Replication, registration, and scientific creativity. *Perspect. Psychol. Sci.* **2018**. [CrossRef] [PubMed]
34. Open Science Collaboration. Estimating the reproducibility of psychological science. *Science* **2015**, *349*, aac4716. [CrossRef] [PubMed]
35. Sternberg, R.J.; Kaufman, J.C.; Pretz, J.E. *The Creativity Conundrum: A Propulsion Model of Kinds of Creative Contributions*; Psychology Press: New York, NY, USA, 2002.
36. Stanovich, K.E. *Rationality and the Reflective Mind*; Oxford University Press: New York, NY, USA, 2010.
37. Stanovich, K.E. *What Intelligence Tests Miss: The Psychology of Rational Thought*; Yale University Press: New Haven, CT, USA, 2010.
38. Stanovich, K.E.; West, R.F.; Toplak, M.E. *The Rationality Quotient: Toward A Test of Rational Thinking*; MIT Press: Cambridge, MA, USA, 2018.
39. Sternberg, R.J. What does it mean to be smart? *Educ. Leadersh.* **1997**, *54*, 20.
40. Sternberg, R.J. Abilities are forms of developing expertise. *Educ. Res.* **1998**, *27*, 11–20. [CrossRef]
41. Sternberg, R.J. Intelligence as developing expertise. *Contemp. Educ. Psychol.* **1999**, *24*, 359–375. [CrossRef] [PubMed]
42. Sternberg, R.J.; Grigorenko, E.L.; Singer, J.L. (Eds.) *Creativity: The Psychology of Creative Potential and Realization*; American Psychological Association: Washington, DC, USA.
43. Markus, H.R.; Conner, A. *Clash! How to Thrive in a Multicultural World*; Plume: New York, NY, USA, 2014.
44. Sternberg, R.J. Schools should nurture wisdom. In *Teaching for Intelligence*, 2nd ed.; Presseisen, B.Z., Ed.; Corwin: Thousand Oaks, CA, USA, 2008; pp. 61–88.

45. Sternberg, R.J. The augmented theory of successful intelligence. In *Cambridge Handbook of Intelligence*, 2nd ed.; Sternberg, R.J., Ed.; Cambridge University Press: New York, NY, USA, in press.

46. Gardner, H. *Frames of Mind: The Theory of Multiple Intelligences*; Basic: New York, NY, USA, 2011.

47. Carroll, J.B. *Human Cognitive Abilities. A Survey of Factor-Analytic Studies*; Cambridge University Press: New York, NY, USA, 1993.

48. McGrew, K.S. The Cattell–Horn–Carroll theory of cognitive abilities: Past, present, and future. In *Contemporary Intellectual Assessment: Theories, Tests, and Issues*; Flanagan, D.P., Genshaft, J.L., Harrison, P.L., Eds.; Guilford: New York, NY, USA, 2005.

49. Sternberg, R.J.; Grigorenko, E.L. (Eds.) *The General Factor of Intelligence: How General Is It?* Lawrence Erlbaum Associates: Mahwah, NJ, USA, 2002.

50. Sternberg, R.J. Human intelligence: The model is the message. *Science* **1985**, *230*, 1111–1118. [CrossRef] [PubMed]

51. Haier, R.J. *The Neuroscience of Intelligence*; Cambridge University Press: New York, NY, USA, 2016.

52. Mudde, C. *Populism: A Very Short Introduction*; Oxford University Press: New York, NY, USA, 2017.

53. Rose, G. Is Democracy Dying? *Foreign Affairs*. Available online: https://www.foreignaffairs.com/articles/2018-04-16/democracy-dying (accessed on 12 September 2018).

54. Eisler, D. Income Inequality and the Rise of U.S. Populism: A Cautionary Tale for Canada. 2016. Available online: https://www.schoolofpublicpolicy.sk.ca/research/publications/policy-brief/income-inequality-and-the-rise-of-us-populism.php (accessed on 12 September 2018).

55. Zhang, X.; Chen, X.; Zhang, X. The impact of exposure to air pollution on cognitive performance. *Proc. Natl. Acad. Sci. USA* **2018**, *115*, 9193–9197. [CrossRef] [PubMed]

56. McGuire, W.J. Resistance to persuasion conferred by active and passive prior refutation of same and alternative counterarguments. *J. Abnorm. Psychol.* **1961**, *63*, 326–332. [CrossRef]

57. McGuire, W.J. The effectiveness of supportive and refutational defenses in immunizing and restoring beliefs against persuasion. *Sociometry* **1961**, *24*, 184–197. [CrossRef]

58. McGuire, W.J. Inducing resistance to persuasion. In *Advances in Experimental Social Psychology*; Berkowitz, L., Ed.; Academic Press: New York, NY, USA, 1964; Volume 1, pp. 191–229.

59. Mitchell, A.; Gottfried, J.; Kiley, J.; Matsa, K.E. Political polarization and media habits. Pew Research Center. 21 October 2014. Available online: http://www.journalism.org/2014/10/21/political-polarization-media-habits/ (accessed on 12 September 2018).

60. Sompayrac, L. *How the Immune System Works*; Wiley-Blackwell: Chichester, UK, 2012.

Journal of
Intelligence

MDPI

Article

Individual Mental Abiities vs. the World's Problems

Jonathan Baron

Department of Psychology, University of Pennsylvania, 3720 Walnut St., Philadelphia, PA 19104, USA;
baron@upenn.edu

Received: 28 February 2018; Accepted: 12 April 2018; Published: 16 April 2018

Abstract: The major problems in the world today are problems of government or the lack of it. Thus, the relevant parts of intelligence are those that make for good citizenship, such as supporting the best candidates and policies. I argue that dispositions, as well as capacities, are part of intelligence, and that some dispositions are the ones most crucial for citizenship, particularly the disposition to engage in actively open-minded thinking (AOT) and to apply it as a standard for the evaluation of the qualifications of authorities and leaders. AOT is a general prescriptive theory that applies to all thinking. It affects the aptness of conclusions and the accuracy of confidence judgments, and it reduces overconfidence when extreme confidence is not warranted. AOT may be affected by different factors from those that affect other components of intelligence and thus may undergo different changes over time. Whatever has happened in the past, we need more of it now.

Keywords: Flynn effect; actively open-minded thinking; cognitive style; political judgment

1. Introduction

The question of this Special Issue is "...why are there so many unresolved and dramatic problems in the world, and what can be done about it?" In particular, what is the role of cognitive abilities in resolving these problems.

As I see them, most of the big ones can be described as failures of government. Here is a rough classification:

1. In many poor countries, government simply does not function [1]. In the so-called Democratic Republic of the Congo, government cannot prevent the rise of a feudalism of gangs and tribes, all heavily armed. And what is left of the government is hopelessly corrupt. Often, in cases such as Venezuela, situations like this have arisen from support for a bad government that took over from a relatively benign one.

2. In less-poor countries, and even some relatively rich ones, the function of government is hampered by widespread corruption, "crony capitalism", and the social norms that support these practices [2,3]. Payola becomes a way of life, and it does not seem so bad to accept it when so many other are doing the same. The system maintains itself as a vicious circle.

3. In other countries, including some of the richest democracies along with others, voters accept unsupportable theories about the nature of their problems (e.g. [4]), leading to the adoption of policies that oppose the well-being of the citizens who supported them.

4. Some of these policies are isolationist: opposition to trade and immigration, unwillingness to participate in international agreements, and so on. These also threaten to create another vicious circle in which nations respond to each other in kind, thus losing the benefits of many kinds of international cooperation. And these policies often cause great harm to outsiders (such as potential refugees), who are simply left out of the moral calculus of the citizens who are in control, and, hence, their government ([5], especially ch. 6; [6], especially ch. 4).

5. At the opposite extreme of (1), world government is also not functioning. We have some international institutions, but they are weak and becoming weaker from increased isolationism of their members, and they do not coordinate with each other. This happens at a time when the human population, and its use of resources, have expanded to the point where their effects on the environment seriously threaten further increases in the world's standard of living [7]. We are now depending on scientific, technological, and administrative advances not yet made, or fully known, in order to provide sufficient food, water, and energy even for the population we have [8].

Omitted from this list is one commonly invoked cause of problems, namely, the behavior of individuals outside of their role as citizens. It is sometimes said, for example, that a solution to global warming is for each of us to reduce our carbon footprint. There are two problems with this idea. First, it is difficult to do this without a lot of help from government, in the form of relevant infrastructure and changes in laws and regulations. Second, the capacity of people to sacrifice their own well-being for the good of others is limited. Of course, it is variable: some people are more willing than others to make sacrifices. But even those people need information about what sacrifices will matter. And it is doubtful that further exhortation from activists will increase the average level to the point where it makes a serious dent in the world's problems. (The exhortation has been going on for a while.) It is not too much to expect people to recycle their trash (even in the absence of penalties for not doing it) or to reduce their water use during a drought. But the level of sacrifice required to prevent continued unsustainable draining of aquifers is much greater. It requires a combination of government coercion and government support of alternative water sources. Likewise, fishers are not going to reduce their catch to the point of sustainability of the fishery unless they are threatened with punishment for over-fishing ([6], ch. 1). We need government.

How can individuals help solve the problems of government? I think that the answer is different for different problems. In particular, the first problem, non-functioning national government, is not easily solved by individual citizens voting for politicians who will fix it. The "system" is too powerful. What is required is something more like revolution. That requires a few courageous and inspiring leaders, like Nelson Mandela, and a large number (although not necessarily a majority) who are willing to put their lives on the line for a cause [9]. The necessary traits thus do not have much to do with the sort of abilities measured by the IQ test, except perhaps in the leaders, and even for them these traits are not the critical ones. Still, after the revolution, the first problem can turn into the second (as has been a danger in South Africa).

In all but the last of these problems, the means for solving the problems are those of ordinary democracy.[1] I have suggested [10] that, in order for a democracy to function well, its citizens need to endorse three social norms, which I called cosmopolitanism, anti-moralism, and actively open-minded thinking (AOT). The first two are specific to politics, so they are not of concern here, except that they may both be facilitated by AOT.[2] The third is the main topic I shall address here, eventually. Note that AOT has many functions. It is an individual disposition, a social norm, and a standard for judgment.

First, a little history from a biased perspective, my own.

2. Dispositions, Abilities, and Intelligence

In 1985, I published *Rationality and Intelligence*, which argued that rational thinking was part of intelligence. This argument had two steps. The first was to define intelligence in a way that did justice

---

[1] It would be convenient for my argument if China did not exist. It is certainly not democratic, yet it is making more progress on most fronts than many well-established democracies. This may be less of a contradiction than it seems. The government pays attention to signals from the people, even if those are in the form of opinion polls rather than voting, and the ruling Communist party is quite large and is somewhat sensitive to the concerns of its members. The government has thus moved to reduce corruption and strengthen the rule of law. In sum, Chinese citizens do have some influence.

[2] Cosmopolitanism is a continuum of breadth of political concern, one end of which is a concern for all humanity (or all sentient life) now and in the future. Anti-moralism is opposition to the imposition of moral principles on others when the principles themselves depend on particular commitments of faith that cannot be defended to those who are affected.

to our use of the term in psychology but was not limited to "whatever the intelligence test measures" and not dependent on the assumption of a g factor (a concept often used to by-pass the need for a clear definition, since its existence seems to imply that "it doesn't matter much how you measure it"). I concluded roughly that intelligence consisted of a bunch of potentially general traits (capacities and dispositions), each of which would help people achieve their rational goals, whatever these goals might be.

"General" meant that their definition was not confined to a particular type of mental task, or a particular subject matter. We could then ask the empirical questions of whether each trait was correlated across different tasks, and whether these different manifestations had common influences, such as transfer of learning in the case of dispositions, or biological substrates in the case of capacities.

Importantly, I saw no reason to exclude thinking dispositions such as perseverance oe open-mindedness. These fit the definition, and they surely influence essentially all manifestations of intelligence. Why should we regard them as artifacts? Measures of intelligence could try to exclude them, but do not. For example, we could attempt to measure pure capacities such as mental speed, or memory storage, using sophisticated cognitive tasks, but we do not do this except in experiments. Yet many writers today implicitly assume that intelligence is the biologically limited part and the contribution of acquired "personality" traits is an artifact (e.g., [11]). If they are separate, then what is intelligence?

Given that dispositions are included, which ones are relevant? To answer this question, we need a theory of rational thinking, defined now as that sort of thinking that helps people pursue their rational goals, whatever these goals might be.[3] I then went on to state a theory of rational thinking, which has been modified a bit over the years, both in my own mind and in my publications (e.g., [12,13]).

The theory includes a simple framework for the description of all thinking, regardless of topic, and then applies standard normative models from decision theory to that framework. The result is a prescriptive model, AOT, which refers to objects available to the thinker, so that, in principle, it is meaningful for someone to try to follow the prescriptions in question. That is, it is not about the criteria of success and failure, but, rather, about the processes under the thinker's control. The model does not require any additional domain-specific knowledge. Of course, good thinking is more effective when such knowledge is available.

AOT has a different purpose than that of other approaches to the analysis of thinking for the purpose of making thinking better. It concentrates narrowly on thinking itself, described in terms that are neutral with respect to content hence not specific to any particular type of thinking. The goal is more to find what is common to all forms of good thinking, and potentially to provide a unifying explanation of why they are useful. Other approaches (e.g., [14]) consider a broader concept, such as wisdom, and try to list all the traits and abilities that contribute to it. Some of these (e.g., tacit knowledge) have little to do with thinking in the more limited sense, and others (e.g., "good judgment") seem to refer to criteria of success rather than prescriptions to be followed.[4]

The proposed framework analyzes thinking into search for various objects (described shortly) and inference from the resulting findings of the search. In ordinary thinking, these two steps are often interleaved through several episodes of search and inference. The objects consist of possibilities (answers to the question that inspired the thinking), evidence (objects that bear on the value of the possibilities), and goals (criteria that determine how each piece of evidence affects the value of each possibility). Search may be directed in various ways, but the main parameters of interest are its extent

---

[3] It would digress too far to deal with the potential circularity of "rational goals" in the definition of "rational thinking". In brief, we can define a subset of rational thinking without this limitation, then discuss the rationality of goals, and so on.

[4] Similarly, a parallel literature on "critical thinking" (e.g., [15]) seems concerned with the full range of skills, some quite specific to certain content, that make for effectiveness in what is understood to be good thinking. Many writers in this tradition take the term "critical" almost literally, so that their concern is to encourage skepticism. Yet, AOT also gives us reasons to trust, as well as to find fault.

and its direction, with direction defined as for or against a currently favored possibility. The direction parameter may also be applied to inference.[5]

Rational thinking determines search and inference. Search is optimal so long as the benefit of additional search is still greater than its cost. Search is "fair" when it optimally distinguishes possibilities (possible answers to the question at hand). For example, it is wasteful to look for reasons why a favored option is best, if one is going to choose that option anyway. Inference depends heavily on the situation, but, again, in order to be fair it must not favor possibilities that are already strong.

Search should be sufficiently extensive for the task at hand. The optimal amount of search is determined by a balance between the cost of search and its potential benefit in terms of increased accuracy. If you know that additional search cannot lead to a change of mind, search is a waste of time. Search is most valuable when you are unsure, when the task is important, and when the prospect of finding something is good. More generally, the potential benefit of search depends on the expected-utility difference between the best possibility and the current favored possibility; this expectation, in turn, depends on the probability that new information will lead to a change in the correct direction (which is lower if the current possibility is more likely to be the best one). The cost of search depends on factors such as time pressure (high cost of delay) and whether the search is enjoyable or painful in its own right. At this point, with a few additional assumptions, the theory is clear enough to be programmed on a computer, although this has never been done.

An important aspect of good thinking, beyond accuracy in choosing the best possibility, is appropriate confidence. Reports of confidence should depend on the difference between the current value (strength) of the favored possibility and the total value of the alternatives. Confidence should depend on the thinking that has been done, or the lack of it. High confidence that one possibility is optimal is justified by extensive examination of the evidence for that possibility and others. (This does not have to be thinking of each citizen. As I shall point out, citizens rely heavily on others. But someone has to have done it.) Confidence should also depend on the balance of arguments for competing possibilities. When evidence is lopsided favoring one possibility, confidence in that one should be higher. Finally, confidence in politics (for example) should be low when little thinking has affected a particular political opinion. In many cases, extensive search is not worth the cost, and people rationally hold opinions that have not been subject to examination. But they should know that they are doing this and thus refrain from confidently accepting their tentative conclusions as justified, and they should refrain from imposing them on others. In the words of a bumper sticker: "Don't believe everything you think."

When we look at how people actually think, we find a few systematic and general departures from this model of rational thinking. Many of these departures are biases that favor conclusions (possibilities) that are already favored. People tend to search selectively for evidence that favors these possibilities, whether they search for external information [16] or internal information based on memory [12,17,18]. For example, Perkins et al. [17] asked students to write down their thoughts on issues that were "genuinely vexed and timely" and that could be discussed on the basis of knowledge that most people have, e.g., "Would providing more money for public schools significantly improve the quality of teaching and learning?" Most students gave more arguments on their favored side, "myside" thoughts, than on the other side. When the students were asked to try harder to think of arguments on each side, they thought of very few additional myside arguments but many additional otherside arguments. Left to their own devices, then, the students looked primarily for reasons to support their initial opinion, but out of biased search rather than lack of ability or knowledge.

---

[5] The direction parameter is not always under the thinker's control. Search of external data sometimes prevents it, and many types of inferences, such as arithmetic calculation, are fixed and cannot be modified.

People also use evidence in a way that supports their pet conclusions [19,20], even to the point of taking the same piece of evidence to favor different conclusions depending on which conclusion they favor [21]. These biases together are called "confirmation bias" or "myside bias" in the literature.[6]

In general, people search too little when search is warranted. We know this mainly from the fact that people who tend to search more do better in a variety of real-world manifestations of intelligence, such as school performance [22] and forecasting [23]. Yet the amount of search need not be correlated with fairness in the direction of search, nor with fairness of inferences, as I shall discuss.

Finally, confidence in judgments is generally too high when judgments are difficult. In most studies of the accuracy of confidence judgments, subjects are asked to provide answers to questions of fact plus a probability that their answer is correct. When the questions are difficult, the mean probability assigned by most subjects to a batch of questions is considerably higher than the proportion that they answer correctly [24]. Political issues, because they are often controversial, are difficult in the relevant sense. AOT reduces overconfidence, especially unjustified extreme confidence [18,25]. People who look for reasons against their favored option are likely to find them and reduce their confidence accordingly.

3. AOT and Politics

All aspects of intelligence are potentially relevant to citizenship of the sort that we need. Smarter people are more able to comprehend some of the issues that they need to understand in order to have informed opinions about policies, especially economic policies (e.g., [4,26]). They are also more likely to get the kind of education that will give them relevant background in many different fields. But AOT plays an outsized role among the aspects of intelligence relevant to politics.

3.1. The Benefits of AOT for Our Own Thinking

First, AOT helps individuals think through the issues on the table. Issues that citizens face tend to be ones with arguments for competing views, if only views about how to overcome the forces of inertia. Openness to arguments on different sides can make citizens more likely to change their mind in the direction of good arguments. Change need not be complete to be beneficial. A little doubt can be a good thing.

Nor does change need not be immediate. When we have thought about something long enough to have reduced confidence, we are more open to additional arguments. Lower confidence rationally increases the utility of additional information, so it is more likely to be sought. Reduced confidence also makes switching more likely when it is warranted by the evidence at hand.

Second, AOT permits better cooperation between political factions. Successful negotiation, in general, usually involves trade-offs on several attributes, such as working hours and salary in the case of labor negotiations [27]. Ideally, each party gives up on those attributes that is of greater concern to the other party. Such "log rolling" (or "integrative bargainins") is more likely when the parties are aware of the weaknesses in their own original positions.

Similarly, AOT ought to reduce the polarization and fanaticism that often ties up political systems in knots. It is extremely unlikely that any political party or pressure group is absolutely right on every issue. Those who realize this are surely more willing to compromise.

3.2. Relation between AOT Norms and Actual Thinking

Baron [28,29] argued that beliefs affect what people do, and supported this with correlations between subjects' beliefs about the nature of good thinking and the subjects' own thinking. Stanovich

---

[6] In the first edition of *Thinking and deciding* (1988), I used the term "myside bias" (which had been used previously by David Perkins) because "confirmation bias" was being used for something that was not a bias. This usage seems to have stopped. Now it seems that we have two terms for the same idea.

and West [30,31] constructed a questionnaire that emphasized similar beliefs. Several papers (reviewed by [32] and [33], Table 1), found correlations between this belief scale and other tests, some of which measured biases described in the literature on judgment and decision making, including (but not limited to): Baserate Neglect, Conjunction Fallacy, Framing Effects, Anchoring Effect, Sample Size Awareness, Regression to the Mean, Temporal Discounting, Gambler's Fallacy, Probability Matching, Overconfidence Effect, Outcome Bias, Ratio Bias, Ignoring P(D/H), Sunk Cost Effect, Risk/Benefit Confounding, Omission Bias, Expected Value Maximization, Hindsight Bias, Certainty Effect, Willingness to pay/Willingness to accept, and Proportion Dominance Effect.

Baron selected items from the Stanovich/West [30,31] scale and added others to make a short form more appropriate for the general population, designed to assess beliefs in particular. Example items are as follows: "People should take into consideration evidence that goes against their beliefs." and "Changing your mind is a sign of weakness." This short form has had considerable success in predicting the results of other tasks such as perceptual judgments and reduced over-confidence in them [34], accuracy in geo-political forecasting [23], utilitarian moral judgment, and problem solving ([35], using a slightly extended version).

The fact that this short belief measure (and others like it) correlates with task performance suggests that efforts to explain to people the value of AOT, thus changing their beliefs to make them more favorable toward AOT, could result in improved performance on many tasks that involve thinking. Gürçay-Morris [18] attempted to do this with a short training module, with some short-term success in reducing overconfidence.

3.3. AOT as a Set of Norms for Evaluation

AOT involves a set of thinking dispositions, but, in those who understand it, it also provides a set of norms (standards) for the evaluation of anyone's thinking, including the thinking of others [36]. Indeed, John Stuart Mill was perhaps the clearest 19th century advocate of what I am calling AOT. In *On liberty* ([37], ch. 2), he writes (as part of a longer argument): "The whole strength and value, then, of human judgment, depending on the one property, that it can be set right when it is wrong, reliance can be placed on it only when the means of setting it right are kept constantly at hand. In the case of any person whose judgment is really deserving of confidence, how has it become so? Because he has kept his mind open to criticism of his opinions and conduct. Because it has been his practice to listen to all that could be said against him; to profit by as much of it as was just, and expound to himself, and upon occasion to others, the fallacy of what was fallacious."

Individual citizens do not have the time or background to delve deeply into policies concerning trade, immigration, crime or almost anything [36]. Partly, this is a function of the low expected-value of spending time informing ourselves, but even if we are passionately involved, we cannot get to the bottom of all the issues we face. Too much is known for any one person to get to the bottom of almost anything. We must rely on the conclusions of others, and we must be able to distinguish relatively trustworthy sources from those that express gut-level intuitions as if they were proven facts or pearls of wisdom [38,39].

For example, science, and many other forms of scholarly inquiry (especially philosophy, these days), are based on actively open-minded thinking (AOT), refining themselves by challenging tentative beliefs. Astronomy differs from astrology because the latter has no standard procedures for thinking critically about its assertions. The same applies to a great deal of religious doctrine. Science, by contrast, engages in AOT at least as a group, if not within the heads of individual scientists. Scientists are rewarded (with publications, grants, promotions, jobs) for finding problems with the conclusions of other scientists. Individual scientists also try (perhaps not always hard enough) to anticipate possible criticisms before they try to publish something. These practices make science effective in approaching truth and understanding ever more closely.

Likewise, the application of the norms of scholarly inquiry, including AOT, in government itself can improve its effectiveness [40]. It would be helpful if citizens understood the value of these advances.

AOT is not just about "critical" thinking; as that term suggests a skeptical attitude, possibly leading critical thinkers to doubt even when they should trust. The understanding of AOT leads to trust insofar as trust is warranted, and this need not involve looking for flaws, as long as we know that others have done so on our behalf.

Populist, and often authoritarian, politicians gain power with the support of those who do not apply the norms of AOT to evaluate their thinking. These politicians are full of confident pronouncements of propositions that others find weak, subject to objections that are sometimes obvious with a little thought. But the air of confidence serves as a false signal of true expertise.

We have no better way. Alternatives such as "faith", "the heart", or acceptance of the word of authority have no built-in mechanism for self-correction. If their conclusions are wrong, we have no way to know, and, therefore, we also have no way to know when they are right.

4. The Flynn Effect and Possible Cultural Effects on AOT

The Flynn effect is a well-documented increase in IQ over several decades and several nations [41]. Recently, it may have hit a ceiling or even begun to decline in some countries (e.g., [42–44]). Of interest here is in which aspects of intelligence changed.

IQ tests are usually thought to measure fluid and crystallized intelligence. Crystallized intelligence is the result of accumulation of knowledge, hence a product of various capacities and environmental influences. Good learners will learn more words throughout their lives, so vocabulary is a reasonable crystallized measure of past learning ability, although of course it is affected by opportunity as well.

Fluid intelligence is usually thought to concern more direct measurement of biologically limited capacities such as mental speed. However, many of the measures of fluid intelligence involve problem solving, such as the Raven's Progressive Matrices, which are also related to measures of cognitive style. For example, many problem-solving tasks show positive correlations between accuracy and response time (e.g., [26,45]). Such results must overcome any negative correlations resulting from any positive influence of mental speed on both accuracy and response *speed*.

All the measures I know that concern cognitive abilities or reflective cognitive style (including measures of AOT) correlate with each other, even when the latter are measured by questionnaires (e.g., [23,46]). Thus, the "positive manifold" that led Spearman to postulate the existence of a g factor seems to extend to dispositions as well as abilities. These correlations may exist for many reasons. High levels of basic capacities (such as mental speed, or durable memory storage) may be helpful in learning to think effectively, just as they help learn almost anything else. Or tests that attempt to measure such capacities might be less pure than they seem. Vocabulary items, for example, sometimes can be solved as problems when words are unknown, and even an apparent speed test such as the digit-symbol task can benefit from a thoughtful approach to choice of a strategy for doing the task. Or environmental influences may themselves be correlated, e.g., good nutrition, health care, and education (of the sort that encourages a more reflective cognitive style), as suggested by Pietschnig and Voracek [41]. Good thinking can even lead to better physical health.

These correlations, and their possible causes, make it difficult to distinguish effects, such as those of historical change, on capacities, acquired knowledge and dispositions. Differences in correlations may result from differences in reliability of measures (or validity in the sense of measuring what they are supposed to measure).

I could find no attempts to examine historical changes in cognitive style. All the evidence suggests that cognitive style is heavily influenced by culture. For example, it is correlated with aspects of religion, which is surely influenced by upbringing (e.g., [35,47]). It thus may be more sensitive to cultural change.

A possible candidate for examination of cultural change is the dimension of reflection/impulsivity (R/I) in problem solving. As argued by [35], this is a measure that can be defined in any problem-solving task. One way to do it is to measure the log of mean response time in the task, and the accuracy rate. (Use of the log makes the distribution closer to normal, thus removing what would otherwise be the excessive influence of long responses.) Then convert both to z scores and take the *sum*. (Note that the *difference* might be seen as a measure of raw mental power, which would consist of speed as well as accuracy.) At one end of the resulting continuum, reflective subjects would be slow and accurate. At the other end, impulsives would be fast and inaccurate. The measure thus assesses the willingness to trade off accuracy for speed (or speed for accuracy). It is quite general across tasks, so long as they do not involve time pressure. In many cases, the response-time measure correlates just as highly (positively) with other results as does the accuracy measure (the one usually used) [35]. Thus, much of the predictive power of problem solving tasks may be the result of the cognitive style of R/I.

One of the problem-solving measures that can be used for this purpose is the Raven's Progessive Matrices. In its standard form, there is little or no time pressure. Yet I was unable to find any articles that reported response times, as well as accuracy. Someone must have relevant data possibly going back as far as 1936, but I could not find them. Such data could allow us to examine historical changes in R/I.[7]

Even if this could be done, though, it is not the best measure of AOT. I have argued (e.g., [29,35]) that reflective thought can be characterized on two dimensions, one of which is R/I, which concerns the tradeoff between the benefits and costs of additional search. The other is direction, specifically whether the thinking is biased toward possibilities that are already strong, both in search and inference, as distinct from being fair.[8] AOT and R/I have different correlates. If we assume that the Cognitive Reflection Test (CRT) is primarily a measure of R/I (insofar as it is sensitive to general dispositions, as distinct from specific knowledge), then it is of interest that it has different correlates from questionnaire measures of AOT. For example, Baron [49] noted that AOT (the short scale) correlates 0.27 with self-reported political liberalism in a representative U.S. sample, while the CRT does not correlate at all in the same sample. Raven's test might be much like the CRT.

AOT does not assume that more thinking is always better. AOT is primarily concerned with direction, and with appropriate confidence. The question of how much thinking is warranted is, as I argued earlier, part of a broader question concerned with the trade-off between amount and confidence. That said, some correlation between AOT and R/I is to be expected, if only because any attempt to be fair will require some search for counter-evidence as well as for evidence, where myside bias requires only the latter. And, even a long search for confirming evidence may turn up counter-evidence instead. Still, it would be nice if we had measures of direction as well as amount.

One possible way to study AOT historically is to use archival scoring of written records. The concept of integrative complexity (e.g., [50]) comes very close to AOT. The scoring system is based on two measures: differentiation and integration. Differentiation is the acknowledgment of multiple views or perspectives. It is essentially equivalent to the idea of fairness in AOT. (This is no coincidence. The concept of AOT has many historical antecedents, and integrative complexity is one of them.) Integration involves some sort of synthesis of the resulting views. It is more difficult to score. And, in fact, differentiation alone does much of the work in accounting for correlations between integrative complexity and other measures. Most studies of integrative complexity involve highly specialized samples of material, such as speeches made by legislators. Of possible relevance here, Thoemmes and Conway [51] found essentially no historical change in the complexity of speeches

---

7   The idea that R/I can be assessed from Raven's test and is part of g is not a radical one. Arthur Jensen [48], a strong defender of the traditional approach to the g factor, writes (pp. 617–619): "Reflective persons tend to delay responses in answering test items involving initial uncertainty, and as a result their performance gains in accuracy. The payoff of a reflective attitude is greatest in tasks that call for careful analysis of possible response alternatives, as is characteristic, for example, of multiple-choice nonverbal tests such as the Raven's Matrices." After noting the correlation between R/I and IQ, he suggests "that much of the correlation may be due to an intrinsic relationship between g and reflectivity, that is, one of the manifestations of g ability is reflectiveness."

8   In principle, thinking could be systematically biased against currently favored possibilities, but I know of no results showing that a general dimension of direction can go "below 0" in this way.

of U.S. presidents from George Washington to George W. Bush, but they did find several possible determinants other than historical time.

Now it is time for a guess. Recently, Emlen Metz, in her PhD dissertation (summarized in [45]) developed measures of AOT for middle-school children (roughly ages 12–13) in the U.S. The schools included private schools for the well-off and public schools in poor neighborhoods, but, it might be said, none of the "Christian" schools in the South, known for their emphasis on strict doctrine and opposition to some of the conclusions of modern science. What surprised everyone about the results of these tests, modeled after the adult versions but also including many items with open-ended answers, was that most students were near the ceiling. The expected correlations with other measures—highly significant because of the very large sample size—were low because of the low variance in all measure of AOT. Some of the open-ended items required students to put themselves in the position of someone holding a position now thought to be untenable, such as the claim that women should not be allowed to vote. Most students were able to do this, even though they disagreed with the conclusion. They had no particular resistance to trying to think of "arguments on the other side" from their own. They also dealt reasonably with hypothetical scenarios involving substantive arguments with peers.

Unfortunately, it was impossible to find historical data even on items taken from tests that have been used extensively over the last few decades. But it seemed likely to me that schools—public, private, rich, and poor—have adopted a norm of respect for others, and this norm has implications for how to deal with people who hold different views. This norm is part of AOT but not all of it. For example, it has little to do with (and may not generalize to) thought processes about individual decisions that do not involve conflicts of opinion, such as those concerning health or how to fix a toilet, and little to do with appropriate confidence.

I also suspect that culture in some parts of the world, and of the U.S., has moved farther from the sort of ideology that encourages AOT. Such "negative" cultural changes may result from the spread of fundamentalist or doctrinaire religions of many sorts (Muslim, Christian, Jewish, and Hindu), even in countries that have in the past embraced liberal, tolerant, doctrines (e.g., Turkey, Indonesia). It is as if more people want to declare their identity through membership in a religious group that regards other doctrines as potentially subversive and in need of suppression. Such cultural defenses may tend to spread, even to the point of discouraging children's natural curiosity about outsiders.

Such cultural attitudes are part of the world's problems. We see this specifically in religious opposition to polio vaccination in Nigeria and Pakistan, in one-issue voting on abortion in the U.S., and in the persistent Hindu/Muslim conflict in South Asia. But the same general attitudes prevent citizens from thinking well about other issues, and, more importantly, distort their evaluation of potential leaders and trusted authorities toward those who are most doctrinaire, those with the most unwarranted confidence.

5. Promoting AOT in Schools

The argument for AOT is thus simple. Errors of judgment, and poor decisions, are common. Especially when judgments of different people conflict, as in beliefs about religion or public policy, at least one of the parties must be incorrect in some way. How can we protect ourselves against such errors? The answer, the essence of AOT, was provided by J. S. Mill in the quote above. And it applies in spades when we judge our leaders.

What is needed is cultural change (or prevention of such change in the wrong direction), perhaps beginning with the norms of the classroom, but also in the news media, in political discourse, and in everyday norms of discussion. Even in classrooms that emphasize respect for the views of others, more is needed. In particular, people must understand the justification of AOT, just as I have sketched it in here. They must learn the basic relation between fair reflection and justified confidence. And they must come to understand how potential leaders and authorities can be evaluated in these terms. Understanding of AOT is not like understanding rocket science. It is more the basic physics of mass, weight, volume, and density (as assessed in "Volume and heaviness" test based on Piaget's discoveries; as described by [44]).

Attempts to teach students, and others, to think better have been going on for some time, perhaps since the Renaissance [36]. Some recent efforts have been designed with the idea of increasing intelligence in mind, such as the "Venezuela project" [52]. Inspired by the writing and political activity of Luis Alberto Machado [53], the aim of this project was to increase intelligence by teaching thinking. An initial experiment in a large number of 7th grade classes was successful in raising IQ scores. But experiment did not lead to lasting changes in Venezuela's political system. A change of government led to the closing of the "Ministry of Intelligence" (headed by Machado), the source of its support within the government. And the Ministry of Education was not equipped to extend the program to new schools by further developing the materials.[9] Some time after the project closed, I attended a small meeting at Yale to discuss other ways of funding similar efforts elsewhere. (Japan and Saudi Arabia were mentioned as possibly interested. If only ...).

But it is not clear to me that this project could have provided an adequate basis for further development. An examination of the curriculum [54] suggests that the approach of this project was to "think of everything that might help and put it all together". This was a perfectly reasonable approach given the primary goal, which was to try to show that intelligence *could* be increased through an educational intervention. Many of the lessons concerned specific subject matter, such as language, mathematics, solving common types of problems, or creative writing. Very little was specifically directed at highly general dispositions such as those I have discussed, although it seems quite likely that many of these dispositions were affected, if only as side effects of instruction in specific tasks.

I think that what is needed now is a method of teaching thinking that is based on a clear and simple theory that teachers can understand, such as the AOT theory I have sketched here (or something similar). A few smaller experiments have tested such ideas. Selz [55] described a few relevant studies in which he directly tried to increase intelligence by training in problem solving. In one, an experimental and a control group of students, aged 11 to 13, were given an intelligence test consisting of completion problems (stories with words left out); word-ordering problems (arranging words into a sentence); verbal-analogy problems; and number-series completions. The experimental group was given training on only the completion problems for 1 h on each of two successive days. The training was designed to make students take into account the requirements of the task, checking each possible answer to see if these requirements were met. Subjects were taught both to explain why answers did not meet the requirements and to justify answers when they seemed to fit. After the training, a second intelligence test was given. The experimental group showed substantial improvement not only on the completion test, on which they were trained, but also on all of the others, to roughly the same extent. Apparently, the students learned to be more critical of initial possibilities, seeking evidence against them as well as looking for alternative possibilities.

Perkins et al. [17] taught high school students to think in an actively open-minded way through a sixteen-session course that emphasized searching thoroughly for arguments on both sides of an issue. Students were taught that the arguments they consider when thinking about a controversial issue should be true (to the best of the thinker's knowledge), relevant to the issue, and complete—that is, all important relevant arguments should be considered. Controversial issues were discussed in class, and students were explicitly encouraged to generate and evaluate (for truth and relevance) arguments on both sides, especially the other side. When students were asked to list arguments, the course nearly doubled the number of arguments that students gave on the other side from their own.

Gaskins and Baron conducted an 8-month training study in her school for reading-disabled children, the Benchmark School [22]. The teachers in the school (including Gaskins) identified three

---

[9] Personal communication from Prof. Jorge Dominguez (Harvard), who helped design the program and has followed education in Venezuela over the years.

cognitive styles that they felt were holding many children back from academic success, even when their initial reading problems had been largely corrected. We called these styles *impulsiveness, rigidity,* and *nonpersistence. Impulsiveness* consisted of failing to think sufficiently on an individual problem or when answering a question. *Rigidity* consisted of an unwillingness to consider alternatives to an initial possibility concerning how something should be done or about the truth of some issue. *Nonpersistence* was the failure to complete extended activities, such as seat-work assignments; it can be taken as a sign of lack of motivation. Our training program was designed to overcome these biases by emphasizing three slogans: "Take time to think"; "Consider alternatives"; and "Keep at it." The program was a success, according to teacher ratings of the styles we tried to train; the experimental group improved considerably and the control group hardly at all. The training also (weakly) affected ratings of academic performance given by teachers of children who had graduated from the Benchmark School and gone to other schools. In addition, children did slow down and take more time to think in a few different laboratory measures using tasks other than those used in training, including syllogisms and arithmetic word problems.

The Gaskins/Baron program was directed at both AOT and R/I, but the two others were directed at AOT. This is no coincidence, because their existence influences the development of the theory I sketched earlier. In sum, it seems that we can successfully teach AOT by encouraging it directly, and explaining to students why it helps.

To some extent, it could be argued that most people would learn how to think well on their own, but for the barriers set up by cultures that survive because they discourage questioning. Curiosity, for example, seems to be a common feature of childhood, yet parents and teachers often discourage it by telling children that certain questions should not be asked.

6. Conclusions

The Flynn effect may result from a kind of g factor of *influences* on IQ, including improvements in economic standard of living, public health, environmental quality, parental investment in children's education, and so on, all of which influence each other and indeed are also influenced by improvements in the entire battery of abilities and dispositions that constitute IQ (along the lines suggested by [41]).

AOT, as one of many components of IQ, may differ from the rest. Low acceptance of AOT is compatible with cultures that do well by the other criteria. (Saudi Arabia comes to mind.) Education can be economically useful without encouraging AOT. Thus, AOT will be subject to other influences, particularly the ebb and flow of the worldwide "culture wars". In those wars, it is on the side of the Enlightenment, and it is opposed by various traditions that emphasize the role of "the heart", "faith", "intuition" and (unquestioned) "authority". If we had been paying attention, we probably would have seen both increases and decreases in AOT in different social environments over the last century.

If AOT is part of a culture war, should its advocates be actively open-minded about the other side? Should we try to be "balanced" in our discussion of alternative ways of coming to have beliefs? There are many manifestations of this question, e.g., the controversy about whether reflective classroom discussion about the theory of evolution must give some time, or equal time, to creationism. Does equal time amount to "false balance"?

My answer is that the most important thing is to teach people to *understand* the arguments about why, and when, AOT is superior to other forms of reasoning. They must understand it as a "design" in Perkins' [56] sense. That is, they must know its purposes (coming up with the best answer, with appropriate confidence), its structure (testing, and revising or replacing, tentative conclusions, maintaining appropriate confidence, and so on) and the arguments about why this structure serves the purposes. Students can understand something without accepting it, so this is not indoctrination in its pure form. Of course, we do know what the outcome will be: if we teach understanding of some concept and test this understanding (as we must do, if we want to teach it effectively), then in fact more students will accept it. But we are applying our incentives to understanding, and acceptance is a beneficial side effect.

If the culture warriors from the other side challenge us, then we must argue with them respectfully, but firmly. Is AOT special in this way? Does instruction in physics and astronomy affect how people think about the cosmos, in ways that might conflict with religious doctrine? And, of course, we must ask why we should accept someone's conclusions if all the arguments for them come from their intuition or from historical longevity.

The benefits of increased AOT may show up in economic progress, but they will have special effects on politics. Citizens do not need to be very "smart" in the usual sense to know when they do not know something, and to figure out which authorities are trustworthy, by understanding what those authorities have done, or not done, to reach their conclusions. As I learned in college when I switched my major to psychology, psychology is easier than real science.

Conflicts of Interest: The author declares no conflict of interest.

References

1. Rice, S.E. Global poverty, weak states and insecurity. In *The Brookings Blum Roundtable. Session I: Poverty, Insecurity and Conflict*; The Brookings Institution: Washington, DC, USA, 2006.
2. Bicchieri, C. *The Grammar of Society: The Nature and Dynamics of Social Norms*; Cambridge University Press: New York, NY, USA, 2006.
3. Fisman, R.; Miguel, E. Corruption, norms, and legal enforcement: Evidence from diplomatic parking tickets. *J. Polit. Econ.* **2007**, *115*, 1020–1048. [CrossRef]
4. Caplan, B. *The Myth of the Rational Voter: Why Democracies Choose Bad Policies*; Princeton University Press: Princeton, NJ, USA, 2007.
5. Bazerman, M.H.; Baron, J.; Shonk, K. *You Can't Enlarge the Pie: The Psychology of Ineffective Government*; Basic Books: New York, NY, USA, 2001.
6. Baron, J. *Judgment Misguided: Intuition and Error in Public Decision Making*; Oxford University Press: New York, NY, USA, 1998.
7. Dasgupta, P.S.; Erlich, P.R. Pervasive externalities at the population, consumption, and environment nexus. *Science* **2013**, *340*, 324–328. [CrossRef]
8. Godfray, H.C.J.; Beddington, J.R.; Crute, I.R.; Haddad, L.; Lawrence, D.; Muir, J.F.; Pretty, J.; Robinson, S.; Thomas, S.M.; Toulmin, C. Food security: The challenge of feeding 9 billion people. *Science* **2010**, *327*, 812–818. [CrossRef]
9. Elster, J. *The Cement of Society: A Study of Social Order*; Cambridge University Press: New York, NY, USA, 1989.
10. Baron, J. Social norms for citizenship. *Soc. Res.* **2018**, *85*, 229–253.
11. Grossmann, I.; Na, J.; Varnum, M.E.W.; Kitayama, S.; Nisbett, R.E. A route to well-being: Intelligence vs. wise reasoning. *J. Exp. Psychol. Gen.* **2013**, *142*, 944–953. [CrossRef]
12. Baron, J. *Rationality and Intelligence*; Cambridge University Press: New York, NY, USA, 1985.
13. Baron, J. *Thinking and Deciding*, 4th ed.; Cambridge University Press: New York, NY, USA, 2008.
14. Sternberg, R.J. A balance theory of wisdom. *Rev. Gen. Psychol.* **1998**, *2*, 347–365. [CrossRef]
15. Halpern, D.F. Teaching critical thinking for transfer across domains. *Am. Psychol.* **1998**, *53*, 449–455. [CrossRef]
16. Hart, W.; Albarracín, D.; Eagly, A.H.; Brechan, I.; Lindberg, M.J.; Merrill, L. Feeling validated versus being correct: A meta-analysis of selective exposure to information. *Psychol. Bull.* **2009**, *135*, 555–588. [CrossRef]
17. Perkins, D.; Bushey, B.; Faraday, M. *Learning to Reason*; Final report, Grant No. NIE-G-83-0028, Project No. 030717; Harvard Graduate School of Education: Cambridge, MA, USA, 1986.
18. Gürçay-Morris, B. The Use of Alternative Reasons in Probabilistic Judgment. Ph.D. Dissertation, Department of Psychology, University of Pennsylvania, Philadelphia, PA, USA, 2016.
19. Lord, C.G.; Ross, L.; Lepper, M.R. Biased assimilation and attitude polarization: The effects of prior theories on subsequently considered evidence. *J. Personal. Soc. Psychol.* **1979**, *37*, 2098–2109. [CrossRef]
20. Meszaros, J.R.; Asch, D.A.; Baron, J.; Hershey, J.C.; Kunreuther, H.; Schwartz-Buzaglo, J. Cognitive processes and the decisions of some parents to forego pertussis vaccination for their children. *J. Clin. Epidemiol.* **1996**, *49*, 697–703. [CrossRef]
21. Baron, J. Belief overkill in political judgments. *Informal Logic* **2009**, *29*, 368–378. [CrossRef]

22. Baron, J.; Badgio, P.; Gaskins, I.W. Cognitive style and its improvement: A normative approach. In *Advances in the Psychology of Human Intelligence*; Sternberg, R.J., Ed.; Erlbaum: Hillsdale, NJ, USA, 1986; Volume 3, pp. 173–220.
23. Mellers, B.A.; Stone, E.; Atanasov, P.; Roghbaugh, N.; Metz, S.E.; Ungar, L.; Bishop, M.B.; Horowitz, M.; Merkle, E.; Tetlock, P.E. The psychology of intelligence analysis: Drivers of prediction accuracy in world politics. *J. Exp. Psychol. Appl.* **2015**, *21*, 1–14. [CrossRef]
24. Lichtenstein, S.; Fischhoff, B. Do those who know more also know more about how much they know? *Organ. Behav. Hum. Perform.* **1977**, *20*, 159–183. [CrossRef]
25. Koriat, A.; Lichtenstein, S.; Fischhoff, B. Reasons for confidence. *J. Exp. Psychol. Hum. Learn. Mem.* **1980**, *6*, 107–118. [CrossRef]
26. Baron, J.; Kemp, S. Support for trade restrictions, attitudes, and understanding of comparative advantage. *J. Econ. Psychol.* **2004**, *25*, 565–580. [CrossRef]
27. Bazerman, M.H.; Neale, M.A. *Negotiating Rationality*; Free Press: New York, NY, USA, 1992.
28. Baron, J. Beliefs about thinking. In *Informal Reasoning and Education*; Voss, J.F., Perkins, D.N., Segal, J.W., Eds.; Erlbaum: Hillsdale, NJ, USA, 1991; pp. 169–186.
29. Baron, J. Myside bias in thinking about abortion. *Think. Reason.* **1995**, *1*, 221–235. [CrossRef]
30. Stanovich, K.E.; West, R.F. Reasoning independently of prior belief and individual differences in actively open-minded thinking. *J. Educ. Psychol.* **1997**, *89*, 342–357. [CrossRef]
31. Stanovich, K.E.; West, R.F. Individual differences in rational thought. *J. Exp. Psychol. Gen.* **1998**, *127*, 161–188. [CrossRef]
32. Toplak, M.E.; West, R.F.; Stanovich, K.E. Rational thinking and cognitive sophistication: Development, cognitive abilities, and thinking dispositions. *Dev. Psychol.* **2014**, *50*, 1037–1048. [CrossRef]
33. Stanovidh, K.E. The comprehensive assessment of rational thinking. *Educ. Psychol.* **2016**, *51*, 23–34. [CrossRef]
34. Haran, U.; Ritov, I.; Mellers, B.A. The role of actively open-minded thinking in information acquisition, accuracy, and calibration. *Judg. Decis. Mak.* **2013**, *8*, 188–201.
35. Baron, J.; Scott, S.; Fincher, K.; Metz, S.E. Why does the Cognitive Reflection Test (sometimes) predict utilitarian moral judgment (and other things)? *J. Appl. Res. Mem. Cogn.* **2015**, *4*, 265–284. [CrossRef]
36. Baron, J. Why teach thinking?—An essay. *Appl. Psychol.* **1993**, *42*, 191–237. [CrossRef]
37. Mill, J. S. *On Liberty*; J. W. Parker & Son: London, UK, 1859.
38. Pennycook, G.; Cheyne, J.A.; Barr, N.; Koehler, D.J.; Fugelsang, J.A. On the reception and detection of pseudo-profound bullshit. *Judg. Decis. Mak.* 2015, 10, 549–563.
39. Pennycook, G.; Cheyne, J.A.; Barr, N.; Koehler, D.J.; Fugelsang, J.A. It's still bullshit: Reply to Dalton (2016). *Judg. Decis. Mak.* **2016**, *11*, 123–125.
40. Sunstein, C.R. Deliberative democracy in the trenches. *Daedalus* **2017**, *146*, 129–139. [CrossRef]
41. Pietschnig, J.; Voracek, M. One century of global IQ gains: A formal meta-analysis of the Flynn effect. *Perspect. Psychol. Sci.* **2015**, *10*, 282–306. [CrossRef]
42. Flynn, J.R.; Shayer, M. IQ decline and Piaget: Does the rot start at the top? *Intelligence* **2018**, *66*, 112–121. [CrossRef]
43. Woodley of Menie, M.A.; Peñaherrera-Aguirre, M.; Fernandes, H.B.F.; Figueredo, A.-J. What causes the anti-Flynn effect? A data synthesis and analysis of predictors. *Evol. Behav. Sci.* **2017**. [CrossRef]
44. Shayer, M.; Ginsburg, G. Thirty years on—a large anti-Flynn effect/(II): 13- and 14-year-olds. Piagetian tests of formal operations norms 1976–2006/7. *Br. J. Educ. Psychol.* **2009**, *79*, 409–418. [CrossRef]
45. Baron, J.; Gürçay, B.; Metz, S.E. Reflection, intuition, and actively open-minded thinking. In *Individual Differences in Judgment and Decision Making from a Developmental Context*; Toplak, M., Weller, J., Eds.; Routledge: New York, NY, USA, 2017; pp. 107–126.
46. Sá, W.C.; West, R.F.; Stanovich, K.E. The domain specificity and generality of belief bias: Searching for a generalizable thinking skill. *J. Educ. Psychol.* **1999**, *91*, 497–510. [CrossRef]
47. Pennycook, G.; Fugelsang, J.A.; Koehler, D.J. Everyday consequences of analytic thought. *Curr. Dir. Psychol. Sci.* **2015**, *24*, 425–432. [CrossRef]
48. Jensen, A.R. *Bias in Mental Testing*; Free Press: New York, NY, USA, 1980.
49. Baron, J. Comment on Kahan and Corbin: Can polarization increase with actively open-minded thinking? *Res. Polit.* **2017**, *4*. [CrossRef]

50. Suedfeld, P.; Tetlock, P.E. Integrative complexity of communications in international crises. *J. Confl. Resolut.* **1977**, *21*, 169–184. [CrossRef]
51. Thoemmes, F.J.; Conway, L.J., III. Integrative complexity of 41 U.S. presidents. *Polit. Psychol.* **2007**, *28*, 193–226. [CrossRef]
52. Herrnstein, R.J.; Nickerson, R.S.; de Sánchez, M.; Swets, J.A. Teaching thinking skills. *Am. Psychol.* **1986**, *41*, 1279–1289. [CrossRef]
53. Machado, L.A. *The Right to Be Intelligent*; Pergamon Press: Oxford, UK, 1980.
54. Adams, M.J. (Ed.) *Odyssey: A Curriculum for Thinking*; Charlesbridge Publishing: Watertown, MA, USA, 1986; Volumes 1–6.
55. Selz, O. Versuche zur Hebung des Intelligenzniveaus: Ein Beitrag zur Theorie der Intelligenz und ihrer erziehlichen Beeinflussung. *Z. Psychol.* **1935**, *134*, 236–301.
56. Perkins, D.N. *Knowledge as Design: Critical and Creative Thinking for Teachers and Learners*; Erlbaum: Hillsdale, NJ, USA, 1986.

Journal of
Intelligence

MDPI

Perspective

The Strengths of Wisdom Provide Unique Contributions to Improved Leadership, Sustainability, Inequality, Gross National Happiness, and Civic Discourse in the Face of Contemporary World Problems

Igor Grossmann [1,*] and Justin P. Brienza [2]

1   Department of Psychology, University of Waterloo, Waterloo, ON N2L 3G1, Canada
2   Lazaridis School of Business and Economics, Wilfrid Laurier University, Waterloo, ON N2L 3C7, Canada;
     jbrienza@wlu.ca
*   Correspondence: igrossma@uwaterloo.ca

Received: 5 February 2018; Accepted: 29 March 2018; Published: 9 April 2018

Abstract: We present evidence for the strengths of the intellectual virtues that philosophers and behavioral scientists characterize as key cognitive elements of wisdom. Wisdom has been of centuries-long interest for philosophical scholarship, but relative to intelligence largely neglected in public discourse on educational science, public policy, and societal well-being. Wise reasoning characteristics include intellectual humility, recognition of uncertainty, consideration of diverse viewpoints, and an attempt to integrate these viewpoints. Emerging scholarship on these features of wisdom suggest that they uniquely contribute to societal well-being, improve leadership, shed light on societal inequality, promote cooperation in Public Goods Games and reduce political polarization and intergroup-hostility. We review empirical evidence about macro-cultural, ecological, situational, and person-level processes facilitating and inhibiting wisdom in daily life. Based on this evidence, we speculate about ways to foster wisdom in education, organizations, and institutions.

Keywords: wisdom; reasoning; virtues; well-being; political polarization; culture; social class; egocentrism; leadership

1. Introduction

As the world is approaching the end of the second decade of the 21st century, human progress in scientific knowledge and medicine has contributed to the lowest levels of disease-based mortality, illiteracy, extreme poverty [1], as well as a shift from patriarchal to emancipative values [2]. For instance, medical advances and success in containing the spread of infectious diseases have been linked to greater gender equality in many countries around the world [3]. At the same time, advances in science and technology have contributed to the increasing complexity of world affairs. Nuclear energy has provided great prosperity to many countries but also provokes worry about the demise of humanity in the case of a nuclear strike. Instant availability and ever-increasing wealth of information through traditional and social media has made us smarter but has also contributed to skepticism of "fake news" and has facilitated partisanship and increasing political polarization in many Western countries [4–7]. As the world entered the year 2018, the Secretary-General of the United Nations, António Guterres issued a "red alert". Guterres pointed out a deepening of conflicts, growing inequalities, increasing xenophobia and nationalism, violations of human rights, and global anxieties of nuclear weapons being at the highest since the end of the Cold War [8].

Arguably, the advances in sciences, medicine, and technology reflect shifts in overall levels of human intelligence. At the same time, as the introductory article to this special issue indicates [9], the ever-increasing complexity of social and political affairs suggest that intelligence alone is not sufficient to solve the contemporary, "ill-defined" problems people are facing on the interpersonal and intergroup levels. These problems are ill-defined (or ill-structured) due to numerous unknown parameters preventing an easy formula-based solution to a problem [10]. As a brief glimpse at the history of the last century indicates, technological and medical advances have often been accompanied by massive-scale suffering and misery. Social critiques point out that the same culture that promoted advances in medicine and technology contributed to a breakdown of ecological systems, species extinction, as well as toxic waste and pollution (e.g., [11]). Balancing gains in intelligence and power requires wisdom—a seemingly ancient, yet empirically understudied concept [12]. Infusing wisdom into the public discourse can provide policy-makers with critical tools for addressing ill-defined challenges facing the world today.

1.1. A Cautionary Preface

Intelligence and wisdom can have many faces. Even specialist scholars exploring either concept cannot reach perfect agreement on the nuances. Intelligence can mean logic, planning, understanding, learning, reasoning, but also self-awareness, emotional knowledge, creativity, and problem solving (e.g., [13,14]), though much of the mainstream science of intelligence focuses on some common underlying cognitive factor(s) (e.g., [15,16]). Similarly, wisdom can refer to cultural norms and values, intuitions, life experience, autobiographic narratives, emotion regulation, and moral concerns (for reviews, see [12,17–19]). In the present article, we use a narrow definition of wisdom, focusing on higher-order cognition. We do this for several reasons. First, by focusing on the reasoning aspects of wisdom affording sound judgment, we aim to unpack key psychological constituents in the Platonian and Aristotelian concepts of wisdom (readily admitting that our narrow attempt will provide only an incomplete portrayal of these philosophical underpinnings [20]). Second, narrowing the focus on cognition allows us to remain in the same realm when comparing psychological processes involved in intelligence and wisdom. Third, cognitive aspects of wisdom appear to be most common to the recent characterizations of wisdom both in psychology and in cross-cultural lay views of wisdom [17] (for an updated review of common characteristics, see [21]). However, we caution the reader that the findings reviewed below do not speak to the notion of wisdom writ large, though arguably some of the processes discussed below may also play an important role for such wisdom-related concepts as effective emotion regulation (for instance, [22], for a review, see [23] and morality, e.g., [24]).

In what follows, we start by drawing a distinction between mainstream views of cognitive processes characterizing intelligence and wisdom in reasoning (wise reasoning from here on). We proceed by highlighting possible societal benefits of wise reasoning for public policy, focusing on five domains: Gross National Happiness, leadership, sustainability, inequality, and civic discourse. At the end, we build on recent evidence about ways to facilitate wise reasoning to showcase how societies can educate for wise reasoning.

1.2. Wisdom Complements Intelligence: A Case for Wise Reasoning

At least since Aristotle, philosophers have speculated that people require certain forms of reflection or reasoning when navigating the complex dilemmas and trade-offs they encounter in social life (for a cross-cultural perspective, see [21], for a selective review, see [25]). One may wonder, however, whether philosophic characterizations of such cognitive processes map on to the mainstream definition of intelligence favored in the behavioral and education sciences. For philosophers like Aristotle, superior reasoning is characterized by its wisdom. What does such wise reasoning entail and how is it distinct from the mainstream definitions of intelligence? Like intelligence, wisdom requires at least a basic level of general knowledge and the application of logic. At the same time, philosophers and some behavioral scientists are quick to point out that neither general knowledge nor logic should be confused with wisdom (e.g., [26–33]). Behavioral scientists have proposed that wisdom uniquely involves context-sensitive processing of knowledge, enabling understanding and navigating the complexities of one's social world [28,30,34]. In ancient Greece, this feature of wisdom has been described by Aristotle as *phronesis* and in the modern scholarship, it is often characterized as a pragmatic capacity to balance and integrate diverse viewpoints in a way that enables one to work through the challenges of social life [35].

When empirical scientists started to become interested in wisdom, scholars were quick to distinguish wise from intelligent (or analytical) reasoning. Scholars like Clayton suggested that mainstream definitions of intelligence focus on abstract symbolic rules and procedures such as propositional logic [30,36]. Abstract logic and other domain-general abilities are advantageous when solving well-structured problems in which all parameters in the evaluative space are known [37]. Thus, in the well-defined situations surrounding financial or technical decisions, features of intelligence such as superior knowledge (e.g., financial literacy, specialized knowledge of physics and engineering) and logic can promote an optimal decision. However, if decisions concern questions of social rather than purely financial or technical nature, these domain-general abilities may be insufficient for a sound decision.

Social issues typically involve other people who may have opinions and interests differing from one's own—they are ill-structured. Ill-structured problems can concern value trade-offs, unclear means or end-goals, or other situations with incomplete information for a decision [38]. Here, features of abstract reasoning such as symbolic rules and propositional logic can be of little help. Instead of applying a general rule, one may rather benefit from ways to enhance one's sensitivity to and integration of contextual contingencies. Under such circumstances, abstract cognition may be augmented by metacognitive strategies affording open, nuanced, and dynamic processing of information [17,25,30,36,39–41]: Epistemic humility, recognition of varied contexts of life and how they change over time, and open-mindedness toward the possibility of multiple outcomes of a situation and the different viewpoints other people bring to the table (see Table 1).

To illustrate this point, consider the following letter sent to an advice columnist Abigail Van Buren:

> My husband is very political, and around election time he becomes engrossed in news shows. He has a habit of showing his favorite political news clips to friends when they visit. I am uncomfortable with this, as I feel our friends are too polite to decline, and they allow my husband to preach politics to them out of courtesy to the host. They are like-minded, politically speaking, and the few who aren't are not going to be swayed by comedy news shows. I excuse myself from the room when he begins his sermons. I have asked him to stop doing this when friends visit, but he refuses. How can I persuade him to just have "friends time" with no politics? (adopted from [41])

A wise reasoning approach to this issue may start by realizing that one may not know enough about the husband's motives or the political issues he aims to promote. One may also consider how such behavior may be temporary, and how the husband acted differently in the past and may again act differently in the future. Finally, one may focus on the perspectives of friends involved in the situation and search for a way to balance both the husband's and their friends' interests. As becomes evident, a wise reasoning approach does not necessarily advocate for a single solution. Instead, it facilitates attention to the bigger picture surrounding the situation and the balance of different perspectives and interests.

An intelligent approach to the same problem could take a similar path. Yet, it is equally plausible too that a *self-focused* intelligent person would start searching for the best pieces of evidence in support of one's request, possibly enumerating the times the husband has demonstrated the disturbing pattern of behavior. Such an approach can result in a fallacy known as a confirmation bias [42], making it antithetical to a wise judgment [43]. Moreover, such an approach can likely backfire, threatening the husband, and possibly motivating him to focus only on friends who endorse his viewpoints or even to start keeping track of all the unpleasant experiences he has with his partner. Instead of bringing the spouses closer and helping figure out a solution that would work for them and their friends, an intelligent approach may, in fact, ruin the respective relationships.

It appears that domain-general cognition does *not necessarily* translate into the context-sensitive processing of information characterized in the wise reasoning approach above. We summarize the common features of the latter approach in Table 1, providing a few examples for a possible manifestation of each feature. Central to these features is their fostering of greater sensitivity to contextual (interpersonal and intertemporal) contingencies, providing greater insight into the complex nature of the uncertain situation at hand. We should note that this conceptualization of wise reasoning aligns with the neo-Piagetian theorizing on features of mature thought in developmental psychology [39,44] and builds on the conceptualization of wisdom-related knowledge advanced by Baltes and colleagues [28,45], avoiding conflation of declarative knowledge with meta-cognitive strategies utilized when working through ill-structured situations/dilemma. It also shared cognitive features with other models of wisdom in the psychological literature [26,46,47] (for a more nuanced comparison of different models of wisdom in behavioral sciences, see [48]).

Table 1. Features, definition, and possible manifestations of wise reasoning in everyday life, represented by frequently co-occurring aspects of cognition.

Feature	Definition	Possible Manifestation
Intellectual humility	Recognition of limits of one's knowledge	• Double-checking whether one's opinion on the situation might be incorrect. • Searching for extraordinary circumstances before forming an opinion
Recognition of uncertainty and change	Recognition that contexts change over time; open-mindedness about direction of change	• Searching for different solutions as the situation evolves • Considering alternative ways a situation may unfold
Perspective-taking of diverse viewpoints	Open-mindedness toward different viewpoints on an issue	• Making effort to take the other persons' perspective(s) • Taking time to get different opinions on the matter before coming to a conclusion
Integration of different viewpoints	Search for a compromise between different interests at stake for the issue	• Considering whether a compromise is possible in resolving the situation • Searching for a solution that could result in most of the interests being satisfied (acknowledging that this may not always be possible)

Using a range of methods to measure these features of reasoning [25,30,41,48,49], the empirical studies provided support the idea that these features of reasoning explain a unique portion of variance on measures of cognitive and personality-related individual differences, showing weak positive relations between wise reasoning and standard measures of intelligence and related physiological processes [43,50–52], as well as established individual difference constructs such as the Big Five personality traits (e.g., "openness to new experiences" or "agreeableness") [49].

2. Policy-Making

Wise reasoning can provide unique societal benefits when facing challenges in intergroup relations, at work, and those faced by members of a society in their personal lives. Below, we point to recent evidence suggesting that reasoning aspects of wisdom may be particularly relevant for coping with social challenges of relevance for public policy. We would like to touch on five domains in which we see wisdom-related insights of particular relevance: Gross National Happiness; leadership, sustainability, inequality, and civic discourse.

2.1. Gross National Happiness

The economic wealth of a nation does not necessarily correspond to the levels of well-being of people living in a given country. This led several countries such as Bhutan to start exploring ways to facilitate the Gross National Happiness—i.e., the well-being of its citizens [53]. Bhutan is not alone. In 2011, the UN passed a resolution "Happiness: towards a holistic approach to development," aiming to encourage political leaders to find ways to promote the well-being of their constituents. Worldwide, surveys such as the OECD Better Life Index or the Social Progress Index by the non-profit Social Process Initiative highlight the rising awareness of societal well-being.

Research from the last two decades has begun to identify a range of unique benefits of wise reasoning for improving well-being. One should note that large-scale studies failed to observe a positive relationship between scores on mainstream intelligence tests and well-being (e.g., [54–56]), suggesting that rising levels of intelligence in many Western nations do not need to correspond to societal shifts in well-being. In contrast, newer empirical scholarship has started to indicate that having a *wiser* outlook on life can yield benefits to well-being. Higher scores on the wisdom-related characteristics reviewed in Table 1 have been positively linked to reports of greater interpersonal well-being [51], superior emotion regulation [57], and lower intensity of negative emotions [51,58]. Until recently, cross-sectional studies could not yield a conclusive picture concerning the relationship between wise reasoning and positive emotions or life satisfaction [51,57,59,60]. However, new national longitudinal data suggests that among U.S. Americans a wise outlook on life (i.e., being intellectually humble, recognizing change in the world, and considering different perspectives) predicts an increase in positive emotions and life satisfaction over the course of 20 years [61]. Overall, these observations support the philosophical model of wisdom as a set of features that promote a "good" life [17,62,63]. These findings suggest that Gross National Happiness can be promoted by fostering and educating for wise reasoning in a society.

2.2. Leadership

We argue that wise reasoning may provide an edge in managing contemporary leadership challenges. Leadership not only requires decision making about regulations and policies. Leaders also serve as models and guides by which business and society can change for the better, thereby impacting people's values, attitudes, and behavior. Throughout history, leaders who demonstrated epistemic humility and an ability to face up to complexity and change, inspired societal cooperation, and showed concern for the greater good have been marked as most influential, admired, and wise (e.g., Gandhi; Martin Luther King, Jr.) [64]. Contemporary leadership requires wisdom to tackle the challenges of life in the 21st century: the increasing rate of change and uncertainty in business, politics and civic affairs, the need to motivate cooperation among and between increasingly diverse stakeholders, and growing concern for bigger-picture, ethical and socially responsible decision making.

Wise leadership. Wisdom-related qualities play a role in overcoming leadership challenges and can contribute to leaders' outstanding success. As an example, consider that Anne Mulcahy is credited with keeping the Xerox Corporation afloat by successfully navigating the financial and ethical challenges the company faced in the early 2000s. Taking over the CEO role, Mulcahy was advised to take the easy route and declare bankruptcy. Taking a bigger-picture perspective, Mulcahy recognized that such a decision could have ruined the company and any long-term prospects for a viable future. She displayed intellectual humility by personally meeting with stakeholders, allowing them to voice their concerns, heeding advice, taking personal responsibility and apologizing for the company's past mistakes. She set a firm commitment to ethics, human rights, and sustainable business practice, including righting past wrongs (e.g., in accounting and social irresponsibility). "By doing the right thing for our stakeholders (i.e., more than just stockholders) and the global community," she said, "we're also doing what's right for our business" [65]. Mulcahy has been widely recognized and praised for her actions (e.g., CEO of the year award, 2008), yet humbly defers credit to her colleagues and subordinates, having said that her success "represents the impressive accomplishments of Xerox people around the world." It appears that Anne Mulcahy's intellectual humility in the face of complex challenges, accommodation of different perspectives, needs, and values, all played a significant role during the critical moment in allowing her to harness positive outcomes for a company in trouble and herself. The company remained stable for a few years after Mulcahy's retirement in 2009, fighting an up-fill battle in the post-print digital age.

Foolish leadership. One can juxtapose such examples of wisdom in leadership (also see the Fortune's 2017 "World's Greatest Leaders" column) [66] with examples of massive failures resulting from leaders' neglect of wisdom-related qualities and an excessive focus on self-promotion. Notably, many of the examples in Fortune's 2016 "Most Disappointing Leaders" [67] find their place in the list explained by factors described in the introduction to this special issue as foundations of foolishness—i.e., the opposite of wisdom [9]. These leaders appear to hold high levels of intelligence, yet fail in their jobs, succumbing to numerous fallacies. We discuss some examples below.

Martin Winterkorn, the former chairman of the board of directors of Volkswagen, seems to have fallen prey to the *omnipotence fallacy* (i.e., a belief that one is invulnerable and can do whatever they want), and the ethical disengagement fallacy (i.e., a belief that ethics are essential for others but not the self) in his handling of the company's diesel fraud case. As Fortune notes, despite a reputation for being a micromanager, Winterkorn denied any wrongdoing or knowledge of wrongdoing. Other examples provided by Fortune similarly fell prey to at least one fallacy. For instance, Michigan Governor Rick Snyder was held responsible for sacrificing public health and safety for economic face-saving and then shifting blame, thereby exhibiting the ethical disengagement fallacy. It appears that the neglect of wisdom in favor of myopic decision making does not support long-term success for the greater community, nor oneself.

Variability in leadership. Even the wisest leaders cannot be wise at all times and in all matters. Indeed, one of the most famous examples, King Solomon, was known for both his wisdom and his foolishness in personal life [68]. This asymmetry is evident in many leaders to whom we typically attribute wisdom (e.g., Gandhi, Martin Luther King, Jr., Mother Theresa).

The observation of variability in wisdom may sound paradoxical: After all, is not "true wisdom" stable? Indeed, in many cultures virtue-based qualities like wisdom are linked to the concept of a morally good "true self" [69,70]—a "robust, invariant tendency to believe that inside every individual there is a "true self" calling them to behave in morally virtuous ways" [71]. Notably, this belief is rooted in psychological essentialism, which is a fundamental cognitive bias assuming that "all entities have deep, unobservable, inherent properties that comprise their true nature" [71], and which may not at all reflect the empirical reality of a virtuous characteristic.

Indeed, in everyday life, people's ability to express wisdom-related epistemic virtues, such as intellectual humility, open-mindedness or the ability to consider a wide range of perspectives on a challenging issue, varies dramatically [57]. As Figure 1 indicates, the variability within a person across several days is at least as large if not larger than the variability between people in their average tendency to express wisdom-related characteristics. This is not to say that there are no trait-level components of wise judgment [49]. Rather, based on the density distribution perspective of individual differences [72], traits may be represented through the unique density distribution profiles of individuals, including unique responses to various situational contingencies [73]. Thus, when discussing wise leadership, is not our intention to discount leaders who are otherwise remarkable and characterize them as fools after singular signs of folly, nor is it our intention to suggest that wise leaders have no faults. Rather, we argue for a pragmatic and evidence-based evaluation of leadership qualities, drawing a connection between the use of wisdom-related attributes and successful leadership (even as judged by sources who are not wisdom scholars), and the relationship between neglect of such attributes and large-scale failure. Moreover, we suggest that awareness of the variability in wisdom-related characteristics and other virtue-based attributes [72] may promote a more contextualized picture of wisdom exemplars in business, politics, and civic discourse.

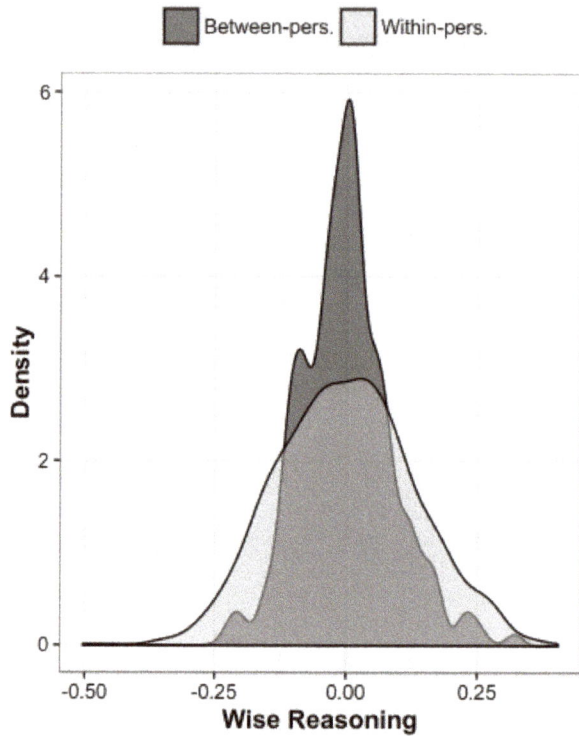

Figure 1. Density distribution of wise reasoning (intellectual humility, consideration of uncertainty/change, perspective-taking) in everyday life, based on reflections about the most challenging issues people encountered across nine days. Within-pers. = Variability of person's scores from their mean. Between-pers. = Between-person variability in person's average responses across nine days. Adopted from [58].

2.3. Sustainability

The current attention to climate change and issues of resource scarcity raise new and urgent questions about how such decisions contribute to integration of short-term and long-term sustainability—i.e., protection of natural resources, while simultaneously improving services and well-being of the most people [74]. The Intergovernmental Panel on Climate Change outlined such concerns in their most recent report, which warned that "delaying global mitigation actions may reduce options for climate-resilient pathways and adaptation in the future" [75].

Questions of sustainability are intertwined with complex social, economic, political, and ecological systems, meaning that they will require more attention to uncertainty, flux, and the bigger picture in which these dilemmas are set [74]. Indeed, as identified at the 2005 World Summit on Social Development, sustainability goals can refer to the balance of economic, environmental, and social goals [76]. Sustainability researchers like Gibson [74] have suggested that a sustainable world view is about intertwined means and ends, embedded in a world of complexity and surprise that requires recognition of links and interdependencies. In Gibson's view, solutions to sustainability dilemmas depend on context. To craft an adaptive style of sustainability capable of addressing modern environmental issues, one may, therefore, benefit from a capacity for wise reasoning, which directly targets the topics of uncertainties, context, complexities, and multiple perspectives in a proactive manner [30], and can help to identify the balance between such diverse interpersonal, interpersonal, and extrapersonal interests [12,49].

2.4. Inequality, Wisdom and Social Class

The driving force behind the global shifts toward greater individualism in industrialized and post-industrial countries appears to involve a rise in the economic prosperity of the country [77,78] (for a review, see [79]). The more affluent a society becomes on average, the higher the shift in the mainstream culture of this society toward greater individualism. Of course, increasing affluence does not equally affect all strata of the population, such that in countries like the U.S., economic inequality is on the rise despite substantial economic growth over the course of the last century [80,81]. Such growing inequality has consequences both for the individual and the society at large, as revealed by many studies concerning the relationship of wisdom and social class.

Research conducted in the U.S., Europe, and East Asia has demonstrated that people with higher socioeconomic status (SES) focus more on the self vs. others [82–87], and attend less to contextual features in their social environment [22,88,89].

Drawing on these observations, recent work starts to indicate substantial class differences in the propensity of applying wisdom in reasoning about interpersonal conflicts. Whereas prior research indicated that higher socioeconomic status typically promotes better performance on standardized intelligence tasks (e.g., [90,91]), this newer work starts to suggest a reverse pattern for wise reasoning.

Brienza and Grossmann [92] hypothesized that people with lower (rather than higher) SES would express wiser reasoning about interpersonal conflict situations as it would provide them with an ecological adaptation to secure survival and success in a resource-poor environment. To test their hypothesis, the researchers conducted two studies, involving (i) personality-style assessment of wisdom-related characteristics with a survey on participants' reflections on recent interpersonal transgressions, and (ii) performance-based assessment of stream-of-thought reflections on standardized interpersonal and intergroup dilemmas [93]. Across both studies, higher SES (Study 1: composite of level of education and income; Study 2: level of education) was associated with significantly lower wise reasoning scores, even when controlling for gender and age, social desirability, emotional intelligence, agreeableness, and abstract cognitive abilities (e.g., executive functioning and crystallized IQ). Moreover, the effect of social class on wise reasoning was at least in part accounted for by a greater sense of social attunement expressed by participants with lower SES.

The observation of social class differences in wise reasoning about interpersonal matters is noteworthy, as it suggests some drawbacks of the contemporary cultural trends in the Western world. As mainstream culture continues shifting toward greater self-focus and individualism, emphasizing uniqueness, individual achievement, and self-serving rationality [94] (but see [95]), it may inadvertently erode wisdom despite the growing complexity of our social world. More specifically, it suggests that people who are more likely to wield the executive power of leadership are especially in danger of making foolish decisions when faced with complex, ill-structured situations. To combat these trends, it appears prudent to (a) allocate more resources to promoting greater inclusiveness of individuals from a broader range of social strata in leadership positions, education, and public policy; and (b) shift societal discourse on social inequality from a "deficiency model," representing lower social class individuals solely as a "deficient" and "vulnerable" group [96–98] to an inclusive model recognizing the unique strengths and vulnerabilities of *each* social strata [99]. Failure to promote inclusivity in such areas as leadership, education, and public policy, and to utilize the strengths and address the vulnerabilities of each social strata, may contribute to further social division, inequality, and societal conflict, and will limit our ability to develop insightful solutions to complex contemporary societal problems.

2.5. Civic Discourse

We believe that one of the threats preventing inclusivity on the societal level concerns shifts in political polarization, tribalism, and apathy observed in the civic discourse in North America and Western Europe over the course of the last several decades [4,6,100]. Here we discuss possible ways wise reasoning could be useful for combating these trends.

Political and other group-related polarization has been heightening globally, inflaming intergroup hostilities. Polarization causes clashes and conflicts and threatens societies from making balanced decisions that benefit the greater good (as opposed to single groups). Political and ideological polarization threaten integrative solutions to issues of utmost importance, including health care, inclusivity and effective diversity management, human rights and infrastructure improvements for lower class citizens, immigration and refuge for victims of war, and the list goes on. We suggest that wise reasoning may broaden one's perspective beyond a limited tribal scope by promoting bipartisanship and attenuating within-group polarization toward solutions that result in shared, collective benefits.

Some initial evidence has shown that wise reasoning may serve such a purpose. As compared to intelligence, wisdom also appears to be uniquely associated with prosocial and eudaimonic tendencies (e.g., cooperative intentions and behavior, growth orientation; [49,101–103]), a willingness to forgive friends and family members one has a dispute with [57], as well as more prosocial behavior in economic transactions [104]. Moreover, and particularly pertinent to intergroup issues, wisdom is associated with reduced political bias [105], reduced intergroup attitude polarization across several heightened intergroup conflicts [106] (unpublished manuscript), and the willingness to consider diverse viewpoints during political elections in the US [107], with such aspects of wise reasoning as an appreciation of diverse viewpoints facilitating accuracy in the forecasting of geopolitical events [108].

In several studies, researchers have also found that wise reasoning relates to reduced intergroup bias [106]. The tests were conducted at times of heightened political, ideological, and other group conflicts, each time finding that wise reasoning related to lower or absence of outgroup hostility, improved positivity toward outgroups and moderated "ingroup love." One study was conducted in the context of the 2015 Baltimore, US, protests, sparked by police violence against Black Americans. In this study, low wise reasoning about the events was linked to extremely unfavorable attitudes toward police among people who identified strongly with the protesters, and unfavorable attitudes toward protesters among people who identified strongly with the police. Conversely, high wise reasoning about the events was linked to less polarized and more balanced intergroup attitudes. This attenuation of polarization did not result in more apathy toward the events or peoples involved: across the different groups, wise reasoning consistently related to greater endorsement that society should use these events as motivation to pursue progress and change rather than the status-quo. Further, reduced polarization via wise reasoning was found to relate to increased acceptance, willingness to associate with, and support for public policy to benefit the (minority) outgroup. These initial findings were replicated across different cultures, ethnicities, and conflicts, and controlling for a host of different demographics (e.g., SES, age, gender) and individual differences in variables known to play a role in intergroup bias (e.g., lay theories of malleability and change in ethnicity).

It is possible that nudging wise reasoning at a societal level could undermine some of the foundations of group polarization. As the classic studies on intergroup conflict indicate, intergroup conflict tends to emerge when members of both groups view resources as a limited zero-sum (for a review, see [109]), whereby resources gained by one party are viewed as losses by another party [110]. By inducing wise reasoning, it is possible that one can shift a view of resources from a zero-sum perspective to a more interdependent, non-zero-sum perspective, as we have recently shown in a related domain of cooperation in a Public Goods Game [104]. It is possible that fostering wise reasoning can help to reduce the tendency to view outgroups as driven by more hate and polarization than ingroups (e.g., [111]), which could result in less reactive intergroup attitudes and behavior (e.g., self-protective aggression). It may also help people to avoid limiting their own perspectives through self-created echo-chambers (e.g., [4]) and increase their open-mindedness to select a broad network of associates with different, more diverse viewpoints.

This emerging work starts to suggest that wise reasoning may play a role for moderating the rampant polarization visible in various parts of the world by broadening people's purview about who or what is deserving of the care and compassion that groups tend only to give to their immediate ingroup or tribe. We suggest that modeling, nudging, as well as promoting wise reasoning (as compared to self-serving rationality [95]) may allow us to overcome polarization in favor of amicable solutions that benefit society at large, and potentially most significantly to the less fortunate.

3. Paths to Wisdom

The unique strengths of wisdom highlighted above suggest potential applications to contemporary individual and societal challenges. They also suggest directions for future research in such domains as leadership, education, and sustainability, and promoting inclusive social-organizational policies and programs meant to maximize the benefits (e.g., progress and innovation) and reduce the pitfalls (e.g., bias and conflict) of an increasingly diverse society. We discuss some of these applications and future directions below.

3.1. Education

Is it possible to educate for wisdom in handling contemporary business and societal problems? Business schools provide courses in organizational behavior and human resource management that attempt to engage students in critical thinking (e.g., about their own biases) and communicate balanced, ethical decisions that benefit the self and the greater good. However interesting and well-meaning these courses may be, their effectiveness for guiding wise decision making may be occluded by a hard focus on the notion of economic, self-interested rationality [95,112] as a chief basis for sound judgment in the majority of courses students are required to complete (e.g., [94]). Social critiques suggest that such unitary focus on de-contextualized, self-interested reasoning and decision-making is widely spread in the Western societies, including in school curricula [113–115], poorly preparing students for facing the uncertainties and complexities of the ill-structured social world. Indeed, empirical work indicates that Western education promotes higher performance on tests of de-contextualized intelligence, but does so at the expense of fostering social responsibility [116].

It may be the case that what is missing in training is the notion of *reasonableness* as discussed by modern philosophers [117–120], which views just decisions as those that balance economic pursuits with humility and concern for the common good. We suggest that instruction on the benefits of wise reasoning (e.g., for education, management and leadership)—care and attention to, and integration of, different perspectives and needs, intellectual humility and acknowledging uncertainty and change, and a bigger-picture outlook—may provide a necessary toolkit that students can use to balance self-interested and cooperative goals. Based on the recent empirical evidence, below we discuss potential methods for inducing or training wise reasoning.

Fostering wisdom by reducing egocentrism. Over the course of the last decade, research has repeatedly shown that one factor can profoundly impact wise reasoning. This factor concerns the degree to which a person focuses on the self. Both in observational and experimental studies, greater self-focus has led to a lower expression of wisdom-related characteristics. For instance, examining diary entries on the most challenging events of a day revealed that people are less likely to reason wisely when they were surrounded by strangers compared to situations involving co-workers, family, or friends as well [57]. Similarly, when presented with interpersonal transgression scenarios concerning infidelity and trust betrayal, people show lower wisdom when transgressions involve them personally as compared to transgressions involving a close friend [121]. In such scenarios, one is particularly in danger of inhibiting one's wisdom about interpersonal and intergroup issues if approaching the situation from an egocentric, first-person perspective (as compared to a third-person perspective [107,121,122]).

The observation that greater self-focus inhibits one's ability to approach interpersonal and intergroup matters wisely may be bad news, given repeated observations about the rise of individualism, self-centeredness, and other related tendencies in many parts of the world. In the US alone, analyses of cultural products such as themes in books, baby naming practices, or household make-up patterns indicate that themes emphasizing personal achievement, uniqueness, preference for single child household, and divorce rates have been on the rise for a good part of the 19th and 20th centuries [77,123,124]. Similar patterns can be observed in other parts of the world, as well [78].

3.2. Cultivating Wisdom

How does one grow wisdom in a time of cultural shifts to more individualism? Randomized control-trial studies of wise reasoning suggest several promising ways of fostering wise reasoning under such conditions, as demonstrated by experimental shifts in wise reasoning about personal challenges involving politics, career choices, or interpersonal conflicts. In one set of studies, Kross and Grossmann [107] instructed participants who were pre-screened for polarized political attitudes to reflect on a contentious political issue concerning the election of a candidate they do not endorse as the next U.S. President. Researchers experimentally assigned half of the participants to adopt a perspective of a U.S. citizen living in the U.S. when reflecting on this issue (psychologically close group). The other half of participants were instructed to adopt a perspective of an Icelandic citizen living in Iceland (psychologically distant group). This simple shift in perspective resulted in a higher degree of epistemic humility and view of the situation as in flux/change, as well as promoting greater open-mindedness, shown through their willingness to meet and discuss political issues in a bipartisan fashion.

In other similar studies, researchers examined the effects of adopting a first- (i.e., psychologically close) vs. third-person (i.e., psychologically distant) perspective when reflecting on their career development at the peak of the 2008 economic recession [107], or when reflecting on the possibility of an infidelity by their partner or a trust betrayal by a close friend [121]. In each of these studies, adopting a psychologically distant perspective resulted in wiser reasoning as compared to adopting a psychologically close perspective. Though this effect is not large, it appears to be reliable and extends to people's reflections on conflicts they experience in their lives [122,125]. Insights about ways to facilitate wisdom-related qualities in the face of political, interpersonal, and personal adversity suggest a possibility of fruitful educational and training programs. For instance, Grossmann [40] has outlined several possibilities for integrating insights about the effects of social and psychological distance on wisdom in the context of educational curricula, though the effectiveness of these and other similar ideas [126] have yet to be evaluated empirically.

Insights about the strategies for promoting wise reasoning suggest that structural changes in the environment and framing of behavioral choices in ways that can encourage wise reasoning in decision making are effective. Similar to "nudges" promoting saving and morally-conscious behavior [127,128], it is foreseeable to develop nudges for wise reasoning through an altering of the structure of organizational and political decision-making. For instance, based on the insights about how solitary decisions (compared to decisions made in the presence of people one cares about) may be less likely to foster wise reasoning, organizations may structure their decision-making environments in a way that would promote interdependent (rather than independent) decisions. For example, organizations could assign individual agents into mentor-mentee pairs to create environments encouraging an open debate among various stakeholders. In such situations, mentors may be more likely to approach contentious issues in a perspective-diverse, open-minded fashion [129]. In situations where solitary decisions are unavoidable, one can also attempt to institute a checklist reminder similar to how checklists are employed to reduce error in medical decision-making [130]. Finally, one can develop context-specific reminders of wisdom-boosting strategies [68] (for a general notion of "boosts," see [128]). We suggest that particularly promising reminders to specific critical events through computerized communication platforms, employing natural language processing and AI algorithms to detect the significance of a communicated message and providing customized, wisdom-fostering reminders to take a step back, consider a wide range of perspectives, and estimate the degree of uncertainty and the consequences of one's decision vis-à-vis plausible alternatives are prudent strategies.

Although these findings and speculations provide some hopeful suggestions for improving wisdom at the societal level, their effectiveness would surely depend on the "political will," and other cultural factors such as a generalized normative acceptance of interdependent decision making and behavior. The current trends in the post-industrial and developing countries indicate that the rise of individualistic attitudes and behavior [78] could represent a mounting hurdle to achieving these ends. Thus, whether these insights about the potential benefits of wise reasoning are able to pan out likely depends to some extent on the societal realization that individual decisions cannot be taken out of context. Recent work suggests that such a realization is growing in certain political circles (e.g., sustainability [76]), giving hope that the rise of individualism will be balanced by an increased realization of systemic interdependence and a greater propensity for wise reasoning.

4. Conclusions

A societal focus on increasing domain-general cognitive abilities (as measured by mainstream intelligence tests) has brought welcome improvements to the world in many domains such as health and technology. However, such forms of intelligence alone appear insufficient when facing large-scale social problems involving intergroup conflicts, sustainability concerns, inequality, as well as ill-defined challenges people encounter in their lives. In the current paper, we distinguished mainstream definitions of intelligence from wise reasoning, proposing that the latter concept is useful for working through societal problems. We bolstered our proposition by drawing on recent empirical evidence on the role of wisdom-related processes in deliberation and judgment about social issues. Features of wise reasoning, such as intellectual humility, the recognition of uncertainty and change, a consideration of diverse perspectives, and the search for an integration of these perspectives can promote societal well-being, and they can improve leaders' ability to provide and guide others toward outcomes that benefit both themselves and the greater good. Further, wise reasoning may help to face societal issues concerning sustainability, inequality, and polarization of the civic discourse. Evidence-based insights start to pave ways to promote wise reasoning in education and strategic decision-making. Whether these insights can be implemented depends on the political will and the societal realization that individual actions can rarely be taken out of social context, making knowledge about ways to situate individual actions into a given situation paramount.

Acknowledgments: The present research was funded by Social Sciences and Humanities Research Council of Canada (435-2014-0685), the Templeton Pathway to Character Project, and the Ontario Ministry of Research, Innovation and Science (Early Researcher Award) to the first author.

Author Contributions: Both authors wrote the paper.

Conflicts of Interest: The authors declare no conflict of interest.

References

1. Pinker, S. *Enlightenment Now: The Case for Reason, Science, Humanism, and Progress*; Viking: New York, NY, USA, 2018.
2. Welzel, C. *Freedom Rising: Human Empowerment and the Quest for Emancipation*; Cambridge Univerisity Press: New York, NY, USA, 2013.
3. Varnum, M.E.W.; Grossmann, I. Pathogen prevalence is associated with cultural changes in gender equality. *Nat. Hum. Behav.* **2016**, *1*, 3. [CrossRef]
4. Bakshy, E.; Messing, S.; Adamic, L.A. Exposure to ideologically diverse news and opinion on Facebook. *Science* **2015**, *348*, 1130–1132. [CrossRef] [PubMed]
5. Halberstam, Y.; Knight, B. Homophily, group size, and the diffusion of political information in social networks: Evidence from Twitter. *J. Public Econ.* **2016**, *143*, 73–88. [CrossRef]

6.   Pew Research Center. The Partisan Divide on Political Values Grows Even Wider. Sharp Shifts among Democrats on Aid to Needy, Race, Immigration. 2017. Available online: http://www.people-press.org/2017/10/05/the-partisan-divide-on-political-values-grows-even-wider/ (accessed on 4 February 2018).

7.   Iyengar, S.; Westwood, S.J. Fear and Loathing across Party Lines: New Evidence on Group Polarization. *Am. J. Polit. Sci.* **2015**, *59*, 690–707. [CrossRef]

8.   CNN UN Chief Issues "Red Alert" for the World. Available online: https://www.cnn.com/videos/world/2017/12/31/un-secretary-general-red-alert-new-year-2018-sot.cnn (accessed on 4 February 2018).

9.   Sternberg, R. Speculations on the Role of Successful Intelligence in Solving Contemporary World Problems. *J. Intell.* **2018**, *6*, 4. [CrossRef]

10.   Newell, A.; Simon, H.A. *Human Problem Solving*; Prentice-Hall: Englewood Cliffs, NJ, USA, 1972.

11.   Espinosa, P.; Horton, R. Study: Climate Change is Damaging the Health of Millions of People. *Time Magazine*. 31 October 2017. Available online: http://time.com/4999425/climate-change-health-2/ (accessed on 9 April 2018).

12.   Sternberg, R.J. Building wisdom and character. In *Health, Happiness, and Well-Being: Better Living through Psychological Science*; Lynn, S.J., O'Donohue, W., Lilienfeld, S., Eds.; Sage: Thousand Oaks, CA, USA, 2014; pp. 296–316.

13.   Gardner, H. *Frames of Mind: The Theory of Multiple Intelligences*; Basic Books: New York, NY, USA, 2011.

14.   Sternberg, R.J. The theory of successful inteligence. In *Cambridge Handbook of Intelligence*; Sternberg, R.J., Kaufman, S.B., Eds.; Cambridge University Press: New York, NY, USA, 2011; pp. 504–527.

15.   Cattell, R.B. *Intelligence: Its Structure, Growth and Action*; Elsevier Science Publishers: Amsterdam, The Netherlands, 1987.

16.   Nisbett, R.E.; Aronson, J.; Blair, C.; Dickens, W.; Flynn, J.; Halpern, D.F.; Turkheimer, E. Intelligence: New findings and theoretical developments. *Am. Psychol.* **2012**, *67*, 130–159. [CrossRef] [PubMed]

17.   Bangen, K.J.; Meeks, T.W.; Jeste, D.V. Defining and assessing Wisdom: A review of the literature. *Am. J. Geriatr. Psychiatry* **2013**, *21*, 1254–1266. [CrossRef] [PubMed]

18.   Staudinger, U.M.; Glück, J. Psychological wisdom research: Commonalities and differences in a growing field. *Annu. Rev. Psychol.* **2011**, *62*, 215–241. [CrossRef] [PubMed]

19.   Walsh, R. What is wisdom? Cross-cultural and cross-disciplinary syntheses. *Rev. Gen. Psychol.* **2015**, *19*, 278–293. [CrossRef]

20.   Kristjánsson, K. Virtue from the Perspective of Psychology. In *The Oxford Handbook of Virtue*; Snow, N., Ed.; Oxford University Press: New York, NY, USA, 2018. [CrossRef]

21.   Grossmann, I.; Kung, F.Y.H. Wisdom and culture. In *Handbook of Cultural Psychology*, 2nd ed.; Kitayama, S., Cohen, D., Eds.; Guilford Press: New York, NY, USA, in press.

22.   Grossmann, I.; Kross, E. The impact of culture on adaptive versus maladaptive self-reflection. *Psychol. Sci.* **2010**, *21*, 1150–1157. [CrossRef] [PubMed]

23.   Gross, J.J. Emotion regulation: Current status and future prospects. *Psychol. Inq.* **2015**, *26*, 1–26. [CrossRef]

24.   Narvaez, D. Moral complexity: The fatal attraction of truthiness and the importance of mature moral functioning. *Perspect. Psychol. Sci.* **2010**, *5*, 163–181. [CrossRef] [PubMed]

25.   Oakes, H.; Brienza, J.P.; Elnakouri, A.; Grossmann, I. Wise reasoning: Converging evidence for the psychology of sound judgment. In *Cambridge Handbook of Wisdom*; Sternberg, R.J., Glück, J., Eds.; Cambridge University Press: New York, NY, USA, in press.

26.   Ardelt, M. Where can wisdom be found? *Hum. Dev.* **2004**, *47*, 304–307. [CrossRef]

27.   Baltes, P.B.; Kunzmann, U. The two faces of wisdom: Wisdom as a general theory of knowledge and judgment about excellence in mind and virtue vs. Wisdom as everyday realization in people and products. *Hum. Dev.* **2004**, *47*, 290–299. [CrossRef]

28.   Baltes, P.B.; Smith, J. The fascination of wisdom: Its nature, ontogeny, and function. *Perspect. Psychol. Sci.* **2008**, *3*, 56–64. [CrossRef] [PubMed]

29.   Jeste, D.V.; Ardelt, M.; Blazer, D.; Kraemer, H.C.; Vaillant, G.; Meeks, T.W. Expert Consensus on Characteristics of Wisdom: A Delphi Method Study. *Gerontologist* **2010**, *50*, 668–680. [CrossRef] [PubMed]

30.   Grossmann, I. Wisdom in Context. *Perspect. Psychol. Sci.* **2017**, *12*, 233–257. [CrossRef] [PubMed]

31.   Kekes, J. Wisdom. *Am. Philos. Quart.* **1983**, *20*, 277–286. [CrossRef]

32.   Sternberg, R.J. A balance theory of wisdom. *Rev. Gen. Psychol.* **1998**, *2*, 347–365. [CrossRef]

33. Vervaeke, J.; Ferraro, L. Relevance, meaning and the cognitive science of wisdom. In *The Scientific Study of Personal Wisdom*; Ferrari, M., Weststrate, N.M., Eds.; Springer: Dordrecht, The Netherlands, 2013; pp. 325–341. [CrossRef]

34. Santos, H.C.; Huynh, A.C.; Grossmann, I. Teaching & Learning Guide for: Wisdom in a Complex World. *Soc. Personal. Psychol. Compass* **2017**, *11*. [CrossRef]

35. Kristjánsson, K. *Aristotelian Character Education*; Routledge: London, UK, 2015.

36. Clayton, V.P. Wisdom and intelligence: The nature and function of knowledge in the later years. *Int. J. Aging Hum. Dev.* **1982**, *15*, 315–321. [CrossRef] [PubMed]

37. Haugeland, J. *Artificial Intelligence: The Very Idea*; Bradford Books/The MIT Press: Cambridge, MA, USA, 1989.

38. Jonassen, D.H. Instructional design models for well-structured and Ill-structured problem-solving learning outcomes. *Educ. Technol. Res. Dev.* **1997**, *45*, 65–94. [CrossRef]

39. Sinnott, J.D. Postformal reasoning: The relativistic stage. *Beyond Form. Oper.* **1984**, *1*, 298–325.

40. Grossmann, I. Wisdom and How to Cultivate It. *Eur. Psychol.* **2017**, *22*, 233–246. [CrossRef]

41. Santos, H.C.; Huynh, A.C.; Grossmann, I. Wisdom in a complex world: A situated account of wise reasoning and its development. *Soc. Personal. Psychol. Compass* **2017**, *11*, e12341. [CrossRef]

42. Nickerson, R.S. Confirmation bias: A ubiquitous phenomenon in many guises. *Rev. Gen. Psychol.* **1998**, *2*, 175–220. [CrossRef]

43. Grossmann, I.; Sahdra, B.K.; Ciarrochi, J. A heart and a mind: Self-distancing facilitates the association between heart rate variability and wise reasoning. *Front. Behav. Neurosci.* **2016**, *10*, 68. [CrossRef] [PubMed]

44. Kitchener, K.S.; Brenner, H.G. Wisdom and reflective judgment: Knowing in the face of uncertainty. In *Wisdom. Its Nature, Origins and Development*; Sternberg, R.J., Ed.; Cambridge Univerisity Press: New York, NY, USA, 1990; pp. 212–227.

45. Baltes, P.B.; Staudinger, U.M. Wisdom: A metaheuristic (pragmatic) to orchestrate mind and virtue toward excellence. *Am. Psychol.* **2000**, *55*, 122–136. [CrossRef] [PubMed]

46. Glück, J.; Bluck, S. The MORE Life Experience Model: A Theory of the Development of Personal Wisdom. In *The Scientific Study of Personal Wisdom*; Ferrari, M., Weststrate, N.M., Eds.; Springer: Dordrecht, The Netherlands, 2013; pp. 75–97.

47. Webster, J.D.; Westerhof, G.J.; Bohlmeijer, E.T. Wisdom and mental health across the lifespan. *J. Gerontol. B Psychol. Sci. Soc. Sci.* **2014**, *69*, 209–218. [CrossRef] [PubMed]

48. Glück, J. Measuring Wisdom: Existing Approaches, Continuing Challenges, and New Developments. *J. Gerontol. Ser. B* **2017**. [CrossRef] [PubMed]

49. Brienza, J.P.; Kung, F.Y.H.; Santos, H.C.; Bobocel, D.R.; Grossmann, I. Wisdom, Bias, and Balance: Toward a Process-Sensitive Measurement of Wisdom-Related Cognition. *J. Personal. Soc. Psychol.* **2017**. [CrossRef] [PubMed]

50. Grossmann, I.; Na, J.; Varnum, M.E.W.; Park, D.C.; Kitayama, S.; Nisbett, R.E. Reasoning about social conflicts improves into old age. *Proc. Natl. Acad. Sci. USA* **2010**, *107*, 7246–7250. [CrossRef] [PubMed]

51. Grossmann, I.; Na, J.; Varnum, M.E.W.; Kitayama, S.; Nisbett, R.E. A route to well-being: Intelligence versus wise reasoning. *J. Exp. Psychol. Gen.* **2013**, *142*, 944–953. [CrossRef] [PubMed]

52. Staudinger, U.M.; Lopez, D.; Baltes, P.B. The psychometric location of wisdom-related performance: Intelligence, personality, and more? *Personal. Soc. Psychol. Bull.* **1997**, *23*, 1200–1214. [CrossRef]

53. Bates, W. Gross National Happiness. *Asian Pac. Econ. Lit.* **2009**, *23*, 1–16. [CrossRef]

54. Sigelman, L. Is ignorance bliss? A reconsideration of the folk wisdom. *Hum. Relat.* **1981**, *34*, 965–974. [CrossRef]

55. Watten, R.G.; Syversen, J.L.; Myhrer, T. Quality of life, intelligence and mood. *Soc. Indic. Res.* **1995**, *36*, 287–299. [CrossRef]

56. Wirthwein, L.; Rost, D.H. Giftedness and subjective well-being: A study with adults. *Learn. Individ. Differ.* **2011**, *21*, 182–186. [CrossRef]

57. Grossmann, I.; Gerlach, T.M.; Denissen, J.J.A. Wise reasoning in the face of everyday life challenges. *Soc. Psychol. Personal. Sci.* **2016**, *7*, 611–622. [CrossRef]

58. Baltes, P.B.; Kunzmann, U. Wisdom. *Psychologist* **2003**, *16*, 131–133.

59. Baltes, P.B.; Staudinger, U.M.; Maercker, A.; Smith, J. People nominated as wise: A comparative study of wisdom-related knowledge. *Psychol. Aging* **1995**, *10*, 155–166. [CrossRef] [PubMed]

60. Mickler, C.; Staudinger, U.M. Personal wisdom: Validation and age-related differences of a performance measure. *Psychol. Aging* **2008**, *23*, 787–799. [CrossRef] [PubMed]

61. Santos, H.C.; Grossmann, I. *Relationship of Wisdom-Related Attitudes and Subjective Well-Being over Twenty Years: Application of the Train-Preregister-Test (TPT) Cross-Validation Approach to Longitudinal Data*; Psychological Science: Waterloo, ON, Canada, 2018.

62. Tiberius, V. *The Reflective Life: Living Wisely with Our Limits*; Oxford University Press: New York, NY, USA, 2008.

63. Kekes, J. *Moral Wisdom and Good Lives*; Cornell University Press: Ithaca, NY, USA, 1995.

64. Weststrate, N.M.; Ferrari, M.; Ardelt, M. The Many Faces of Wisdom. *Personal. Soc. Psychol. Bull.* **2016**, *42*, 662–676. [CrossRef] [PubMed]

65. Canada Newswire Xerox Marks Human Rights and Environmental Progress in Annual Citizenship Report [Press release]. Available online: https://en-news.xerox.ca/news/CAN_News_11_12_2007 (accessed on 4 Feburary 2018).

66. Colvin, G. Worlds Greatest Leaders. Available online: http://fortune.com/worlds-greatest-leaders/ (accessed on 4 Feburary 2018).

67. Fortune Editors. The World's 19 Most Disappointing Leaders. Available online: http://fortune.com/2016/03/30/most-disappointing-leaders/ (accessed on 4 Feburary 2018).

68. Grossmann, I.; Kross, E. Exploring "Solomon's paradox": Self-distancing eliminates the self-other asymmetry in wise reasoning about close relations in younger and older adults. *Psychol. Sci.* **2014**, *25*, 1571–1580. [CrossRef] [PubMed]

69. De Freitas, J.; Sarkissian, H.; Newman, G.E.; Grossmann, I.; De Brigard, F.; Luco, A.; Knobe, J. Consistent Belief in a Good True Self in Misanthropes and Three Interdependent Cultures. *Cogn. Sci.* **2017**. [CrossRef] [PubMed]

70. Strohminger, N.; Knobe, J.; Newman, G. The True Self: A Psychological Concept Distinct From the Self. *Perspect. Psychol. Sci.* **2017**, *12*, 551–560. [CrossRef] [PubMed]

71. De Freitas, J.; Cikara, M.; Grossmann, I.; Schlegel, R. Origins of the Belief in Good True Selves. *Trends Cogn. Sci.* **2017**, *21*, 634–636. [CrossRef] [PubMed]

72. Fleeson, W.; Furr, R.M.; Jayawickreme, E.; Meindl, P.; Helzer, E.G. Character: The Prospects for a Personality-Based Perspective on Morality. *Soc. Personal. Psychol. Compass* **2014**, *8*, 178–191. [CrossRef]

73. Mischel, W.; Shoda, Y. A cognitive-affective system theory of personality: Reconceptualizing situations, dispositions, dynamics, and invariance in personality structures. *Psychol. Rev.* **1995**, *102*, 244–268. [CrossRef]

74. Gibson, R. *Sustainability Assessment: Criteria and Process*; Routledge: New York, NY, USA, 2005.

75. The Core Writing Team. *IPCC, 2014: Climate Change 2014. Synthesis Report. Summary for Policymakers*; Pachauri, R.L., Meyer, L.A., Eds.; The Core Writing Team: Geneva, Switzerland, 2015.

76. Adams, W.M. The Future of Sustainability: Re-thinking Environment and Development in the Twenty-first Century. In *Report of the IUCN Renowned Thinkers Meeting*; IUCN: Gland, Switzerland, 2006.

77. Grossmann, I.; Varnum, M.E.W. Social structure, infectious diseases, disasters, secularism, and cultural change in America. *Psychol. Sci.* **2015**, *26*, 311–324. [CrossRef] [PubMed]

78. Santos, H.C.; Varnum, M.E.W.; Grossmann, I. Global Increases in Individualism. *Psychol. Sci.* **2017**, *28*. [CrossRef] [PubMed]

79. Varnum, M.E.W.; Grossmann, I. Cultural Change: The How and the Why. *Perspect. Psychol. Sci.* **2017**, *12*, 956–972. [CrossRef] [PubMed]

80. Heathcote, J.; Perri, F.; Violante, G.L. Unequal we stand: An empirical analysis of economic inequality in the United States, 1967–2006. *Rev. Econ. Dynam.* **2010**, *13*, 15–51. [CrossRef]

81. Saez, E.; Zucman, G. Wealth Inequality in the United States since 1913: Evidence from Capitalized Income Tax Data. *Quart. J. Econ.* **2016**, *131*, 519–578. [CrossRef]

82. Grossmann, I.; Varnum, M.E.W. Social class, culture, and cognition. *Soc. Psychol. Personal. Sci.* **2011**, *2*, 81–89. [CrossRef]

83. Stephens, N.M.; Markus, H.R.; Townsend, S.S.M. Choice as an act of meaning: The case of social class. *J. Personal. Soc. Psychol.* **2007**, *93*, 814–830. [CrossRef] [PubMed]

84. Grossmann, I.; Huynh, A.C. Where Is the Culture in Social Class? *Psychol. Inq.* **2013**, *24*, 112–119. [CrossRef]

85. Kraus, M.W.; Piff, P.K.; Keltner, D. Social Class as Culture. *Curr. Direct. Psychol. Sci.* **2011**, *20*, 246–250. [CrossRef]

86. Kraus, M.W.; Côté, S.; Keltner, D. Social class, contextualism, and empathic accuracy. *Psychol. Sci.* **2010**, *21*, 1716–1723. [CrossRef] [PubMed]

87. Stellar, J.E.; Manzo, V.M.; Kraus, M.W.; Keltner, D. Class and compassion: Socioeconomic factors predict responses to suffering. *Emotion* **2012**, *12*, 449–459. [CrossRef] [PubMed]

88. Na, J.; Grossmann, I.; Varnum, M.E.W.; Kitayama, S.; Gonzalez, R.; Nisbett, R.E. Cultural differences are not always reducible to individual differences. *Proc. Natl. Acad. Sci. USA* **2010**, *107*, 6192–6197. [CrossRef] [PubMed]

89. Dietze, P.; Knowles, E.D. Social Class and the Motivational Relevance of Other Human Beings. *Psychol. Sci.* **2016**, *27*, 1517–1527. [CrossRef] [PubMed]

90. Varnum, M.E.W.; Blais, C.; Hampton, R.S.; Brewer, G.A. Social class affects neural empathic responses. *Cult. Brain* **2015**, *3*, 122–130. [CrossRef]

91. Bridges, J.W.; Lillian, E.C. The relation of intelligence to social status. *Psychol. Rev.* **1917**, *24*, 1–31. [CrossRef]

92. Witkin, H.A. Social Influences in the Development of Cognitive Style. In *Handbook of Socialization Theory and Research*; Goslin, D.A., Ed.; Rand McNally: New York, NY, USA, 1969.

93. Brienza, J.P.; Grossmann, I. Social class and wise reasoning about interpersonal conflicts across regions, persons and situations. *Proc. R. Soc. B Biol. Sci.* **2017**, *284*. [CrossRef] [PubMed]

94. Frank, R.H.; Gilovich, T.; Regan, D.T. Does studying economics inhibit cooperation? *J. Econ. Perspect.* **1993**, *7*, 159–171. [CrossRef]

95. Grossmann, I.; Koyama, J.; Eibach, R.P. *Internalized Standards of Sound Judgment: The Rational vs. the Reasonable*; Psyarxiv.com: Waterloo, ON, Canada, 2017.

96. Rist, R.C. Student Social Class and Teacher Expectations: The Self-fulfilling Prophecy in Ghetto Education. *Harv. Educ. Rev.* **2000**, *70*, 257–301. [CrossRef]

97. Stephens, N.M.; Fryberg, S.A.; Markus, H.R. When choice does not equal freedom: A sociocultural analysis of agency in working-class American contexts. *Soc. Psychol. Personal. Sci.* **2011**, *2*, 33–41. [CrossRef]

98. Ellis, B.J.; Bianchi, J.; Griskevicius, V.; Frankenhuis, W.E. Beyond Risk and Protective Factors: An Adaptation-Based Approach to Resilience. *Perspect. Psychol. Sci.* **2017**, *12*, 561–587. [CrossRef] [PubMed]

99. Stephens, N.M.; Markus, H.R.; Fryberg, S.A. Social class disparities in health and education: Reducing inequality by applying a sociocultural self model of behavior. *Psychol. Rev.* **2012**, *119*, 723–744. [CrossRef] [PubMed]

100. Oxenham, S. The rise of political apathy in two charts. *Nature* **2017**. [CrossRef]

101. Huynh, A.C.; Oakes, H.; Shay, G.R.; McGregor, I. The Wisdom in Virtue: Pursuit of Virtue Predicts Wise Reasoning About Personal Conflicts. *Psychol. Sci.* **2017**, *28*, 1848–1856. [CrossRef] [PubMed]

102. Kunzmann, U.; Baltes, P.B. Wisdom-related knowledge: Affective, motivational, and interpersonal correlates. *Personal. Soc. Psychol. Bull.* **2003**, *29*, 1104–1119. [CrossRef]

103. Wink, P.; Staudinger, U.M. Wisdom and Psychosocial Functioning in Later Life. *J. Personal.* **2016**, *84*, 306–318. [CrossRef] [PubMed]

104. Grossmann, I.; Brienza, J.P.; Bobocel, D.R. Wise deliberation sustains cooperation. *Nat. Hum. Behav.* **2017**. [CrossRef]

105. Leary, M.R.; Diebels, K.J.; Davisson, E.K.; Jongman-Sereno, K.P.; Isherwood, J.C.; Raimi, K.T.; Hoyle, R.H. Cognitive and Interpersonal Features of Intellectual Humility. *Personal. Soc. Psychol. Bull.* **2017**, *43*, 793–813. [CrossRef] [PubMed]

106. Brienza, J.P.; Franki, Y.; Kung, H.; Chao, M.M. *Wise Reasoning Reduces Intergroup Bias*; Unpublished; 2018.

107. Kross, E.; Grossmann, I. Boosting wisdom: Distance from the self enhances wise reasoning, attitudes, and behavior. *J. Exp. Psychol. Gen.* **2012**, *141*, 43–48. [CrossRef] [PubMed]

108. Tetlock, P.E. *Expert Political Judgement: How Good Is It?* Princeton University Press: Princeton, NJ, USA, 2005.

109. Brewer, M.B. The Psychology of Prejudice: Ingroup Love and Outgroup Hate? *J. Soc. Issues* **1999**, *55*, 429–444. [CrossRef]

110. Von Neumann, J.; Morgenstern, O. *Theory of Games and Economic Behavior*; Princeton University Press: Princeton, NJ, USA, 1947.

111. Waytz, A.; Young, L.L.; Ginges, J. Motive attribution asymmetry for love vs. hate drives intractable conflict. *Proc. Natl. Acad. Sci. USA* **2014**, *111*, 15687–15692. [CrossRef] [PubMed]

112. Bowles, S. Policies Designed for Self-Interested Citizens May Undermine "The Moral Sentiments": Evidence from Economic Experiments. *Science* **2008**, *320*, 1605–1609. [CrossRef] [PubMed]

113. Maxwell, N. *From Knowledge to Wisdom: A Revolution in the Aims and Methods of Science*; Blackwell: Oxford, UK, 1984.
114. Sternberg, R.J. Why schools should teach for wisdom: The balance theory of wisdom in educational settings. *Educ. Psychol.* **2001**, *36*, 227–245. [CrossRef]
115. McGilchrist, I. *The Master and His Emissary: The Divided Brain and the Making of the Western World*; Yale University Press: New Haven, CT, USA, 2009.
116. Jukes, M.C.H.; Zuilkowski, S.S.; Grigorenko, E.L. Do Schooling and Urban Residence Develop Cognitive Skills at the Expense of Social Responsibility? A Study of Adolescents in the Gambia, West Africa. *J. Cross Cult. Psychol.* **2018**, *49*, 82–98. [CrossRef]
117. Rawls, J. *The Law of Peoples*; Harvard University Press: Cambridge, MA, USA, 1999.
118. Rawls, J. *Political Liberalism*, Expanded Edition; Columbia University Press: New York, NY, USA, 2005.
119. Gewirth, A. The rationality of reasonableness. *Synthese* **1983**, *57*, 225–247. [CrossRef]
120. Sibley, W.M. The rational versus the reasonable. *Philos. Rev.* **1953**, *52*, 554–560. [CrossRef]
121. Grossmann, I.; Kross, E. Exploring Solomon's Paradox: Self-Distancing Eliminates the Self-Other Asymmetry in Wise Reasoning about Close Relationships in Younger and Older Adults. *Psychol. Sci.* **2014**, *25*, 1571–1580. [CrossRef] [PubMed]
122. Grossmann, I.; Oakes, H. *Wisdom of Yoda and Mr. Spock: The Role of Emotions and the Self*; Psyarxiv.com: Waterloo, ON, Canada, 2017.
123. Greenfield, P.M. The changing psychology of culture from 1800 through 2000. *Psychol. Sci.* **2013**, *24*, 1722–1731. [CrossRef] [PubMed]
124. Twenge, J.M.; Abebe, E.M.; Campbell, W.K. Fitting in or standing Out: Trends in American parents' choices for children's names, 1880–2007. *Soc. Psychol. Personal. Sci.* **2010**, *1*, 19–25. [CrossRef]
125. Huynh, A.C.; Yang, D.Y.-J.; Grossmann, I. The Value of Prospective Reasoning for Close Relationships. *Soc. Psychol. Personal. Sci.* **2016**, *7*, 893–902. [CrossRef]
126. Sternberg, R.J.; Jarvin, L.; Reznitskaya, A. Teaching for Wisdom Through History: Infusing Wise Thinking Skills in the School Curriculum. In *Teaching for Wisdom*; Ferrari, M., Potworowski, G., Eds.; Springer: Dordrecht, The Netherlands, 2008; pp. 37–57. [CrossRef]
127. Thaler, R.H.; Sunstein, C.R. *Nudge: Improving Decisions about Health, Wealth, and Happiness*; Penguin: New York, NY, USA, 2009.
128. Hertwig, R.; Grüne-Yanoff, T. Nudging and Boosting: Steering or Empowering Good Decisions. *Perspect. Psychol. Sci.* **2017**, *12*, 973–986. [CrossRef] [PubMed]
129. Huynh, A.C.; Santos, H.; Tse, C.; Grossmann, I. *The Socrates Effect: How a Teacher's Mindset Impacts Political Reasoning*; Psyarxiv.com: Waterloo, ON, Canada, 2017.
130. Hales, B.M.; Pronovost, P.J. The checklist—A tool for error management and performance improvement. *J. Crit. Care* **2006**, *21*, 231–235. [CrossRef] [PubMed]

Journal of
Intelligence

MDPI

Article

Creativity as a Stepping Stone toward a Brighter Future

James Kaufman

Neag School of Education, University of Connecticut, 2131 Hillside Road, Unit 3007, Storrs, CT 06269-3007, USA; james.kaufman@uconn.edu

Received: 2 February 2018; Accepted: 21 March 2018; Published: 4 April 2018

Abstract: If IQs continue to rise over generation, why has the world been unable to solve basic recurrent problems? This paper argues that creativity, which is overlooked in IQ tests and showing no signs of a similar increase, may be part of the reason of why the Flynn Effect has not led to a better world. Creativity's predictive power for traditional positive outcomes, such as school or work performance, is significant but slight. However, there are other ways that creativity can help to make a better world. Two exemplar ways that are discussed in this paper are how creativity can (a) help people lead happier and more meaningful lives and (b) focus a spotlight on talented members of underrepresented groups who are overlooked by traditional measures. Both of these directions can lead to a world that is better equipped to solve larger issues.

Keywords: creativity; IQ; meaning; fairness; ethnicity

1. Introduction

It is easy to glamorize the "good old days". Many times in the past appeal to people. Some are nostalgic for eras they lived through themselves, whereas others may wonder about life in ancient Rome. However, the past held quite a few downsides. Most past generations lived in a world that was unpleasant and dangerous for people who were not wealthy men. It is also easy to forget the comforts of air conditioning, penicillin, basic safety regulations, and prenatal care (e.g., [1]). That said, there is nonetheless a feeling among many people that the world is not moving in the right direction. Although the current state of the world may still represent an improvement over past horrors, it nonetheless seems worse than a multitude of possible worlds that might exist under the same conditions. If our current global situation were a Choose Your Own Adventure book, then there is a distinct feeling that a wrong decision was made several pages back.

As this special issue asks, why are we not living in the best of times? The Flynn Effect [2,3] has consistently shown that IQ is increasing at approximately three points per decade. We are, presumably, getting smarter over time. Yet even if we are not living in the imagined future of vacationing on Venus, should not we have solved some basic problems by now? Why do hunger, lack of proper medical care, and homelessness remain predominant issues after so many years? The "duck and cover" school routine (in preparation for potential nuclear war) is gone, but it has been replaced by the equally terrifying "lockdown" routine (in preparation for a school shooter).

The obvious answer is that there's more to life than IQ, even if our society's priorities do not reflect this concept. The idea that we value the concepts we are able to measure dates back more than 100 years to Lord Kelvin (e.g., [4]). IQ tests have a long and varied history, and over the last 150 years there have many bursts of development and inspiration, from Wechsler's combination of verbal and non-verbal assessments into one battery to the push in the 1980's to develop theory-based IQ tests [5]. Yet, innovations are still the exception, and there has been little advancement in the last decade or two. Technological advances have enabled a new world of testing possibilities (e.g., [6]), yet IQ tests have been content to remain stagnant. Increasing IQs may be notable, but they may be less related to our ability as a population to cope with ever-changing problems and possibilities.

What do IQ tests miss? In the pages that follow, I will explore why creativity's absence from IQ tests (and, therefore, any Flynn effect boost) is a key reason that the world is not on a strong forward trajectory. It is important to note before I discuss creativity that just as IQ alone is not enough to solve global problems, neither is creativity. They are but two of many constructs (many discussed in this issue, such as wisdom or rational thought) that are needed to create the leaders and humanitarians of tomorrow [7]. I am under no myopic illusion that all problems would be solved if everyone magically woke up tomorrow being twice as creative as they are today. Indeed, creativity is not always benevolent [8]. J. Robert Oppenheimer was an incredibly creative (and smart) scientist who oversaw the Manhattan Project [9]. It is possible to argue that nuclear weapons have done much good for the world (i.e., avoiding potential world wars), but it is impossible to argue that nuclear weapons have not unleashed destruction and death. Positive creative actions can be used to prevent negative creative actions, such as current anti-terrorism units [10]. However, the potential misuse of creativity cannot be ignored. Although I will focus this article on the positive potential of creativity, I am quite aware that creativity can (and has) been used to make the world worse, as well.

Another important note, that whereas IQ may be increasing, creativity is probably not. In a well-publicized study, Kim [11] analyzed archival data on the figural form (i.e., drawing) of the Torrance Tests of Creative Thinking from six normative samples between 1966 and 2008. She found that as of 1990, scores began to decline. Unfortunately, scores from the verbal form were not analyzed. Creativity is a complex construct that manifests itself differently depending the domain [12,13]. A subsequent study analyzed actual creative writing and visual art that were published between 1990 and 2011 [14]. In contrast to Kim's [11] study, many components of visual art (such as complexity and unconventionality) showed an increase over the two decades. However, the creative writing was rated as more formulaic and conventional. Without significantly more research, it is hard to reach any conclusion about trends, but there is little evidence that any Flynn-like effect is occurring in creativity.

When creativity is studied, the vast majority of researchers (more than 70%) focus on how to predict or increase creativity [15]. This work is important, but it leaves a gap for someone trying to argue creativity's importance in potentially solving world problems. There are many papers describing the personality, motivational, cognitive, or situational traits that can increase (or decrease) creativity. Yet, few consider how creativity can predict positive outcomes. One initial suggestion is to increase this type of work.

When this predictive research is conducted, however, the desirable outcomes that were studied tend to be standard, such as academic achievement [16], job performance [17], or employee satisfaction [18]. Although creativity is positively related to these variables, school and work success are better predicted by intelligence and conscientiousness [19,20].

If we want to talk about how creativity can change the world, we need to consider new pathways. An argument that focuses on easily-measured school or work performance can be quickly countered: why go through the hassle of testing creativity when there are more established assessments of intelligence (and personality) that are better predictors? Further, there is much more to life than GPA or a supervisor's rating. I will discuss ways in which creativity can help to solve the world's problems at all levels—from personal to global [21]. With further empirical studies to add to our base of knowledge, creativity may be better used to help people.

2. Changing the World in New Ways

It is instinctual to think of large-scale, genius-level interventions when we think about changing the world, such as the development of the internet or the Polio vaccine. Certainly, with world leaders and political parties in seemingly perpetual states of disagreement and inability to work together, a successful mediator would need creative solutions. In addition, creativity is a driving force behind most of the advances we have made [22]. But greatness does not suddenly materialize. Child prodigies, for example, are only barely more like to develop into adult geniuses than anyone else [23]. Although we know a great deal about which variables predict Big-C, or creative geniuses [24]. Millions of people may have the same perfect blend of familial and cultural environments and ideal individual factors yet accomplish nothing meaningful. A top-down approach may not be the best way to identify how creativity can help to change the world.

One place to start is that there is no Big-C without mini-c (personal creativity), little-c (everyday creativity), or Pro-c (expert-level creativity; [25,26]). If creativity is not nurtured in school at the K-12 [27] and collegiate [28] level, then it will be much less prevalent in adults. In addition, creativity has a multitude of benefits beyond low-level correlations with school and work performance. For example, in our daily lives, creativity is associated with being seen as more sexually desirable [29], better physical health [30], and higher career satisfaction [31].

I will now address two understudied, bottom-up ways in which creativity can lead to a better world: through providing and maintaining meaning in life and by increasing equity and fairness.

2.1. Meaning and Well Being

Creativity has long been a key part of humanistic (e.g., [32,33]) and positive psychology [34,35]. Creative activity can not only help people experience personal growth and be more likely to contribute to the world; it can also help to prevent them from focusing on the looming certainty that everyone is eventually going to die [36]. Lifton [37] suggests there are many ways that people can accept their own mortality by focusing on what may keep their memory or presence alive after death. In addition to such possibilities as family or spiritual beliefs, one way is through creative activity. As Kaufman [38] suggests, there are many ways that creativity can help people find meaning in life. Writing narratives or memoirs, creating art, or finding a unique creative passion may help someone make sense of their own life [39], experience joy in the present moment [40], manage existential worries about death [41], and leave a legacy for future generations [42].

In addition to enhancing someone's meaning in life on a larger scale, creativity can help hold on to meaning after experiencing a traumatic event. Being creative is associated with people who continue to thrive and grow after experiencing a traumatic event [43]. Although culture and individual differences play an important role, these general connection has been found with survivors of such large-scale disasters as the Rwandan massacre [44] or Hurricane Katrina [45]. On a smaller scale, creativity can help reduce stress [46], lift psychological burdens [47], and replenish a person after a difficult day at work [48]. The exact underlying nature of creativity's contribution to these positive outcomes does need more study [49].

It is reasonable to question how creativity leading to personal meaning and well-being can impact the world. It turns out that happy people are much more likely to engage in behaviors that are beneficial to other people. For example, general well-being is associated with being more likely to participate in general prosocial activities [50]. Happier people are specifically more likely to help the environment [51], donate to charities [52], and be more productive at work [53]. They are also less likely to engage in criminal or delinquent activity [54]. The impact of general well-being on society is strong enough that Maccagnan, Wren-Lewis, Brown, and Taylor [55] suggest that it may be just as important to accurate assess and nurture the happiness of a society as it is to consider more traditional measures of a country's success, such as its GDP (gross domestic product).

2.2. Equity and Fairness

Most measures of ability and achievement (IQ tests, SATs, GREs, and many others) show significant differences by ethnicity [56,57], with White and Asian Americans tending to receive higher scores than other groups. Achievement tests show differences by gender, with women receiving lower scores on math-related measures [58]. This topic is both controversial and nuanced, and as such beyond the scope of the current paper. Many questions of potential bias have been raised, and I have discussed this issue in more detail elsewhere [59,60].

As I have noted before [61,62], measures of creativity either show virtually no differences by ethnicity [63–65] or a slight advantage for underrepresented groups [66–69]. Gender differences are inconsistent and are generally rare [70]. On the few occasions that creativity assessments have been used to supplement (not replace) more traditional measure for college admissions, underrepresented groups have been more likely to be admitted to college—and the average SAT scores of accepted students actually increased [71]. Indeed, students accepted to Tufts who completed the supplemental measures (including creativity) were more likely to get better grades than those who did not (controlling for high school GPA and SAT scores); they were also more likely to get involved in leadership or extracurricular activities [72].

There are many obstacles to using creativity as a high-stakes measure, whether for college [61] or gifted [73] admissions. Current creativity assessments tend be either outdated or require extensive financial or personnel resources (e.g., [74]). Consider, however, the strong possibility of discovering exciting new candidates who might score lower on traditional measures. The chance to attend more prestigious colleges will offer members of underrepresented groups better access to more important and higher status jobs. Substantial research indicates that groups that are comprised of different ethnicities are more creative, effective, and produce higher quality work [75–77]. If we want to have better large-scale ideas in our organizations, we need to start recognizing a broader array of talents much earlier. As Wordsworth said, "the child is the father of the man" ([78], p. 7).

Another intriguing possibility is the link between getting people to counter stereotypes and an increase in creativity [79–81]. Although most studies are more focused on how these interventions can increase creativity, it has been proposed that the reverse angle may be equally true. In other words, helping people to increase their creativity may lead to the rejection of stereotypical thinking [82,83].

3. Concluding Thoughts

Is creativity an automatic pathway toward solving our world's many problems? Of course not. But, if we move beyond the links between creativity and school and workplace performance, some intriguing possibilities emerge. Existing studies suggest that higher levels of creativity may enable people to have more meaning in their life and to be happier. Including creativity tests as part of gifted or college admissions may recognize talented members of underrepresented groups. Interventions to increase creativity may increase tolerance. Much more research is needed to establish the best ways in which creativity can enhance fairness and meaning, as well as identifying new positive outcomes that can be nurtured by creativity.

These steps will not suddenly end world hunger, climate change, or growing hatred between cultural, ethnic, and political groups. Investing in creativity is rarely a short-term solution. But, over time, people who are happier, more engaged with life, interacting with diverse groups, and more tolerant of others will be the ones who can bring us closer to the world that many of us might imagine only as a fantasy. Creativity represents a solid starting point for the future.

Conflicts of Interest: The author declares no conflict of interest.

References

1. Pinker, S. *The Better Angels of Our Nature*; Viking: New York, NY, USA, 2011.
2. Flynn, J.R. The mean IQ of Americans: Massive gains 1932 to 1978. *Psychol. Bull.* **1984**, *95*, 29–51. [CrossRef]
3. Flynn, J.R. Searching for justice—The discovery of IQ gains over time. *Am. Psychol.* **1999**, *54*, 5–20. [CrossRef]
4. Tunbridge, P. *Lord Kelvin: His Influence on Electrical Measurements and Units*; Peter Peregrinus: London, UK, 1992.
5. Kaufman, A.S. *IQ Testing 101*; Springer: New York, NY, USA, 2009.
6. Shute, V.J.; Ventura, M. *Measuring and Supporting Learning in Games: Stealth Assessment*; MIT Press: Cambridge, MA, USA, 2013.

7. Sternberg, R.J. Speculations on the role of Successful Intelligence in solving contemporary world problems. *J. Intell.* **2018**, *6*, 4. [CrossRef]
8. Cropley, D.H.; Kaufman, J.C.; Cropley, A.J. Malevolent creativity: A functional model of creativity in terrorism and crime. *Creat. Res. J.* **2008**, *20*, 105–115. [CrossRef]
9. Hecht, D.K. *Storytelling and Science: Rewriting Oppenheimer in the Nuclear Age*; University of Massachusetts Press: Amherst, MA, USA, 2015.
10. Gill, P.; Horgan, J.; Hunter, S.T.; D Cushenbery, L. Malevolent creativity in terrorist organizations. *J. Creat. Behav.* **2013**, *47*, 125–151. [CrossRef]
11. Kim, K.H. The creativity crisis: The decrease in creative thinking scores on the Torrance Tests of Creative Thinking. *Creat. Res. J.* **2011**, *23*, 285–295. [CrossRef]
12. Kaufman, J.C.; Glăveanu, V.; Baer, J. (Eds.) *Cambridge Handbook of Creativity Across Domains*; Cambridge University Press: New York, NY, USA, 2017.
13. Kaufman, J.C.; Pumaccahua, T.T.; Holt, R.E. Personality and creativity in realistic, investigative, artistic, social, and enterprising college majors. *Pers. Ind. Differ.* **2013**, *54*, 913–917. [CrossRef]
14. Weinstein, E.C.; Clark, Z.; DiBartlomomeo, D.J.; Davis, K. A decline in creativity? It depends on the domain. *Creat. Res. J.* **2014**, *26*, 174–184. [CrossRef]
15. Forgeard, M.J.C.; Kaufman, J.C. Who cares about imagination, creativity, and innovation, and why? A review. *Psychol. Aesthet. Creat. Arts* **2016**, *10*, 250–269. [CrossRef]
16. Gajda, A.; Karwowski, M.; Beghetto, R.A. Creativity and academic achievement: A meta-analysis. *J. Educ. Psychol.* **2016**. [CrossRef]
17. Harari, M.B.; Reaves, A.C.; Viswesvaran, C. Creative and innovative performance: A meta-analysis of relationships with task, citizenship, and counterproductive job performance dimensions. *Eur. J. Work Organ. Psychol.* **2016**, *25*, 495–511. [CrossRef]
18. Kim, T.; Hon, A.Y.; Crant, J.M. Proactive personality, employee creativity, and newcomer outcomes: A longitudinal study. *J. Bus. Psychol.* **2009**, *24*, 93–103. [CrossRef]
19. Poropat, A.E. A meta-analysis of adult-rated child personality and academic performance in primary education. *Br. J. Educ. Psychol.* **2014**, *84*, 239–252. [CrossRef] [PubMed]
20. Schmidt, F.L.; Hunter, J.E. The validity and utility of selection methods in personnel psychology: Practical and theoretical implications of 85 years of research findings. *Psychol. Bull.* **1998**, *124*, 262–274. [CrossRef]
21. Kaufman, J.C.; Beghetto, R.A. Beyond big and little: The Four C Model of Creativity. *Rev. Gen. Psychol.* **2009**, *13*, 1–12. [CrossRef]
22. Florida, R. *The Rise of the Creative Class-Revisited: Revised and Expanded*; Basic Books: New York, NY, USA, 2014.
23. Winner, E. Child Prodigies and Adult Genius: A Weak Link. In *The Wiley Handbook of Genius*; Simonton, D.K., Ed.; Wiley: Oxford, UK, 2014; pp. 297–320.
24. Simonton, D.K. *Genius 101*; Springer: New York, NY, USA, 2009.
25. Beghetto, R.A.; Kaufman, J.C. Toward a broader conception of creativity: A case for "mini-c" creativity. *Psychol. Aesthet. Creat. Arts* **2007**, *1*, 13–79. [CrossRef]
26. Beghetto, R.A.; Kaufman, J.C. Fundamentals of creativity. *Educ. Leadersh.* **2013**, *70*, 10.
27. Beghetto, R.A.; Kaufman, J.C.; Baer, J. *Teaching for Creativity in the Common Core Classroom*; Teachers College Press: New York, NY, USA, 2014.
28. Sternberg, R.J. *College Admissions for the 21st Century*; Harvard University Press: Cambridge, MA, USA, 2010.
29. Kaufman, S.B.; Kozbelt, A.; Silvia, P.; Kaufman, J.C.; Ramesh, S.; Feist, G.J. Who finds Bill Gates sexy? Creative mate preferences as a function of cognitive ability, personality, and creative achievement. *J. Creat. Behav.* **2016**, *50*, 294–307. [CrossRef]
30. Stuckey, H.L.; Nobel, J. The connection between art, healing, and public health: A review of current literature. *Am. J. Public Health* **2010**, *100*, 254–263. [CrossRef] [PubMed]
31. Seibert, S.E.; Kraimer, M.L.; Crant, J.M. What do proactive people do? A longitudinal model linking proactive personality and career success. *Pers. Psychol.* **2001**, *54*, 845–874. [CrossRef]
32. Maslow, A.H. A theory of human motivation. *Psychol. Rev.* **1943**, *50*, 370–96. [CrossRef]
33. Rogers, C. *On Becoming a Person*; Houghton Mifflin: Boston, MA, USA, 1961.
34. Seligman, M.E.P. *Flourish: A Visionary New Understanding of Happiness and Well-Being*; Simon and Schuster: New York, NY, USA, 2012.

35. Seligman, M.E.P.; Csikszentmihalyi, M. Positive psychology: An introduction. *Am. Psychol.* **2000**, *55*, 5–14. [CrossRef] [PubMed]
36. Heine, S.J.; Proulx, T.; Vohs, K.D. The Meaning Maintenance Model: On the coherence of social motivations. *Personal. Soc. Psychol. Rev.* **2006**, *10*, 88–110. [CrossRef] [PubMed]
37. Lifton, R.J. *Witness to an Extreme Century: A Memoir*; Free Press: New York, NY, USA, 2011.
38. Kaufman, J.C. Finding meaning with creativity in the past, present, and future. *Perspect. Psychol. Sci.* **2018**, in press.
39. Pennebaker, J.W.; Seagal, J.D. Forming a story: The health benefits of narrative. *J. Clin. Psychol.* **1999**, *55*, 1243–1254. [CrossRef]
40. Csikszentmihalyi, M. *Creativity: Flow and the Psychology of Discovery and Invention*; HarperCollins: New York, NY, USA, 1996.
41. Perach, R.; Wisman, A. Can creativity beat death? A review and evidence on the existential anxiety buffering functions of creative achievement. *J. Creat. Behav.* **2018**, in press. [CrossRef]
42. Sligte, D.J.; Nijstad, B.A.; De Dreu, C.K. Leaving a legacy neutralizes negative effects of death anxiety on creativity. *Personal. Soc. Psychol. Bull.* **2013**, *39*, 1152–1163. [CrossRef] [PubMed]
43. Forgeard, M.J.C. Perceiving benefits after adversity: The relationship between self-reported posttraumatic growth and creativity. *Psychol. Aesthet. Creat. Arts* **2013**, *7*, 245–264. [CrossRef]
44. Forgeard, M.J.C.; Mecklenburg, A.C.; Lacasse, J.J.; Jayawickreme, E. Bringing the whole universe to order: Creativity, healing, and posttraumatic growth. In *Creativity and Mental Illness*; Kaufman, J.C., Ed.; Cambridge University Press: New York, NY, USA, 2014; pp. 321–342.
45. Metzl, E.S. The role of creative thinking in resilience after hurricane Katrina. *Psychol. Aesthet. Creat. Arts* **2009**, *3*, 112–123. [CrossRef]
46. Nicol, J.J.; Long, B.C. Creativity and perceived stress of female music therapists and hobbyists. *Creat. Res. J.* **1996**, *9*, 1–10. [CrossRef]
47. Goncalo, J.A.; Vincent, L.C.; Krause, V. The liberating consequences of creative work: How a creative outlet lifts the physical burden of secrecy. *J. Exp. Soc. Psychol.* **2015**, *59*, 32–39. [CrossRef]
48. Eschleman, K.J.; Madsen, J.; Alarcon, G.M.; Barelka, A. Benefiting from creative activity: The positive relationships between creative activity, recovery experiences, and performance-related outcomes. *J. Occup. Organ. Psychol.* **2014**, *87*, 579–598. [CrossRef]
49. Forgeard, M.J.; Elstein, J.G. Advancing the clinical science of creativity. *Front. Psychol.* **2014**, *5*, 613. [CrossRef] [PubMed]
50. Thoits, P.A.; Hewitt, L.N. Volunteer work and well-being. *J. Health Soc. Behav.* **2001**, *42*, 115–131. [CrossRef] [PubMed]
51. Sulemana, I. Are happier people more willing to make income sacrifices to protect the environment? *Soc. Indic. Res.* **2016**, *127*, 447–467. [CrossRef]
52. Priller, E.; Schupp, J. Social and economic characteristics of financial and blood donors in Germany. *DIW Econom. Bull.* **2011**, *6*, 23–30.
53. Barsane, S.G.; Gibson, D. Why does affect matter in organizations? *Acad. Manag. Perspect.* **2007**, *21*, 36–59. [CrossRef]
54. Buunk, A.; Peiro, J.M.; Rocabert, E.; Dijkstra, P. Life satisfaction and status among adolescent law offenders. *Crim. Behav. Ment. Health* **2016**, *26*, 94–100. [CrossRef] [PubMed]
55. Maccagnan, A.; Wren-Lewis, S.; Brown, H.; Taylor, T. Wellbeing and society: Towards quantification of the co-benefits of wellbeing. *Soc. Indic. Res.* **2018**. [CrossRef]
56. Bleske-Rechek, A.; Browne, K. Trends in GRE scores and graduate enrollments by gender and ethnicity. *Intelligence* **2014**, *46*, 25–34. [CrossRef]
57. Edwards, O.W.; Oakland, T.D. Factorial invariance of Woodcock-Johnson III scores for Caucasian Americans and African Americans. *J. Psychoeduc. Assess.* **2006**, *24*, 358–366. [CrossRef]
58. Ackerman, P.L.; Kanfer, R.; Calderwood, C. High school advanced placement and student performance in college: STEM majors, non-STEM majors, and gender differences. *Teach. Coll. Rec.* **2013**, *115*, 1–43.
59. Kaufman, J.C. Non-biased assessment: A supplemental approach. In *Children's Handbook of Multicultural School Psychology*; Frisby, C.L., Reynolds, C.R., Eds.; Wiley: New York, NY, USA, 2005; pp. 824–840.
60. Kaufman, J.C. *Creativity 101*, 2nd ed.; Springer: New York, NY, USA, 2016.

61. Kaufman, J.C. Using creativity to reduce ethnic bias in college admissions. *Rev. Gen. Psychol.* **2010**, *14*, 189–203. [CrossRef]
62. Kaufman, J.C. Why creativity isn't in IQ tests, why it matters, and why it won't change anytime soon . . . .Probably. *J. Intell.* **2015**, *3*, 59–72. [CrossRef]
63. Glover, J.A. Comparative levels of creative ability in black and white college students. *J. Gen. Psychol.* **1976**, *128*, 95–99. [CrossRef] [PubMed]
64. Kaufman, J.C.; Baer, J.; Gentile, C.A. Differences in gender and ethnicity as measured by ratings of three writing tasks. *J. Creat. Behav.* **2004**, *38*, 56–69. [CrossRef]
65. Kaufman, J.C.; Niu, W.; Sexton, J.D.; Cole, J.C. In the eye of the beholder: Differences across ethnicity and gender in evaluating creative work. *J. Appl. Soc. Psychol.* **2010**, *40*, 496–511. [CrossRef]
66. Ivcevic, Z.; Kaufman, J.C. The can and cannot do attitude: How self estimates of ability vary across ethnic and socioeconomic groups. *Learn. Ind. Differ.* **2013**, *27*, 144–148. [CrossRef]
67. Kaufman, J.C. Self-reported differences in creativity by gender and ethnicity. *J. Appl. Cognit. Psychol.* **2006**, *20*, 1065–1082. [CrossRef]
68. Torrance, E.P. Are the Torrance Tests of Creative Thinking biased against or in favour of disadvantaged groups? *Gifted Child Q.* **1971**, *15*, 75–80. [CrossRef]
69. Torrance, E.P. Non-test indicators of creative talent among disadvantaged children. *Gifted Child Q.* **1973**, *17*, 3–9. [CrossRef]
70. Baer, J.; Kaufman, J.C. Gender differences in creativity. *J. Creat. Behav.* **2008**, *42*, 75–106. [CrossRef]
71. Sternberg, R.J. Applying psychological theories to educational practice. *Am. Educ. Res. J.* **2008**, *45*, 150–165. [CrossRef]
72. Sternberg, R.J.; Bonney, C.R.; Gabora, L.; Merrifield, M. WICS: A model for college and university admissions. *Educ. Psychol.* **2012**, *47*, 30–41. [CrossRef]
73. Luria, S.R.; O'Brien, R.L.; Kaufman, J.C. Creativity in gifted identification: Increasing accuracy and diversity. *Ann. N. Y. Acad. Sci.* **2016**, *1377*, 44–52. [CrossRef] [PubMed]
74. Kaufman, J.C.; Plucker, J.A.; Russell, C.M. Identifying and assessing creativity as a component of giftedness. *J. Psychoeduc. Assess.* **2012**, *30*, 60–73. [CrossRef]
75. Cady, S.H.; Valentine, J. Team innovation and perceptions of consideration what difference does diversity make? *Small Group Res.* **1999**, *30*, 730–750. [CrossRef]
76. McLeod, P.L.; Lobel, S.A.; Cox, T.H. Ethnic diversity and creativity in small groups. *Small Group Res.* **1996**, *27*, 248–264. [CrossRef]
77. Milliken, F.J.; Martins, L.L. Searching for common threads: Understanding the multiple effects of diversity in organizational groups. *Acad. Manag. Rev.* **1996**, *21*, 402–433.
78. Wordsworth, W. *The Complete Poetical Works of William Wordsworth*; Troutman Hayes: Philadelphia, PA, USA, 1852.
79. Gocłowska, M.A.; Baas, M.; Crisp, R.J.; De Dreu, C.K.W. Whether social schema violations help or hurt creativity depends on need for structure. *Personal. Soc. Psychol. Bull.* **2014**, *40*, 959–971. [CrossRef] [PubMed]
80. Gocłowska, M.A.; Crisp, R.J. On counter-stereotypes and creative cognition: When interventions for reducing prejudice can boost divergent thinking. *Think. Skills Creat.* **2013**, *8*, 72–79. [CrossRef]
81. Gocłowska, M.A.; Crisp, R.J.; Labuschagne, K. Can counter-stereotypes boost flexible thinking? *Group Processes Intergroup Relat.* **2013**, *16*, 217–231. [CrossRef]
82. Luria, S.R.; Kaufman, J.C. Examining the relationship between creativity and equitable thinking in schools. *Psychol. Schools* **2017**, *54*, 1279–1284. [CrossRef]
83. Luria, S.R.; Sriraman, B.; Kaufman, J.C. Enhancing equity in the classroom by teaching for mathematical creativity. *Int. J. Math. Educ.* **2017**, *49*, 1033–1039. [CrossRef]

Journal of
Intelligence

MDPI

Commentary

Inequality, Education, Workforce Preparedness, and Complex Problem Solving

Patrick C. Kyllonen

Educational Testing Service, Princeton, NJ 08648, USA; pkyllonen@ets.org; Tel.: +1-609-734-1056

Received: 19 March 2018; Accepted: 19 June 2018; Published: 16 July 2018

Abstract: Economic inequality has been described as the defining challenge of our time, responsible for a host of potential negative societal and individual outcomes including reduced opportunity, decreased health and life expectancy, and the destabilization of democracy. Education has been proposed as the "great equalizer" that has and can continue to play a role in reducing inequality. One means by which education does so is through the development of complex problem solving skills in students, skills used to solve novel, ill-defined problems in complex, real-world settings. These are highly valued in the workforce and will likely continue to be so in the future workforce. Their importance is evident in results from employer surveys, as well as by their inclusion in large scale international and domestic comparative assessments. In this paper, I review various definitions of complex problem solving and approaches for measuring it, along with findings from PISA 2003, 2012, and 2015. I also discuss prospects for teaching, assessing, and reporting on it, and discuss the emerging importance of collaborative problem solving. Developing and monitoring complex problem solving skills, broadly defined, is a critical challenge in preparing students for the future workforce, and in overcoming the negative effects of inequality and the diminishment of individual opportunity.

Keywords: inequality; problem solving; complex problem solving; PISA; National Assessment of Educational Progress; collaborative problem solving; skills; general ability; cognitive ability; general fluid ability

1. Introduction

In 2013, former U.S. president Barack Obama argued that reducing economic inequality and improving upward mobility was "the defining challenge of our time" [1]. This is not a uniquely American perspective. Similar sentiments have been expressed by Prime Minister Justin Trudeau of Canada [2] and the topic has been central in recent elections in Germany, Italy, and France. Best sellers by the economists Thomas Piketty [3] and Joseph Stiglitz [4] chronicle the growing concentration of income and wealth and its implications for reducing opportunity, decreasing health and life expectancy, and destabilizing democracy.

Since Horace Mann [5], education has been seen as the "great equalizer," a sentiment later echoed by Obama's Secretary of Education, Arne Duncan [6]. For example, log wages go up linearly with years of education, from 7th grade to Ph.D. [7]; estimates of the causal effects of education on earnings suggest roughly 10% per year of education [8] with even higher returns to those from disadvantaged backgrounds [7])[1]. Thus, among the remedies to the growing inequality problem proposed by Obama was increasing educational attainment. He proposed doing this through greater spending on high-quality pre-school, emphasis on career and technical education, and making higher

---

[1] Card [7] identified several approaches to estimating causal effects of education, including use of instrumental variables (e.g., minimum school leaving age, tuition costs, and geographic school proximity) and within family (e.g., sibling and twin) comparisons of members with different amounts of education.

education more affordable. Education not only affects earnings, but brings a host of other benefits, including increased life satisfaction, trust, and social interaction, and improved decision making about choices related to health, marriage, and parenting [9].

It is important to consider what it is about education that serves to deliver these positive benefits. A way to think about this is that education serves two functions that are extremely valuable in the workplace and in life generally. Education teaches domain-specific skills, particularly mathematics and language skills, but also more specialized curricular skills such as those associated with particular occupations (in career and technical education) or college majors. In addition, education teaches domain-general skills such as problem-solving, communication skills, and conscientiousness.[2] Certainly mathematics and language skills are essential core skills for continued education and they are the focus of many large-scale surveys designed to report on the quality of nations' education systems (e.g., NAEP and PISA), and workforces (PIAAC). However, a theme here is that an emphasis on domain-specific skills may be disproportionate, at the expense of the domain-general skills. Consider that there are many occupations at various levels that require minimal mathematics skills (e.g., court reporters, law clerks, radio announcers, and historians) or minimal language skills (janitors, sewing machine operators, and watch repairers). Further, many people are employed in jobs outside their academic major—Robts [12] found that 45% of college graduates reported that their job was only partially related or not related to their field of study. He also found that the costs of working in an out-of-field job were lowest for liberal arts majors, that is, those probably most likely to learn domain-general skills.

Another issue pertaining to the relative importance of domain-specific vs. general skills is that the workforce keeps changing, primarily due to technology, and the pace of change appears to be accelerating. For example, technologies such as the telephone and electricity took four to six decades from invention to 40% market penetration, whereas tablets and smartphones accomplished this within a decade [13]. This has implications for the nature of work in the future workforce. A National Research Council workshop and report [14] on the future labor force highlighted the importance of broad general skills (social, interpersonal, and problem solving) as initially defined in the Department of Labor's Secretary's Commission on Achieving Necessary Skills (SCANS) report [15]. Their importance was not limited to college, but included Career and Technical Education (CTE) as well. Ken Kay, a speaker at the workshop said that today's students will need broad skills (communication, creativity, problem solving), to prepare for "multiple careers and multiple jobs" [14] (p. 88), and as a "self-defense mechanism" in case of displacement or layoffs due to disruptions in the workforce.

In sum, education is the "great equalizer" that can mitigate the deleterious effects of inequality and the concentration of wealth on society and on individual opportunity. A proposal is that a mechanism by which education does so is through the development of general, complex problem solving skills, which may at least partly be a byproduct of instruction in science, technology, engineering, and mathematics, which occurs in K-12 [16], community college [17], higher education [18,19], and in career and technical education [20]. In this commentary, I explore definitions of problem solving and complex problem solving, review its importance, discuss its malleability, and conclude with suggestions on how it might be monitored and developed in school so as to enhance the great equalizing effects of school.

---

[2]   There is a potential third alternative: years in school or a degree signals to potential employers that a person who achieved this level of education has the general cognitive ability, communication skills, and conscientiousness to have made it this far [10]). Discussion of this issue lies outside the scope of this commentary [11].

2. Complex Problem Solving

Complex problem solving (CPS) skills may be defined broadly as those "used to solve novel, ill-defined problems in complex, real-world settings" [21].[3] Complex problem solving describes the activities associated with some of the most demanding and highly financially valued and rewarded occupations in the workforce, such as chief executives, emergency management directors, judges, physicists, surgeons, biomedical engineers, and neurologists (based on data from the U.S. Department of Labor's Occupational Information Network, O*NET [21]). There is every indication that complex problem solving skills are likely to continue to be valued in the future workforce [22]. Students with strong complex problem solving skills are in demand by employers for entry level positions [23,24] and jobs requiring complex problem solving are the ones that pay the most throughout one's career [21].

However, before considering issues of how to develop and evaluate complex problem solving (CPS) skills in students, there is a question about what exactly complex problem solving skill is. Can CPS even be considered a general skill, or is it simply a name for a broad set of specialized skills in diverse knowledge domains. Both the chief executive and surgeon draw on CPS skills, according to evaluations by job experts, but what do skills in the two domains have in common, if anything? If one acquires complex problem solving skills in one domain, through school or elsewhere, to what extent do such skills transfer to different knowledge domains? While complex problem solving skills are most important in occupations such as chief executives, physicists, and chemical engineers (for these jobs "complex problem solving" has a rated importance level of 78 to 85 on a 0–100 scale [21]), complex problem solving is also rated as important, just not as important, in a broad variety of other occupations such as art directors, fashion designers, biologists, materials engineers, and survey researchers (importance level 66 on a 0–100 scale), and even in so called middle-skills jobs such as medical assistants, license clerks, crane operators, and retail salespersons (importance level 47 on a 0–100 scale). What is common about complex problem solving skills across both domains and levels of occupations? Is "CPS skills" even a coherent psychological construct or is it simply a shorthand label, similar to "expertise," for unrelated activities which have only in common that they are difficult?

The answers to these questions have implications for how complex problem solving can be taught and developed, and whether CPS skills should be targeted for instruction generally, or in the context of specific knowledge or curricular domains. If complex problem solving skill is a general skill, then perhaps it makes sense to teach it directly, using examples from different knowledge domains. If complex problem solving skill is simply a label for a diverse set of activities that have nothing in common, other than a label, that suggests that there will be little transfer of skill, neither from school to the workplace, nor from one job domain or subject matter domain to another.

The issue of the domain specificity of what appears to be a very general skill is a hotly debated topic, not yet settled, with advocacy on both sides of the issue. In this article, I address the issue of the nature of complex problem solving skill, and the issue of the degree to which it may be developed in school, in training, or on the job. I begin with a summary of the indications that it is a highly valued skill, based primarily on surveys and other informal reports.

3. Employers Seek Complex Problem-Solving Skills Now and Likely in the Future

Several surveys have been conducted, which ask employers what skills they look for in recent graduates during hiring or what employers' greatest needs are. The National Association of Colleges and Employers annually surveys its U.S. employer members on a variety of topics to project the market for new college graduates. Table 1 presents the 2017 findings. "Problem solving skills" is the second most important skill category (behind "ability to work in a team"). Findings on the skills employers

---

[3] This is the definition of CPS skills; O*NET [21] also provides the more specific definition of complex problem solving as "identifying complex problems and reviewing related information to develop and evaluate options and implement solutions."

are looking for do not vary much from year to year, regardless of wording. For example, on the 2015 survey, the two highest "candidate skills/qualities" were "ability to work in a team structure" and "ability to make decisions to solve problems," both of which received average ratings of 4.61 on a 1 ("not at all important") to 5 ("extremely important") scale [23] A similar survey [25], Table 2; 431 employers identified "critical thinking/problem solving" as among the top five "very important" applied skills for job success for new workforce entrants at all education levels (High school, two-year and four-year graduates).

Table 1. Most important skills sought by employers.

NACE 2017 [a]	"Importance" [b]	McKinsey [c]	"Importance" [d]
Ability to work in a team	78%	Work ethic	80%
Problem-solving skills	77%	Teamwork	79%
Written communication skills	75%	Oral communications	73%
Strong work ethic	72%	Local language	73%
Verbal communication skills	71%	Hands-on-training	69%
Leadership	69%	Problem solving	66%
Initiative	66%	Written communications	64%

Sources: National Association of Colleges and Employers ([23], Figure 2). McKinsey Center for Government [24] (Exhibit 15, p. 44). [a] N = 169 US employers, 17% return rate; [b] a Survey question is to rate the importance of candidate skills/qualities on a 5-point scale, where 1 = Not at all important, 2 = Not very important, 3 = Somewhat important, 4 = Very important, and 5 = extremely important; [c] N = 2832 employers, stratified by sector, size, and distributed across nine countries (Brazil, Germany, India, Mexico, Morocco, Saudi Arabia, Turkey, UK, and USA); [d] Survey question is "Please rate how important these skills are for new hires to have in order to be effective at your company . . . on a scale of 0 to 10, where . . . 10 means extremely important"; Listed is percentage responding 8 or higher out of 10.

These results are similar to those obtained by the Department of Labor and the states. For example, North Carolina's Association of Workforce Development Boards [26] conducted a survey of employers (1152 respondents) that identified the greatest need to be soft skills, particularly communication/interpersonal skills (59%), critical and analytical thinking (47%), and problem solving (45%). Table 1 shows that a similar list of skills was obtained in a much larger study by McKinsey & Company, which surveyed employers from nine socioeconomically and culturally diverse countries (including the U.S.). Here, again, "problem solving" was rated as among the most important skills employers look for in recent hires.

The U.S. Department of Labor's O*NET program surveys employers, job incumbents, and occupational experts and analysts continuously[4] on the abilities, interests, values, work styles, skills, tasks, education requirements, and other factors associated with 974 occupations covering the entire U.S. economy [27]. Among the over 200 ratings completed on each occupation are ones on the importance and level required of "complex problem solving"[5] one of several cross-functional skills.[6] Across all jobs, CPS is one of 14 skills (of 35) considered relevant to all occupations [28] (Table 1). The importance of CPS for an occupation is highly correlated with earnings for that occupation $r = 0.42$ with log median wages; [29], comparable to the relationship with general ability/general fluid ability

---

[4] On average, two thirds of the 900 plus occupations are updated each year.

[5] Job analysts make independent judgments about the importance and level of skills required for each occupation; there have been 16 ratings cycles which enables calculating interrater reliabilities. For CPS importance, single-rater reliabilities, ICC(C,1) = 0.37, 8-rater reliabilities, ICC(C,8) = 0.83; for CPS level, ICC(C,1) = 0.52, ICC(C,8) = 0.90 [28], Table 3, p. 8. These tend towards the lower end of agreement, with categories such as equipment maintenance, science, troubleshooting, and operation and control at the higher end of agreement.

[6] In addition to complex problem solving skills, cross-functional skills also include the categories of social skills, technical skills, systems skills, and resource management skills, each of which includes 3–11 subskills; cross-functional skills are members of a larger category of worker requirements, which also include basic skills, knowledge, and education. Worker requirements are related to worker characteristics, which include abilities, occupational interests, work values, and work styles, each of which has numerous subcategories.

(r = 0.39). Burrus et al. [30] identified a problem solving factor (primarily defined by complex problem solving and judgment and decision making ratings) from a factor analysis of all of the O*NET skills and abilities ratings. The problem solving factor had the second highest correlation with wages (r = 0.58) behind a communication skills factor (r = 0.60), but ahead of achievement/innovation (r = 0.46) and fluid intelligence (r = 0.41).

The preceding analysis suggests that complex problem solving skill is considered a very important skill in the workforce and among the most highly compensated skills. What about the future workforce? Autor, Levy, and Murnane [22] showed that, since the advent of computers and widespread automation, circa 1980, some jobs have grown and some declined, explained by computers substituting for human workers in performing routine cognitive and manual tasks (ones accomplished by following explicit rules), but complementing workers in "carrying out problem-solving and complex communication activities ('non-routine' tasks)" [22] (p. 128), a phenomenon known as job polarization. Subsequent research has reinforced those findings with other data sources, and emphasized the mutual importance of both [31,32]. As technology improves, it increasingly replaces work that can be automated. What remains are tasks that are difficult to automate, those requiring "flexibility, judgment, and common sense" [33], or "generalist occupations requiring knowledge of human heuristics, and specialist occupations involving the development of novel ideas and artifacts" with examples being chief executives, lawyers, and engineering and science occupations [34] (p. 40).[7]

If we adopt the definition of complex problem solving as skills used to solve novel, ill-defined problems in complex, real-world settings, then it would seem that these are indeed the skills most resistant to automation, and therefore likely to continue to be rewarded in the workplace. It is difficult to predict technology developments and their impact on the future workforce.[8] However, there does seem to be some consensus around the idea that complex problem solving, broadly defined, and particularly when paired with communication skills, is likely to continue to be a valued skill, a conclusion in line with recommendations going as far back as the 1991 report of the Secretary of Labor's Commission on Achieving Necessary Skills (SCANS [13]), though to a National Research Council workshop on future skill demands [12], and up to the current views reviewed here.

4. What Is Complex Problem Solving?

To this point, the terms problem solving and complex problem solving have been treated almost interchangeably. This partly reflects common usage in employer surveys and the economics literature, which typically do not make a distinction between them. However, there is a distinction in their usage within the psychological literature. It is useful to describe both terms and highlight the distinctions.

4.1. Traditional Problem Solving

Traditional problem solving has a long history in psychology. Problem solving tasks include classic insight problems, ones characterized by an "aha" experience when realizing the correct answer [38], often found in riddles and puzzles books. Examples include retrieving out-of-reach bananas [39] (a study of monkeys), connecting nine dots with four lines [40], and attaching a burning candle to a wall with a box [41]. Problem solving tasks also include non-insight problems, or analytic problems, which are characterized as having a search space (with a starting state, goal state, and operators), such as Tower of Hanoi, Rubik's cube, Chess, and missionaries and cannibals. They also include optimization problems such as the traveling salesman problem; inductive reasoning problems such as rule induction;

---

[7] OECD [35] also provides a useful projection methodology based on cross-walking job tasks with skills measured in PIAAC, including problem solving, concluding that only a small percentage of workers use skills daily that go beyond current computer capabilities, suggesting a possible mistargeting of education.

[8] According to David Leonhardt [36,37], at a 1992 conference on the economy convened by Bill Clinton shortly after his election, no one mentioned the Internet.

and deductive reasoning problems such as verbal arithmetic (also, cryptarithmetic, [42]).[9] There is some evidence for a lack of a distinction between insight and analytic problems, as Raven's Progressive Matrices scores have been found to predict solution on the two types equally well [43].

Studies of problem solving have identified phenomena that impede or facilitate solution such as functional fixedness, mental set, and the importance of problem representation, and problem-solving strategies such as means-ends analysis, breadth vs. depth first search, working backwards, divide-and-conquer, trial-and-error, and reasoning by analogy [44]. A focal point of traditional problem solving research has been on teaching problem solving by making students aware of these kinds of phenomena and problem solving methods, which began with George Polya [45]. He focused on mathematical problem solving, and proposed that it follows the steps: (a) understand the problem; (b) devise a plan; (c) carry out the plan; and (d) review and extend the method used. Bransford and Stein [46] proposed a similar model, IDEAL (Identify, Define, Explore, Act, Look), designed to help schools and organizations teach problem solving.

These methods, distinctions, and problem solving strategies have served as the basis for frameworks and test specifications for OECD's PISA problem solving assessment in several cycles, PISA 2003 [47], 2012 [48] and 2015 [49]. It is instructive to study PISA's definition and implementation of problem solving assessments because: (a) the definitions are constructed by problem solving expert groups (which tend to change membership from cycle to cycle to some degree) representing international scientific consensus; and (b) the definitions and implementations are agreed to by the participating nations, OECD and non-OECD. Thus, PISA represents a fairly broad and common understanding, both scientifically and from a policy making perspective of what problem solving is.

In PISA 2003, problem solving was defined as follows:

"Problem solving is an individual's capacity to use cognitive processes to confront and resolve real, cross-disciplinary situations where the solution path is not immediately obvious and where the literacy domains or curricula areas that might be applicable are not within a single domain of mathematics, science or reading" [47] (p. 154).

The definition highlights several features of problem solving as it is tested in PISA, both in the 2003 cycle and beyond, and as it is probably largely understood outside of PISA, by policy makers and stake holders in education and in the workforce communities internationally. The definition highlights: (a) "real situations" as opposed to more abstract formulations of problem solving, reflecting PISA's position as a literacy examination emphasizing transferable skills; (b) the "non-obvious" nature of solutions, reflecting a general requirement for a task to be considered problem solving, and reflecting the non-routine nature of problem solving; and (c) the cross-curricular or domain-independent focus of the assessment, which draws on diverse (though not inaccessible) knowledge for problem solution.

In PISA 2003, the problem solving framework was organized by problem types (decision making, system analysis and design, and troubleshooting), contexts (personal life, work and leisure, community and society), disciplines (math, science, literature, social studies, technology), processes (*understanding*, characterizing, *representing*, *solving*, *reflecting*, and communicating) (steps overlapping Polya's [45] are italicized), and reasoning skills (analytic, quantitative, analogical, and combinatorial reasoning). The actual test included multiple choice, closed constructed response, and open constructed response item types, enabling both right-wrong and partial-credit scoring.

PISA 2012 adopted a definition similar to that from PISA 2003 (see Appendix A, which lists problem solving definitions through several PISA cycles as well as the PIAAC definition), and the framework was largely the same. However, there were two major changes. One was that computer administration, enabling human–computer interactions, was implemented. The other was that a certain kind of interactive task, known as MicroDYN [50] and MicroFin [51], was introduced to constitute

---

[9] All of the analytic problems listed here have associated Wikipedia articles (https://en.wikipedia.org/wiki/\T1\ textless{}problem-name\T1\textgreater{}).

about two thirds of the assessment items. These item types involve manipulating variables to determine effects on outcomes, for example, manipulating temperature and water to observe effects on plant growth (these are example tasks from the U.S. National Assessment of Educational Progress, Interactive Computer Tasks (Science) assessment [52]). Despite these changes in the assessment, problem solving again correlated highly with the Mathematics, Reading, and Science assessments, the correlations being $r = 0.81, 0.75$, and 0.78, respectively [53]. Despite the high correlations, there were differences. The countries doing better in problem solving than expected (based on their Math, Reading, and Science scores, and expressed in standard deviations) were Korea (+0.12 points), Japan (+0.11), Serbia (+0.11), the U.S. (+0.10), and Italy (+0.10). Those doing worse than expected were Bulgaria (-0.54), Shanghai (China) (-0.51), Poland (-0.42), UAE (-0.42), and Hungary (-0.33).

PISA 2015 also largely adopted the problem solving approach and framework from the earlier assessments, but introduced a collaborative component. The major problem solving stages were retained (Exploring and understanding; Representing and formulating; Planning and executing; and Monitoring and reflecting), but now crossed with collaborative competencies (Establishing and maintaining shared understanding; Taking appropriate action to solve the problem; and Establishing and maintaining group organization). The collaboration was not truly authentic: The collaborator was a computer agent, and the test taker communicated with the agent by selecting multiple-choice responses in a chat window on the display screen, but it was collaboration nevertheless. Collaborative problem solving scores were, similar to previous assessments, highly correlated with Math, Reading, and Science scores, $r = 0.70, 0.74$, and 0.77, respectively (note that the correlations with Reading and Science were almost identical to the correlations found with the non-collaborative problem solving of PISA 2012, but with math, lower). In addition, the countries that did better and worse than expected were similar: Japan (+0.23), Australia (+0.23), U.S. (+0.22), New Zealand (+0.21), and Singapore (+0.17), vs. Russia (-0.22), Turkey (-0.19), Montenegro (-0.18), Tunisia (-0.17), and China (-0.17) [49] (p. 80). An intriguing finding was that the collaborative version of problem solving (in PISA 2015) differed dramatically from the non-collaborative (PISA 2012) version in one respect: in non-collaborative problem solving, boys outperformed girls in most countries; in collaborative problem solving, girls outperformed boys in every country by an average effect size of 0.3 [49] (p. 95).

PISA provides the common, consensus understanding of problem solving, and to some extent how it can be assessed in individuals. There is an alternative approach to understanding problem solving, and that is to observe how it is treated in the human abilities literature [54]. Specifically, to what extent do measures of problem solving correlate with other ability measures and how is that represented in factor analyses of abilities? Many tasks that might be considered traditional problem solving tasks, such as rule induction, were in fact included in Carroll's [54] comprehensive analyses of abilities tests, and from those analyses problem solving would appear to be close conceptually to fluid ability, or general fluid ability (Gf) [29]. In addition, the problem solving tests used in PISA are typically highly correlated with the other tests of mathematics, reading, and science. As such, this indicates that problem solving is a fairly general factor, as would be expected to the degree that it aligned with general fluid ability. For example, PISA 2003 [47] (p. 189) problem solving scores correlated $r = 0.89, 0.82$, and 0.78 with mathematics, reading, and science scores, respectively (latent correlations), which places problem solving at the center of the four domains in the sense of having the highest average correlations with the other three domains. This, again, is consistent with the idea that problem solving and general fluid ability are closely related [29].

4.2. Complex Problem Solving

There are at least three definitions of complex problem solving. One is that it is the same as problem solving, but perhaps emphasizing task complexity or item difficulty, in the way that complex mathematics problems are difficult ones (see [55] for a discussion of the difficulty-complexity distinction). Arguably, PISA treats the concepts of problem solving and complex problem solving in this way. A second definition is implied in O*NET's use of the term complex problem solving, quoted at the beginning of this article, which emphasizes "complex, real-world settings" as would be found in a job, such as CEO or surgeon. This is appropriate for O*NET, in which analysts rate the degree to which a job requires complex problem solving. The complex problem solving rating scale provides rating anchors: at the low end are jobs that require one to "layout tools to complete a job," at the middle level to "redesign a floor layout to take advantage of new manufacturing techniques," and at the high end to "develop and implement a plan to provide emergency relief for a major metropolitan area."

A third definition of complex problem solving is a particular one that has emerged as a school of research, primarily in Germany [56,57] and it is useful to explore this definition in more detail. Dörner and Funke [58] characterize the distinction between regular and complex problem solving as one between well-defined and ill-defined problems, with well-defined ones having "a clear set of means for reaching a precisely described goal state" and ill-defined ones having "no clear problem definition, their goal state is not defined clearly, and the means of moving towards the (diffusely described) goal state are not clear." Investigations of complex problem solving under this definition primarily involve computer simulated microworlds (as in the PISA 2012 MicroDYN and 2009 NAEP Science interactive computer task problems described above). Funke [59] argued that for problem solving to be considered truly complex, it should: (a) involve many variables; (b) that have mutual dependency; (c) be dynamic (changing over time); (d) at least partly intransparent (not possible to know the value of all variables at any one time); and (e) polytelomous, that is that there can be multiple and even conflicting goals for the problem solver. Newer definitions add even more features, such as: (f) involving self-regulation; (g) creativity; (h) combining solutions; and (i) in a high-stakes setting [58]. There is an issue of how this "German school" definition of complex problem solving aligns with a consensus definition (as illustrated in the PISA discussion, and as used in O*NET surveys). It may in some sense simultaneously be too narrow (not all complex problem solving has these features) and too wide (particularly with the latter feature additions, it may describe complex cognition rather than complex problem solving), but the exercise is informative and has led to considerable research activities exploring various notions of complex problem solving.

There are microworlds built based on the "German school" definition, particularly aspects "a" through "e," but such microworlds tend to take a long time for students to learn and to get useful performance measures from. For example, microworlds from "the early years" were systems with between 20 and 2000 variables [58]. Consequently, shortened versions of microworlds that sacrifice some of these features (e.g., MicroDYN) have taken their place in PISA and other research contexts. A pertinent question asked by Dörner and Funke [58] is "what can we learn about BIG P by studying little p?" meaning what can we learn about complex problem solving in the complex, ill-defined, sense (BIG P) by studying shortened, simplified problem solving tasks (little p)?

5. Potential Uses of Complex Problem Solving Assessments

It is useful to review potential uses of a complex problem solving assessment. One is to monitor student growth and development, as PISA and PIAAC do for nations and systems over time, and as NAEP, PISA or a NAEP or PISA-like assessment could do in a longitudinal study to track student skills growth over grades. Another is to use complex problem solving assessments as selection instruments for college admissions, college placement, scholarships, military selection and classification, and employment screening. A third is to use complex problem solving assessments as formative assessments to aid in teaching problem solving skills.

Regarding the monitoring growth and facilitating comparisons use (e.g., PISA and NAEP), it would seem that we learn quite a bit with the little p versions of complex problem solving tasks that is useful for educational policy. In PISA, for example, we have learned that although there is a high correlation between problem solving and content test scores (Mathematics, Reading, and Science) nations differentiate themselves on their relative accomplishment in problem solving, in ways that are not predictable from scores on the other assessments. The U.S.'s relatively strong performance on problem solving (compared to its performance in the other content domains), or more generally, the relatively strong performance in problem solving of the high-functioning economies, suggests that students from those economies are acquiring more general problem solving skills (relative to other skills) in school compared to students from weaker economies. That difference does not show up so clearly in content skills. The fact that girls tend to outperform boys in all nations on collaborative problem solving is also an interesting finding. Would we learn more with more complex problem solving tasks, that is, BIG P tasks? Perhaps, but the evidence that would warrant such an investment that it would take to find out is lacking.

Regarding the selection use of problem solving: The high correlation between problem solving and other measures suggests that problem solving assessments, which might have greater face validity, and perhaps content validity, might be viable substitutes for traditional IQ tests. However, regarding the question of whether BIG P assessments should replace little p ones, it is the case that selection applications have historically been sensitive to the time devoted to them. Thus, here again, the evidence that longer, more complex problem solving assessments would add value beyond the shorter versions, particularly given the additional testing time required, is lacking.

With regard to the formative assessment use, it is here that the more complex, longer-lasting BIG P microworlds are likely to provide unique value beyond what can be had with their shorter, little p counterparts. Formative assessment and student diagnosis uses are ideally suited to longer explorations from students engaging with microworlds. Such applications are currently being researched in various domains [60], although not general complex problem solving, to our knowledge. In any event, this is likely to remain a fruitful pursuit.

Designing complex problem solving tasks that best meet these various purposes will be challenging, because the purposes are different. Reckase [61] provided a compelling perspective on this design challenge, distinguishing two perspectives on test design.[10] One he referred to as the psychological perspective, and the other, the educational perspective. The psychological perspective leads to tests that use homogeneous tasks to place people along a continuum. Trait and ability testing fits this notion, and much of test theory assumes this perspective—selection and monitoring uses align best with this perspective.

In contrast, the educational perspective employs a domain sampling approach to indicate the amount of the domain the test taker has mastered. Simple examples are spelling or vocabulary tests in which words are randomly sampled from a dictionary, but more complex examples can be drawn from any domain, as long as there is a sampling strategy that adequately represents the domain. Reckase [61] argued that monitoring growth aligns with a unidimensional view and the continuum model, but diagnostic uses (determining on which topics students are doing well and poorly), and formative assessment uses (using the test to teach the material) align with a multidimensional view and the domain-sampling approach. Further, Reckase argued that to make good instructional (formative) items requires more complex items than are typically used. The BIG P, complex problem solving microworld approach, as outlined by Dorner and Funke [58] would seem to be well suited to this task.

If complex problem solving can be thought of as a combination of general fluid ability and knowledge, then a hybrid continuum and domain-sampling model might be a useful assessment and reporting strategy. Complex problem solving tasks in various domains could be developed, which would enable reporting on both the general complex problem-solving skill, and the domain-specific aspects of it ([61] provides several examples of how these can be combined).

6. Can Complex Problem Solving Skills Be Developed?

There are two persistent myths on the development and education of general cognitive ability. Complex problem solving skill certainly is a kind of general cognitive ability, particularly insofar as it

---

[10] These are related to the formative–reflective measurement model distinction in psychometrics, see [29], for a discussion of how this is related to two perspectives on measuring complex problem solving.

largely reflects general fluid (Gf) ability [29]. One myth is that general cognitive ability is immutable. This was an argument presented by Jensen [62] Hernstein and Murray [63] and others, but it has attained the status of conventional wisdom. The argument for its immutability is typically based on two kinds of findings. One is the strength of test-retest correlations over time, such as the finding that IQ tested at age 11 had a correlation of 0.54 (0.67 when adjusted for range restriction) with IQ tested at age 90 [64]. The other is on the heritability of IQ [65] based on twin studies (identical twins reared apart), which typically estimate the heritability of intelligence to be from 20% in infancy to 80% in later adulthood.

However, both these findings leave plenty of room for environmental effects on general cognitive ability. The Flynn effect, that IQ has increased by about three points (0.2 standard deviations) per decade [66], is one piece of evidence. Another is the effects of school on IQ, which tends to be about 2–5 points per year of school (e.g., [67,68]). This estimate is based on studies that vary widely in their methodology, and on the degree to which the evidence may be considered causal rather than correlational (the strongest causal evidence may be the natural experiment on changing the age of mandatory schooling [69]), but the fact that the estimate is approximately the same regardless of method increases confidence that there is an effect of schooling on IQ. Another piece of evidence is the fact that achievement test scores, which are not assumed to be immutable (they are used in school accountability, for example, [70]), show the same test–retest stability as general cognitive ability tests do [71].

The other persistent myth is that even if general cognitive skills are directly trained, that training will not transfer. This idea comes from several sources. One is a body of literature in experimental psychology that illustrates the difficulty of transfer from one setting to another. A classic study [72] showed that reading a story about a military strategy (separate, surround, and converge) did not help students solve a tumor problem that could be solved by an analogous strategy. There are many illustrations of this phenomenon in real life contexts, such as shoppers who are poor at standardized math problems doing well in calculating good deals in the supermarket [73], or bettors who perform complex mental calculations to assess race-track odds performing poorly on standardized tests [74]. This has led to the situated cognition view [75] that knowledge is bound to the context in which it is acquired, making transfer difficult or impossible.

If the situated learning perspective is correct (along with the related concept of authentic assessment [76]), that would bring into question the benefits of using the short problem solving measures used in PISA, and would suggest that the benefits of using even the longer ones advocated by Dorner and Funke [58] were limited. However, Anderson, Reder, and Simon [77] challenged the situated learning perspective, arguing that there were many demonstrations of transfer of arithmetic skills from the classroom to the real world, or transfer of learning from say one text editor to another. They argued that training abstract principles, particularly when combined with concrete examples, was a powerful means of preparing students for future unpredictable performance tasks.

The view that transfer is impossible is belied by substantial and varied evidence from different corners as well. In the economics literature [78] it can be shown that workers accumulate knowledge and skill (human capital) in an occupation, which is reflected in their growing earnings. When they switch occupations, that acquired knowledge and skill goes with them. The degree of earnings loss experienced is directly related to the similarity of the old and new occupations, a kind of portable skills transfer gradient. In organizations, over $125 billion is spent annually on training, a colossal waste if transfer does not occur. However, meta-analyses have shown that training in organizations does transfer [79] and the substantial literature that exists focusses on the conditions that foster transfer. Those conditions include trainee characteristics such as cognitive ability and conscientiousness, as well as being motivated; supportive work environments; and training interventions that promote knowledge, self-efficacy, and broad skills such as leadership and perhaps, complex problem solving. In education, there have been several reports that assume transfer and have focused on the learning and instructional conditions that facilitate it [12,14].

If we accept the notion that complex problem solving skill can be developed, and that it can transfer to real-world problem solving, a question is how best to teach it and how best to monitor its development over time. There was considerable research in the 1980s that explored the value of direct instruction of general problem-solving skills [80–82]. Despite some successes [83], much of this line of research fell out of favor for not showing large gains in general problem-solving skills. This led to a movement back towards domain-specific (curricular-focused) instruction. However, with the new-found emphasis on transfer and domain-general abilities, such as problem solving in PISA, or NAEP's 2014-2016 technology and engineering literacy assessment [84] or student learning outcomes assessment in higher education [85] there may be a renewed interest in direct instruction efforts. Direct problem-solving instruction may be particularly acceptable if nested in a formative instructional context, as suggested in the previous section [61].

7. Conclusions

Economic inequality is recognized as a barrier to economic growth and access to quality education [86]. In addition, wealth inequality has been increasing over the past 30 years [87]. Americans tolerate the problem, perhaps because they fail to recognize its magnitude; when given a choice, they dramatically (92% vs. 8%) prefer the wealth distribution of Sweden (36% for the top quintile, 11% for the bottom) over that of the U.S. (84% for the top quintile, 0.1% for the bottom) when those distributions are unlabeled [88]. Various methods have been proposed to address the problem of income and wealth inequality, including progressive income taxation, estate taxation, more open immigration policies, strengthened unions, financial literacy, increased social spending (health and welfare), and pension reform [3]. However, increased education has long been considered the "great equalizer" and, in this commentary, I review some of the evidence on the economic returns to investments in education. There are social, cultural, and health benefits as well. Piketty argued that "in the long run, the best way to reduce inequalities with respect to labor as well as to increase the average productivity of the labor force and the overall growth of the economy is surely to invest in education" [3] (pp. 306–307). Policy makers acknowledge this role of education and therefore continue to support increased educational attainment goals.

A question is the mechanism by which education delivers these benefits. A widely accepted view is that of a race between education and technology in which technology change fuels economic growth, but also "creates winners and losers" leading to increased inequality [89]. However, "if workers have flexible skills and if the educational infrastructure expands sufficiently, the supply of skills will increase as demand (due to technology changes) increases for them" [89] (p. 26).

What does it mean to have flexible skills? Domain-specific (curricular) skills are important, but, in this commentary I have tried to make a case for the importance of general, domain-independent skills, in particular, complex problem solving. Complex problem-solving skill is a name for a construct used in the workforce literature as a characterization of certain job skills. It is also used in the educational testing and cognitive psychological literatures to characterize the abilities required to solve certain kinds of problems. There are debates in the literature on the boundaries of this definition and the best methods for assessing complex problem solving, but a useful definition involves the ability to solve novel, ill-defined problems in complex, real-world settings.

Employers seek and reward individuals possessing complex problem-solving skills. Due to technology advances, it is likely that such skills will remain valued, and perhaps increase in value, particularly in combination with communication skills. This suggests that collaborative problem-solving skill is likely to be an important skill for the future workforce. In recognition of this prospect, assessments of collaborative problem-solving skill have been developed already in PISA [49], and such assessments are being planned for NAEP [90] (see [91], for a discussion of associated assessment and measurement issues).

A wide range of tasks has been put forward for measuring complex problem solving, and it can be argued that the most appropriate task will depend on the particular use—student or employee selection, student development monitoring, or formative assessment. Relatively short, psychometrically efficient tasks are required for the former two uses, but longer, microworld-based tasks [58] may be usefully employed in a formative assessment context. Doing so may entail new task design, analysis, and reporting strategies as outlined by Reckase [61]. It is important for schools at all levels, K-12, community college, career and technical education, and college and university, to recognize the importance of general, complex problem-solving skills for students as part of a strategy to prepare students for the workforce and to thereby reduce the insidious effects of wealth concentration on future opportunities for all.

Conflicts of Interest: The author declares no conflict of interest.

Appendix A. Definitions of Problem Solving in PISA and PIAAC

PISA 2003

"Problem solving is an individual's capacity to use cognitive processes to confront and resolve real, cross-disciplinary situations where the solution path is not immediately obvious and where the literacy domains or curricula areas that might be applicable are not within a single domain of mathematics, science or reading" [47] (p. 154).

PISA 2012

"Problem solving competency is an individual's capacity to engage in cognitive processing to understand and resolve problem situations where a method of solution is not immediately obvious. It includes the willingness to engage with such situations in order to achieve one's potential as a constructive and reflective citizen" [53] (p. 12).

"For the purposes of the PISA 2012 problem solving assessment, the processes involved in problem solving are taken to be Exploring and understanding; Representing and formulating; Planning and executing; and Monitoring and reflecting" [53] (p. 20–21).

PISA 2015

"Three major collaborative problem-solving competencies are identified and defined for measurement in the assessment. These three major CPS competencies are crossed with the four major individual problem-solving processes to form a matrix of specific skills. The specific skills have associated actions, processes and strategies that define what it means for the student to be competent ... The three major CPS competencies are ... (1) Establishing and maintaining shared understanding ... (2) Taking appropriate action to solve the problem ... (3) Establishing and maintaining group organization" [48] (pp. 12–13).

PIAAC

"In PIAAC, problem solving in technology-rich environments is defined as: using digital technology, communication tools and networks to acquire and evaluate information, communicate with others and perform practical tasks. The first PIAAC problem solving survey will focus on the abilities to solve problems for personal, work and civic purposes by setting up appropriate goals and plans, accessing and making use of information through computers and computer networks" [53] (p. 47).

References

1. Obama, B. *Remarks by the President on Economic Mobility (THEARC)*; The White House, Office of the Press Secretary: Washington, DC, USA, 2013. Available online: https://obamawhitehouse.archives.gov/the-press-office/2013/12/04/remarks-president-economic-mobility (accessed on 16 July 2018).
2. Trudeau, J. Remarks at the Charlottetown Confederation Centre on the Canada's 150th Anniversary. 23 November 2017. Available online: https://www.theglobeandmail.com/news/politics/trudeau-targets-income-inequality-in-canadian-confederation-speech/article37062498/ (accessed on 16 July 2018).
3. Piketty, T. *Capital in the 21st Century*; Belknap Press of Harvard University Press: Cambridge, MA, USA, 2014.
4. Stiglitz, J.E. *The Price of Inequality: How Today's Divided Society Endangers Our Future*; W. W. Norton & Company: New York, NY, USA, 2012.
5. Mann, M. *Life and Works of Horace Mann, Volume III*; Horace B. Fuller: Boston, MA, USA, 1868. Available online: https://archive.org/stream/lifeworksofhorac03manniala#page/670/mode/2up/search/equalizer (accessed on 16 July 2018).
6. U.S. Department of Education. Homeroom: The Official Blog of the U.S. Department of Education. 2011. Available online: https://blog.ed.gov/2011/12/in-america-education-is-still-the-great-equalizer/ (accessed on 16 July 2018).
7. Card, D. The Causal Effect of Education on Earnings. In *Handbook of Labor Economics*; Ashenfelter, O., Card, D., Eds.; Elsevier Science: Amsterdam, The Netherlands, 1999; Volume 3A, pp. 1801–1863.
8. Psacharopoulos, G.; Patrinos, H.A. Returns to investment in education: A further update. *Educ. Econ.* **2004**, *12*, 111–134. [CrossRef]
9. Oreopoulos, P.; Salvanes, K.G. *How Large Are Returns to Schooling? Hint: Money Isn't Everything*; NBER Working Paper Series; Working Paper 15339; National Bureau of Economic Research: Cambridge, MA, USA, 2009. Available online: http://www.nber.org/papers/w15339 (accessed on 16 July 2018).
10. Spence, M. Job Market Signaling. *Q. J. Econ.* **1973**, *87*, 355–374. [CrossRef]
11. Lange, F.; Topel, R. The social value of education and human capital. In *Handbook of the Economics of Education*; Hanushek, E., Welch, F., Eds.; Elsevier: Amsterdam, The Netherlands, 2006; pp. 459–509.
12. Robst, J. Education and Job Match: The Relatedness of College Major and Work. *Econ. Educ. Rev.* **2007**, *26*, 397–407. [CrossRef]
13. DeGusta, M. Are Smart Hones Spreading Faster than Any Technology in Human History? *MIT Technology Review*, 9 May 2012. Available online: https://www.technologyreview.com/s/427787/are-smart-phones-spreading-faster-than-any-technology-in-human-history/ (accessed on 16 July 2018).
14. National Research Council; Division of Behavioral and Social Sciences and Education; Center for Education. *Research on Future Skill Demands: A Workshop Summary*; Hilton, M., Ed.; The National Academies Press: Washington, DC, USA, 2008.
15. U.S. Department of Labor. *What Work Requires of Schools. A SCANS Report for America 2000. The Secretary's Commission on Achieving Necessary Skills*; U.S Department of Labor: Washington, DC, USA, 1991.
16. National Research Council; Division of Behavioral and Social Sciences and Education; Board on Science Education; Board on Testing and Assessment; Committee on Defining Deeper Learning and 21st Century Skills. *Education for Life and Work: Developing Transferable Knowledge and Skills in the 21st Century*; Pellegrino, J.W., Hilton, M.L., Eds.; The National Academies Press: Washington, DC, USA, 2013.
17. National Research Council; National Academy of Engineering; Engineering Education Program Office; Division of Behavioral and Social Sciences and Education; Teacher Advisory Council; Board on Science Education; Division on Earth and Life Studies; Board on Life Sciences, Policy and Global Affairs; Board on Higher Education and Workforce; Planning Committee on Evolving Relationships and Dynamics between Two- and Four-Year Colleges and Universities. *Community Colleges in the Evolving STEM Education Landscape: Summary of a Summit*; Olson, S., Labov, J.B., Eds.; The National Academies Press: Washington, DC, USA, 2012.
18. National Research Council; Division of Behavioral and Social Sciences and Education; Center for Education; Board on Science Education. *Exploring the Intersection of Science Education and 21st Century Skills: A Workshop Summary*; Hilton, M., Ed.; The National Academies Press: Washington, DC, USA, 2010.

19. National Research Council; Board on Testing and Assessment; Division of Behavioral and Social Sciences and Education; Committee on the Assessment of 21st Century Skills. *Assessing the 21st Century Skills: Summary of a Workshop*; Koenig, J.A., Ed.; The National Academies Press: Washington, DC, USA, 2011.
20. Stone, J.R., III; Lewis, M.V. *College and Career Ready in the 21st Century*; Teachers College Press: New York, NY, USA, 2012.
21. U.S. Department of Labor. Occupational Information Network (O*NET). Employment and Training Administration (USDOL/ETA). 2018. Available online: https://www.onetcenter.org/ (accessed on 16 July 2018).
22. Autor, D.H.; Levy, F.; Murnane, R.J. The skill content of recent technological change: An empirical exploration. *Q. J. Econ.* **2003**, *118*, 1279–1334. [CrossRef]
23. National Association of Colleges and Employers Job Outlook 2017. Available online: http://www.naceweb.org/talent-acquisition/candidate-selection/the-attributes-employers-seek-on-a-candidates-resume/ (accessed on 16 July 2018).
24. McKinsey Center for Government. *Education to Employment: Designing a System That Works*; McKinsey Center for Government: New York, NY, USA, 2012; Available online: https://www.mckinsey.com/industries/social-sector/our-insights/education-to-employment-designing-a-system-that-works (accessed on 16 July 2018).
25. Casner-Lotto, J.; Barrington, L. *Are They Really Ready to Work? Employers' Perspectives on the Basic Knowledge and Applied Skills of New Entrants to the 21st Century U.S. Workforce*; The Conference Board, Partnership for 21st Century Skills, Corporate Voices for Working Families, Society for Human Resources Management: Washington, DC, USA, 2006.
26. North Carolina Association of Workforce Development Boards. Closing the Gap: 2012 Skills Survey of North Carolina Employers, Summary and Findings. 2012. Available online: http://www.ncawdb.org/wp/wp-content/uploads/2013/05/2012SkillsSurveyWDBFinal.pdf (accessed on 16 July 2018).
27. Research Triangle Institute O*NET Data Collection Program. 2018. Available online: https://onet.rti.org/ (accessed on 16 July 2018).
28. Reeder, M.C.; Tsacoumis, S. *O*NET Analyst Occupational Skills Ratings: Analysis Cycle 16 Results*; O*NET Resource Center, Final Report; National Center for O*NET Development: Raleigh, NC, USA, 2015.
29. Kyllonen, P.C.; Carrasco, C.A.; Kell, H.J. Fluid ability (Gf) and complex problem solving (CPS). *J. Intell.* **2017**, *5*, 28. [CrossRef]
30. Burrus, J.; Jackson, T.; Xi, N.; Steinberg, J. *Identifying the Most Important 21st Century Workforce Competencies: An Analysis of the Occupational Information Nework (O*NET)*; ETS Research Report No. ETS RR-13-21; Educational Testing Service: Princeton, NJ, USA, 2013.
31. Deming, D.J. The Growing Importance of Social Skills in the Labor Market. *Q. J. Econ.* **2017**, *132*, 1593–1640. [CrossRef]
32. Weinberger, C.J. The increasing complementarity between cognitive and social skills. *Rev. Econ. Stat.* **2014**, *96*, 849–861. [CrossRef]
33. Autor, D.H. Why are there still so many jobs? The history and future of workplace automation. *J. Econ. Perspect.* **2015**, *29*, 3–30. [CrossRef]
34. Frey, C.B.; Osborne, M.A. The Future of Employment: How Susceptible Are Jobs to Computerization? Thesis, Oxford Martin School, Oxford, UK, 17 September 2013.
35. Elliott, S.W. *Computers and the Future of Skill Demand*; OECD Publishing: Paris, France, 2017.
36. Leonhardt, D. The Depression: If Only Things Were That Good. *New York Times*, 8 October 2011. Available online: http://www.nytimes.com/2011/10/09/sunday-review/the-depression-if-only-things-were-that-good.html?pagewanted=all (accessed on 16 July 2018).
37. Brynjolfsson, E.; McAfee, A. *Race against the Machine: How the Digital Revolution Is Accelerating Innovation, Driving Productivity, and Irreversibly Transforming Employment and the Economy*; Digital Frontier Press: Lexington, MA, USA, 2011.
38. Webb, M.E.; Little, D.R.; Cropper, S.J. Once more with feeling: Normative data for the aha experience in insight and noninsight problems. *Behav. Res. Methods* **2017**, 1–22. [CrossRef] [PubMed]
39. Kohler, W. *The Mentality of Apes*; Liveright: New York, NY, USA, 1925.

40. Lung, C.; Dominowski, R.L. Effects of strategy instructions and practice on nine-dot problem solving. *J. Exp. Psychol. Learn. Mem. Cogn.* **1985**, *11*, 804–811. [CrossRef]
41. Duncker, K. On problem solving. *Psychol. Monogr.* **1945**, *58*, i-113. [CrossRef]
42. Newell, A.; Simon, H.A. *Human Problem Solving*; Prentice-Hall: Englewood Cliffs, NJ, USA, 1972.
43. Webb, M.E.; Little, D.R.; Cropper, S.J. Insight is not in the problem: Investigating Insight in problem solving across task types. *Front. Psychol.* **2016**, *7*, 1–13. [CrossRef] [PubMed]
44. Anderson, J.R. *Cognitive Psychology and Its Implications*, 8th ed.; Worth Publishers: New York, NY, USA, 2015.
45. Polya, G. *How to Solve It*; Originally Published in 1945 by Princeton University Press; Doubleday: Garden City, NY, USA, 1957.
46. Bransford, J.D.; Stein, B.S. *The Ideal Problem Solver*; W. H. Freeman and Company: New York, NY, USA, 1993; Volume 46. Available online: https://digitalcommons.georgiasouthern.edu/ct2-library/46 (accessed on 16 July 2018).
47. Organisation for Economic Co-Operation and Development (OECD). *PISA 2003 Technical Report*; OECD Publishing: Paris, France, 2005.
48. Organisation for Economic Co-Operation and Development (OECD). Assessing problem-solving skills in PISA 2012. In *PISA 2012 Results: Creative Problem Solving (Volume V)*; OECD Publishing: Paris, France, 2014; pp. 25–46.
49. Organisation for Economic Co-Operation and Development (OECD). *Pisa 2015 Results in Focus*; 2226–0919; Organisation for Economic Co-Operation and Development (OECD): Paris, France, 2016.
50. Greiff, S.; Funke, J. Measuring complex problem solving: The MicroDYN approach. In *The Transition to Computer-Based Assessment. New Approaches to Skills Assessment and Implications for Large-Scale Testing*; Scheuermann, F., Björnsson, J., Eds.; Office for Official Publications of the European Communities: Luxembourg, 2009; pp. 157–163.
51. Funke, J.; Greiff, S. Dynamic problem solving: Multiple-item testing on minimally complex systems. In *Competence Assessment in Education, Methodology of Educational Measurement and Assessment*; Leutner, D., Fleischer, J., Grunkorn, J., Kleime, E., Eds.; Springer: Berlin, Germany, 2017; pp. 427–443.
52. U.S. Department of Education; Institute of Education Sciences; National Center for Education Statistics; National Assessment of Educational Progress (NAEP). *National Science Assessment*; National Center for Education Statistics: Washington, DC, USA, 2009.
53. Organisation for Economic Co-Operation and Development (OECD). *Literacy, Numeracy and Problem Solving in Technology-Rich Environments: Framework for the OECD Survey of Adult Skills*; OECD Publishing: Paris, France, 2012.
54. Carroll, J.B. *Human Cognitive Abilities: A Survey of Factor Analytic Studies*; Cambridge University Press: Cambridge, UK, 1993.
55. Beckman, J.F.; Birney, D.P.; Goode, N. Beyond Psychometrics: The Difference between Difficult Problem Solving and Complex Problem Solving. *Front. Psychol.* **2017**, *8*, 1739. [CrossRef] [PubMed]
56. Frensch, P.A.; Funke, J. *Complex Problem Solving: The European Perspective*; Routledge: Abingdon, UK, 1995.
57. Sternberg, R.J.; Frensch, P.A. *Complex Problem Solving: Principles and Mechanisms*; Routledge: Abingdon, UK, 1991.
58. Dörner, D.; Funke, J. Complex problem solving: What it is and what is not. *Front. Psychol.* **2017**, *8*, 1153. [CrossRef] [PubMed]
59. Funke, J. Complex problem solving. In *Encyclopedia of the Sciences of Learning*; Seel, N.M., Ed.; Springer: Heidelberg, Germany, 2012; Volume 38, pp. 682–685.
60. Shute, V.J.; Emihovich, B. Assessing problem-solving skills in immersive environments. In *International Handbook on IT in Primary and Secondary Education*; Gibson, D., Ifenthaler, D., Webb, M., Eds.; Springer: New York, NY, USA, 2018.
61. Reckase, M.D. *A Tale of Two Models: Sources of Confusion in Achievement Testing*; ETS Research Report No. RR-17-44; Education Testing Service: Princeton, NJ, USA, 2017; ISSN 2330-8516. Available online: https://sharepoint.etslan.org/rd/rrpts/RR/RR-17-44.pdf#search=reckase (accessed on 16 July 2018).
62. Jensen, A. *The g Factor: The Science of Mental Ability*; Greenwood Publishing Group: Westport, CN, USA, 1998.

63. Hernstein, R.J.; Murray, C. *The Bell Curve: Intelligence and Class Structure in American Life*; Free Press: New York, NY, USA, 1994.

64. Deary, I.J.; Pattie, A.; Starr, J.M. The stability of intelligence from age 11 to age 90 years: The Lothian birth cohort of 1921. *Psychol. Sci.* **2013**, *24*, 2361–2368. [CrossRef] [PubMed]

65. Plomin, R.; Deary, I. Genetics and intelligence differences: Five special findings. *Mol. Psychiatry* **2015**, *20*, 98. [CrossRef] [PubMed]

66. Trahan, L.H.; Stuebing, K.K.; Fletcher, J.M.; Hiscock, M. The Flynn effect: A meta-analysis. *Psychol. Bull.* **2014**, *140*, 1332–1360. [CrossRef] [PubMed]

67. Ceci, S.J. How much does schooling influence general intelligence and its cognitive components? A reassessment of the evidence. *Dev. Psychol.* **1991**, *27*, 703–722. [CrossRef]

68. Cliffordson, C.; Gustafsson, J.-E. Effects of age and schooling on intellectual performance: Estimates obtained from analysis of continuous variation in age and length of schooling. *Intelligence* **2008**, *36*, 143–152. [CrossRef]

69. Brinch, C.N.; Galloway, T.A. Schooling in adolescence raises IQ scores. *Proc. Natl. Acad. Sci. USA* **2011**, *109*, 425–430. [CrossRef] [PubMed]

70. Wiliam, D. Standardized tests and school accountability. *Educ. Psychol.* **2010**, *45*, 107–122. [CrossRef]

71. Deary, I.J.; Brett, C.E. Predicting and retrodicting intelligence between childhood and old age in the 6-day sample of the Scottish Mental Survey 1947. *Intelligence* **2015**, *50*, 1–9. [CrossRef] [PubMed]

72. Gick, M.L.; Holyoak, K.J. Analogical problem solving. *Cogn. Psychol.* **1980**, *12*, 306–355. [CrossRef]

73. Lave, J. *Cognition in Practice: Mind, Mathematics and Culture in Everyday Life (Learning in Doing)*; Cambridge University Press: Cambridge, UK, 1988; ISBN 0-521-35734-9.

74. Ceci, S.J.; Liker, J.K. A day at the races: A study of IQ, expertise, and cognitive complexity. *J. Exp. Psychol. Gen.* **1986**, *115*, 255–266. [CrossRef]

75. Lave, J.; Wenger, E. *Situated Learning: Legitimate Peripheral Participation*; Cambridge University Press: Cambridge, UK, 1991; ISBN 0-521-42374-0.

76. Messick, S. The interplay of evidence and consequences in the validation of performance assessments. *Educ. Res.* **1994**, *23*, 13–23. [CrossRef]

77. Anderson, J.R.; Reder, L.M.; Simon, H.A. Situated learning and education. *Educ. Res.* **1996**, *25*, 5–11. [CrossRef]

78. Gathmann, C.; Schonberg, U. How general is human capital? A task-based approach. *J. Labor Econ.* **2010**, *28*, 1–49. [CrossRef]

79. Blume, B.D.; Ford, J.K.; Baldwin, T.T.; Huang, J.L. Transfer of training: A metaanalytic review. *J. Manag.* **2010**, *36*, 1065–1105. [CrossRef]

80. Nickerson, R.S.; Perkins, D.N.; Smith, E.E. *The Teaching of Thinking*; Erlbaum: Hillsdale, NJ, USA, 1985.

81. Segal, J.W.; Chipman, S.F.; Glaser, R. *Thinking and Learning Skills, Volume 1, Relating Instruction to Research*; Routledge: Abingdon, UK, 2014.

82. Chipman, S.F.; Segal, J.W.; Glaser, R. (Eds.) *Thinking and Learning Skills. Volume 2: Research and Open Questions*; Lawrence Erlbaum Associates: Hillsdale, NJ, USA, 1985.

83. Hernstein, R.J.; Nickerson, R.S.; de Sánchez, M.; Swets, J.A. Teaching thinking skills. *Am. Psychol.* **1986**, *41*, 1279–1289. [CrossRef]

84. U.S. Department of Education; Institute of Education Sciences; National Center for Education Statistics; National Assessment of Educational Progress (NAEP). *The Nation's Report Card: Technology and Engineering Literacy*; National Center for Education Statistics: Washington, DC, USA, 2016.

85. Liu, O.L.; Frankel, L.; Roohr, K.C. *Assessing Critical Thinking in Higher Education: Current State and Directions for Next-Generation Assessment*; ETS Research Report Series, RR-14-10; Educational Testing Service: Princeton, NJ, USA, 2014.

86. Cingano, F. *Trends in Income Inequality and Its Impact on Economic Growth*; OECD Social, Employment and Migration Working Papers No. 163; OECD Publishing: Paris, France, 2014.

87. Goldin, C.; Katz, L.F. *The Race between Education and Technology*; Harvard University Press: Cambridge, MA, USA, 2008.

88. Norton, M.I.; Ariely, D. Building a better America—One wealth quintile at a time. *Perspect. Psychol. Sci.* **2011**, *6*, 9–12. [CrossRef] [PubMed]

89. National Center for Education Statistics. *The Nation's Report Card: 2014 Technology and Engineering Literacy*; National Center for Education Statistics: Washington, DC, USA, 2016.

90. National Center for Education Statistics. *Collaborative Problem Solving: Considerations for the National Assessment of Educational Progress*; National Center for Education Statistics: Washington, DC, USA, 2017.

91. Von Davier, A.A.; Zhu, M.; Kyllonen, P.C. *Innovative Assessment of Collaboration*; Springer: Cham, Switzerland, 2017; ISBN 978-3-319-33261-1.

Journal of
Intelligence

MDPI

Article

When Irrational Biases Are Smart: A Fuzzy-Trace Theory of Complex Decision Making

Valerie Reyna

Department of Human Development, Human Neuroscience Institute, Cornell University, Ithaca, NY 14850, USA;
vr53@cornell.edu

Received: 14 March 2018; Accepted: 29 May 2018; Published: 8 June 2018

Abstract: I take a decision-making approach to consider ways of addressing the "unresolved and dramatic problems in the world". Traditional approaches to good decision-making are reviewed. These approaches reduce complex decisions to tradeoffs between magnitudes of probabilities, and outcomes in which the quantity and precision of information are key to making good decisions. I discuss a contrasting framework, called "fuzzy-trace theory", which emphasizes understanding the simple gist of options and applying core social and moral values. Importantly, the tendency to rely on meaningful but simple gist increases from childhood to adulthood (or, in adulthood, as people gain experience in a domain), so that specific irrational biases grow with knowledge and experience. As predicted theoretically, these violations of rationality in the traditional sense are associated empirically with healthier and more adaptive outcomes. Thus, interventions that help decision makers understand the essential gist of their options and how it connects to core values are practical approaches to reducing "unresolved and dramatic problems in the world" one decision at a time.

Keywords: gist; wisdom; biases; heuristics; Allais paradox; framing effects; rationality

---

In this article, I take a process-oriented approach to applying the brain and behavioral sciences to consider ways of reducing the "unresolved and dramatic problems in the world".[1] The logic is the same as for any science that is applied to solve problems: By understanding and intervening in causal processes, outcomes can be changed. In particular, I focus on decision making because laypersons, professionals, and policy makers have the ability to reduce problems in the world by making better decisions. As others have argued, more than intelligence—as is conventionally conceived—is required to make good decisions (e.g., [1]). By conventionally conceived, I refer to such abilities as holding and manipulating large amounts of information in working memory, processing it precisely, and inhibiting effects of context. Some extensions of conventional concepts of intelligence have emphasized the importance of processing context. However, I discuss an ability that complements, but differs from, prior extensions of the concept of intelligence [2,3].

Drawing on fuzzy-trace theory (FTT), I argue that there is another way to be smart, namely, by relying on simple meaningful representations of information called "gist" to make good decisions (see Table 1). However, getting the gist of information is still not sufficient to make good decisions. Decision makers must implement social and moral values, too. By implementing social and moral values, I mean retrieving them from long-term memory and applying them to representations of options to determine choices (see below). Paradoxically, gist representations underlie specific cognitive biases

---

[1] The charge given to authors for this special issue is, "If intelligence is truly important to real-world adaptation, and IQs have risen 30+ points in the past century (Flynn effect), then why are there so many unresolved and dramatic problems in the world, and what can be done about it?"

that emerge predictably with development, but are, nevertheless, associated with healthy and prosocial choices. Below, I describe how cognitive representations of gist and social values combine to promote adaptive decision making, and how their implementation for the greater good can be facilitated.

Table 1. Determining Potential Gist Representations that are Likely to be Encoded for a Particular Decision or Situation.

- Questions to ask to begin the derivation of gist

  - What information about the options is relevant and important to make this particular decision?
  - What is the essence of this decision (what is it really about)?
    - Example: Is the O.J. Simpson case basically about domestic violence or about racism and corruption?
  - What do the options boil down to?
  - What quantities are essentially "nil"?
  - What quantities are essentially "the same" as opposed to qualitatively (meaningfully) different?
  - Which outcomes are irretrievable?
    - Examples: once in a lifetime allowable election of long-term care benefits; losing one's home to fire without being able to afford to replace it; irreversible joint damage from arthritis; instantaneous death from a pulmonary embolism; being sentenced to life in prison without the possibility of parole
  - Which categorical or ordinal distinctions can be made by comparing options (e.g., only one option offers the possibility of nothing as compared to something)?
  - Which distinctions are arbitrary or trivial (and thus should be ignored or assimilated to other outcomes)?

- Operational definitions of gist [4]

  - Ask people to summarize the gist (the essential bottom line) of the decision.
  - Ask people to recall the decision information after a long-term retention interval.
  - Ask people to recognize verbatim and gist representations of information under different instructional conditions designed to disentangle verbatim and gist representations (see [5]).
  - Ask people to provide a title for a narrative relevant to the decision.

- Examples of categorical gist

  - No chance to live vs. a chance to live
  - Extending life (a chance to live longer) vs. not extending life
  - Not really living (e.g., comatose or sedated) vs. really living (e.g., conscious and able to communicate)
  - Saving some lives vs. not saving lives
  - Gaining money vs. gaining no money
  - Gaining money vs. losing money
  - Having a life vs. not having a life
    - Accepting a plea bargain means that the defendant can resume his career and it gives him a chance at a life.

- Examples of ordinal gist

  - Gaining more money vs. gaining less money
  - Saving more lives vs. saving fewer lives
  - Higher quality of life vs. lower quality of life
  - Serving fewer years in prison vs. serving more years in prison
  - Living more years vs. living fewer years

Note: For more extensive and formal descriptions of gist derivation, see Broniatowski and Reyna ([6], Table 1) and Reyna ([7], Figures 1 and 2). Note that people with different levels of expertise or background knowledge, different experience in a domain, or cultural or background differences may have different gist representations. Multiple gist representations are typically extracted for the same information and can all be consistent with that information. The "correct" gist is both accurate (not contradicted by the information) and relevant to the task at hand (e.g., to the question being asked). The O. J. Simpson example is drawn from a question posed by a presenter at the International Bar Association, Chicago, Illinois on 17 May 2018. Orenthal J. (a former professional football player known as "O. J.") Simpson was accused of murdering his ex-wife (whom he had abused) in a 1995 trial in Los Angeles Superior Court in which attorneys argued that police were racially biased.

Specifically, I set the stage by discussing good and bad decisions and how they are related to problems in the world, concluding that understanding the causal processes that underlie decisions, not merely outcomes, offers hope for resolving world problems. I then introduce major theories of decision making, each of which contributes to understanding decision processes and quality. Although classical theories hold that decision makers should choose options that pay off advantageously on average and that decisions should be governed by rules of consistency that eschew effects of context, FTT emphasizes categorical differences between options (rather than averaging over outcomes that are qualitatively distinct) and the beneficial effects of processing qualitative meaning in context. This FTT framework is then applied to several domains of decision making, such as clinicians' decisions to prescribe antibiotics when they know that an illness is probably viral (and, hence, not responsive to antibiotics). The clinician's perspective centers primarily on the individual patient, and only secondarily on society at large, whereas the public health perspective centers on population averages (i.e., expected values). Thus, FTT provides a descriptive and prescriptive approach to understanding decisions that are made by individuals under common circumstances in which probabilistic expectations do not credibly apply. Even when such expectations can apply, as when choices are made repeatedly, FTT offers an alternative to compensatory trading off of risk and reward that represents the essential, non-compensatory bottom line of options.

1. Background: Is This the Best of Times or the Worst of Times?

What is meant by unresolved and dramatic problems? Is this the best of times or the worst of times? In decision making, the paradox of whether human decision making is generally good or bad is well known and is often phrased in terms that juxtapose our triumphs and tragedies [8]. For example, how could the same human race have succeeded in reaching the moon but have failed to recognize Hitler's threat until it was almost too late (e.g., that appeasement would be futile)?[2] Reaching the moon and not recognizing a threat could be described as apples and oranges, but some observers have emphasized the good apples, whereas others have emphasized the bad oranges.

With respect to apples, what little data are available suggest that human beings are making progress in that violence has declined enormously over long periods of time [9]. Institutions, such as the United Nations, provide alternatives to war. News reporters risk death to bring the public information that can motivate people to act. Policy-makers acknowledge that they often first learn of trouble spots around the globe from cable news channels that did not exist decades ago. The miracles of vaccination and antibiotics have saved many millions from death, and infant mortality is at an all-time low. According to the National Institutes of Health, infant death rates in the United States (US) have dropped 15% in the last decade and more than 70% since 1962. Evidence-based decision making has a great deal to do with the progress in health and medicine.

At the same time, evidence-based policy making is not routine despite federal mandates (i.e., GPRA, Government Performance and Results Act of 1993, Pub.L. 103–62; see also the Coalition for Evidence-Based Policy [10]). Violence, such as mass shootings, seems prevalent and preventable, vaccination refusal has put many lives at risk even among the educated and affluent nations that have access to vaccinations, and patients frequently, expect antibiotics—and physicians prescribe them against their better judgment—when illnesses are viral, creating antibiotic-resistant infections that are now commonplace in hospitals [11,12]. Ironically, the news coverage of bad events that provides

---

[2] One could write volumes about whether going to the moon or appeasing Hitler were good or bad decisions, and there are many other decisions that could be selected. My point is that there are momentous decisions that can be used to illustrate the vast stupidity or impressive wisdom of human decision making, which has been the focus of recurrent post hoc debates. Evaluating such decisions involves more than checking a box about good-bad valence of outcomes and they differ in many ways. Contexts, consequences, and uncertainties surrounding these decisions are among the considerations that have to be taken into account, which I touch on only glancingly. Because they differ in so many ways, reaching the moon and not recognizing Hitler's threat could be described as apples and oranges. However, causal theories unpack these differences that should allow, in principle and after much data-gathering, decision makers to improve outcomes.

needed information to make good decisions also exaggerates the perceived probability of negative events beyond objective reality (called the "availability heuristic", [13]).

Regardless of whether these are the best of times or the worst of times, there is certainly substantial room for improvement in decision making, particularly because policy makers have taken so little advantage of scientific evidence regarding the brain and behavior. Superstitions, speculations, and stereotypes usurp the place of data. Even among those who use data, often they are descriptive data, with misleading confounds (e.g., between race and poverty) that obscure causal mechanisms.

For example, is the significant increase in opioid-overdose death rates in Florida from 2015 to 2016 because the state has an inordinate illicit drug problem (that might be addressed with better interdiction and treatment), or because it has a growing number of older people who are prescribed opioids for chronic pain (e.g., for arthritis) or for some other reason [14,15]. Age "explains" many social and economic problems inasmuch as the proportion of younger or older people in a population drives base rates (e.g., of crime, such as illicit drug use or opioid prescriptions; [16,17]). However, age is only the beginning because that, too, is mainly descriptive—but it does allow some triangulation because there are factors that differ by age that are plausibly linked to behavioral problems (e.g., addiction; [18,19]). In short, the solutions to issues, such as the opioid epidemic, depend on its causes, and there are many gaps in knowledge about neurobehavioral causes in addiction and other societal problems. Below, I describe how theories explain the causal mechanisms behind good and bad decisions, and how the latter, in turn, produce many world problems.

2. Theories of Decision Making

FTT incorporates elements of prior theories of decision making, each of which has built on one another. In the beginning of decision theory, Blaise Pascal (see [20]) proposed a mathematical approach to capture how people think about gambles. Subsequently, theories of how people make decisions and how they should make decisions were fused. However, in the latter part of the twentieth century, a schism opened between the real and the ideal. Many contemporary theorists now look back to the origins of decision theory to judge ideal or rational decision making, but they do not claim that people are really rational. Thus, it is important to understand the sequence of empirical challenges that the theories were designed to explain to separate what is considered good and bad decision making.

2.1. Expected Value and Expected Utility Theory

Theories of decision making build on the core concept of expected value: probabilities multiplied by outcomes yield the overall value of an option. In this view, good decision making amounts to choosing the option with the greater value. For example, a gamble option with 0.5 probability of gaining $20 should be preferred to a sure option to gain $9 because $0.5 \times \$20 = \$10$, which is greater than $9.

However, it was recognized early on that most people's choices deviate from expected value. People are generally risk averse. In other words, they would choose the sure $9. Risk aversion is accounted for by assuming that expected utility (a subjective function of expected value) is not linear with objective value; it is negatively accelerated (increases more slowly than the objective numbers, such as dollars, do) as objective value goes up. Thus, the subjective difference between $0 and $100 is greater than the same objective difference between $100,000 and $100,100.

Von Neumann and Morgenstern [21] showed that, as long as an individual's choices consistently reflected true preferences (i.e., they obeyed certain rules of ordinal consistency), they would maximize rational self-interest (i.e., maximize expected utility). This theory of expected utility (EUT) remains popular in many areas of economics (see [22]). The implication of this theory is that being well-informed about the options, consistent about choices, and self-interested are sufficient for good decision making (cf. [23]).

In 1953, Allais challenged EUT with the following paradox in two parts [24]. The first part is:

A. $1 million for sure.

B.   0.89 probability of $1 million, 0.10 probability of $5 million, and 0.01 probability of $0.

Many people choose A, illustrating risk aversion [6]. In fact, the expected value of B is $390,000 higher than A. Imagine that these options represented investment strategies for retirement. On average, people would be arguably better off if they chose Option B, and society could be better off too because retirees could meet their financial needs without help from taxpayers. However, if these estimates are accurate, some people would end up with nothing, a catastrophic outcome for an individual. According to EUT, it is still rational to be risk averse and choose A, so long as a decision maker has consistent preferences.

Consider the following options, the second part of the Allais paradox:

C.   0.11 probability of $1 million and 0.89 probability of $0.

D.   0.10 probability of $5 million and 0.90 probability of $0.

The risk-averse option is C (because there is a greater probability of a payoff, and thus, less uncertainty), but now many of the same people who choose B tend to choose D. Because this pattern of preferences violates consistency—the same people are risk averse and risk seeking—their choices are not rational.

2.2. Prospect Theory

Tversky and Kahneman [25] offered a theory to explain both the Allais paradox plus inconsistencies elicited by the following "framing" problem that ask the decision maker to imagine that he or she is a policy maker:

Imagine that the U.S. is preparing for the outbreak of an unusual Asian disease, which is expected to kill 600 people. Two alternative programs to combat the disease have been proposed. Assume that the exact scientific estimate of the consequences of the programs are as follows:

If Program A is adopted, 200 people will be saved.
If Program B is adopted, there is 1/3 probability that 600 people will be saved, and 2/3 probability that no people will be saved.

Which of the two programs would you favor?

Assume the same preamble (i.e., 600 people are expected to be killed), but the options are framed as follows:

If Program C is adopted 400 people will die.
If Program D is adopted there is 1/3 probability that nobody will die, and 2/3 probability that 600 people will die.

Which of the two programs would you favor?

Although most people chose Program A, demonstrating risk aversion, another group of similar respondents chose Program D, demonstrating risk seeking, when the objectively identical options were framed as losses. Again, people's risk attitudes are inconsistent, violating EUT and rationality. The pattern can be elicited when gains and losses are presented to the same person, although the framing effect is weakened because some respondents notice that the gain and loss problems are mathematically equivalent versions of one another. Once they notice that gain and loss decisions are connected, they censor or inhibit inconsistent responses [26,27].

To explain gain-loss framing biases, Tversky and Kahneman [25] introduced prospect theory (PT), which accepts people's irrational biases as a fundamental feature of cognition. PT explains framing effects by assuming that decision makers perceive outcomes (e.g., the number of lives saved or lost) and the probabilities of those outcomes nonlinearly, much like EUT. However, different from EUT, decision makers are assumed to distinguish outcomes as gains or losses relative to a reference point (e.g., the status quo), and respond more intensely to losses than to gains. Thus, in PT, the perceptions of gains, losses, and probabilities explain diminished overall value for a risky gain when compared to a sure gain and for a sure loss when compared to a risky loss, accounting for the Allais paradox and the framing effect.

2.3. Fuzzy Trace Theory

Although I discussed the Allais paradox in terms of risk aversion and risk seeking to highlight its psychological similarities to framing effects, the deeper point is that the Allais paradox illustrates FTT's central construct of meaning in context. The two Allais gambles are identical except that an 89% chance of $1 million in each option in the first problem is replaced by an 89% chance of $0 in each option in the second problem. According to EUT, in particular, the axiom of the independence of irrelevant alternatives, adding these alternatives to both options should not matter. Like all of the axioms of EUT, this rule that adding the same thing to different options should not change preferences seems appealing on its face.

However, this manipulation of context—the seemingly irrelevant but dominated alternative—changes the categorical contrast between options. That is, the categorical gist of the options depends on the categories in each option: Zero and non-zero outcomes differ qualitatively because they represent presence versus absence of a category. Thus, any manipulation that turns on making zero outcomes explicit and characteristic of only one or some options, but not others, falls under the purview of predictions of FTT (cf. [28]).

FTT builds on traditional theories by incorporating analysis of precise representations of the surface form of information called "verbatim", such as numerical probabilities and outcomes, as one stream of information processing that occurs in parallel with intuitive qualitative processing of gist [7]. Thus, the expected value of each option (as discussed for the Allais paradox problems) is one factor in decision-making. Even young children are able to calculate something like expected value when they are presented with numbers.

In contrast to verbatim representations that are literal and precise, the gist of the options captures the simple bottom-line meaning, providing another perspective on the same decision options. The gist of options is not some post hoc speculation about what the representations must be to fit with results (see [6,29], for formal models of how verbatim and gist representations of decisions are derived and processed). Instead, research on mental representations (that tested theoretical predictions) guides the derivation of gist for different forms of information: words, narratives, pictures, and numbers (e.g., [5]).

To derive gist, human information processors make the simplest, meaningful cut along dimensions, such as dollars, that distinguishes options. (This process occurs unconsciously). For example, in the first Allais problem, the simplest meaningful distinction is between no money and some money. Thus, the categorical gist of the first Allais problem is that it is a choice between some money for sure (Option A) versus taking a chance on getting some money or no money (Option B). Naturally, because some money is valued more than no money, the sure option (Option A) is preferred. The same assumptions explain framing effects: Saving some people is better than saving none (predicting risk-averse choices for gains), and no one dying is better than some people dying for sure (predicting risk-seeking choices for losses).

The second Allais problem does not allow discrimination between options using this simplest categorical gist because both options offer the possibility of some money or no money. Therefore, decision makers must make a finer ordinal distinction between less money (e.g., $1 million) and more money (e.g., $5 million), favoring option D. The predicted shift from relying on categorical (the first Allais problem) to ordinal representations (the second Allais problem) explains the Allais paradox [30]. In gist, outcomes are represented (e.g., some money or none; less money or more), but what about their probabilities? According to FTT, categorically distinct outcomes are represented at the simplest gist level as possibilities rather than probabilities.

A "fuzzy-processing" preference—a tendency to rely on the simplest representation that discriminates options—guides decision making for most adults, which is why the simplest categorical gist representation tends to win out over more precise representations, such as expected value. Expected value is processed; it affects degree of preference for the gist-favored option [6,7,31]. (That is, gist-based preferences are decreased when expected value conflicts with gist, such as when 1/3 probability of saving 630 lives is substituted for Program B in the example above; the degree of suppression depends on individual differences in numeracy and other factors).[3] Similarly, verbatim processing of words and sentences occurs in parallel with gist processing of those words and sentences. However, even when knowledge, memory, and procedural skills make precise processing doable, FTT predicts (and research supports) that reliance on gist processing increases with development, as I now discuss.

2.4. Developmental Differences and the Wisdom of Experience

Insight into what is meaningful—subjectivity, including context, as opposed to purely literal objectivity—is central to wise decision making in FTT [32]. Support for this position comes from developmental evidence that subjective biases, such as the Allais paradox and framing effects (as well as false memories and conjunction fallacies), increase from childhood to adulthood [33,34]. FTT predicts that specific so-called "heuristics and biases" increase with age during this period when they are due to a developmental increase in gist processing. (So-called, because what are called "heuristics and biases" in the current judgment and decision-making literature are often explained by gist-based intuition, as opposed to heuristics in the sense of mental shortcuts). As discussed, process models derived from FTT implicate predicted processes, such as greater reliance with age on simple categorical distinctions (e.g., between no quantity and some quantity as in no risk is better than some risk), rather than more precise tradeoffs (e.g., between degrees of risk and reward), from childhood to adulthood (e.g., [35]).

Thus, FTT research has shown that framing effects emerge with age from childhood to adulthood. Children choose roughly, according to expected value so long as probabilities and outcomes are depicted with concrete props (e.g., spinners and toy prizes on sections of spinners; [36,37]. They tend to be risk-seeking overall, but modulate preferences based on the sizes of outcomes and probabilities. As they get older, the context matters increasingly; losing prizes from a stash of prizes—despite net gains—begins to matter when heretofore only net gains and probabilities mattered. In other words, being given five toys for sure as an option and then losing two toys from that stash begins to feel like a loss rather than a gain (i.e., it does not feel like a net gain of three toys). Consequentialism, the number of toys one has in the end, gives way to subjectivism as categorical gist dominates, at first, when there are only small differences between outcomes (facilitating assimilating outcomes that are not identical to one another, such as 200 saved and 600 saved in the Asian disease problem, to a common category of "some").[4] By adulthood, people are no longer consistent in their risk preferences for gains and objectively identical net gains that emerge from losses.

Similar developmental trajectories are observed for other gist-based biases in that objectivity gives way to subjective biases (e.g., conjunction fallacies; [38,39]). In particular, moral-reasoning biases, which have been contrasted with consequentialism, also increase during this same period.

---

[3]   Note that choosing the mathematically superior option of 1/3 probability of saving 630 lives is conventionally intelligent (i.e., the expected value is 210 lives which exceeds the expected value of the sure option, 200 lives), but it is not necessarily intelligent in the gist-based sense discussed in this article.

[4]   An example of a decision problem in which differences between outcomes is small is choosing between a sure win of \$1 versus a 1/2 probability of \$2 and 1/2 probability of \$0. An example of a decision problem in which differences between outcomes is large is choosing between a sure win of \$100 versus a 1/2 probability of \$200 and 1/2 probability of \$0.

The subjective bias to donate more money (or candies in the case of children) to one needy child, as opposed to a group of children that includes the one child, goes up with age [40]. Younger children give more to the group than to the one child, but this preference gradually reverses for older children, and ultimately, adults who exhibit the "singularity" bias. Also consistent with FTT, those who show the bias are not cognitively inferior; in fact, children with more advanced theories of mind are more likely to show the bias, as compared to those who lack a sophisticated theory of mind.

FTT does not claim that "there is a general increase in heuristics/biases as children move from quantitative-verbatim to gist-based processing" (p. 75, [37]). Instead, FTT distinguishes heuristics and biases that are rooted in gist (bottom-line or simple meaning in context, e.g., framing effects) from those that reflect motivational biases or limited brute-force computational capacity, the latter referring to the ability to hold more details in memory and engage in more computationally exhaustive processing (e.g., [29,41,42]).

Naturally, sometimes judgment and decision making benefits from brute-force computational capacity and this ability improves in childhood. Psychologists and neuroscientists also tend to create artificial tasks that can only be solved through arbitrary associations that demand computational capacity. However, real-world decision making benefits from having insight and wisdom, which includes a gist-based information-processing style that is not "in the weeds" and is not just pragmatic or knowledge-based [3]. Getting the gist and relying on it in decision making have been shown to explain unique variance in both laboratory and real-world decision making, beyond differences in knowledge (e.g., for literature reviews, see [6,43,44]). In other words, knowing a list of facts and relying on the gist of those facts are not the same thing [45]. Thus, according to FTT, rote stimulus-response learning from experience (i.e., experiencing outcomes that are reinforced or not) differs from learning from experience that produces insight into the essential meaning of decision options [32].

3. Choosing the Best Option

3.1. Are Irrational Biases Smart?

It is important to understand how theories characterize decision making because of their implications for improving it. As examples, decision theorists have pointed to widespread low numeracy as a source of judgment biases and poor decision making (e.g., [46,47]). Thus, perceiving numbers objectively and being able to perform simple computations (e.g., calculating medicine dosage by weight for a child) are seen as remedies. Others have noted the inability to recognize the "advantageous" options, those that offer higher expected value [31,48]. Still others suggest that combining probabilities with outcomes (or consequences) can be made more coherent, reducing irrational inconsistencies. Such programs have been offered to members of the public and even to high school students to instill deliberative, precise, and multiplicative processing of relevant probabilities and outcomes to aid in decision-making (e.g., [49]).

Indeed, decision aids in medicine and other fields typically assume the truth of EUT—and ignore the well-known inconsistencies that motivated PT—in an effort to help people make better decisions (see [50]). That is, the aim of decision aids is to help people make choices that agree with their true preferences. However, the EUT assumptions are a problem that is not just one of a difference between descriptive (what people actually do) and prescriptive (what they should do to improve their decisions) adequacies. Traditional decision aids rely on *in*consistent human judgments to determine the prescriptively best option, despite the fact that consistent judgments are required to apply EUT to derive the best option for that individual.

FTT suggests that choosing the best option is not a matter of selecting the option with the highest expected value or expected utility, but, rather, of understanding the essential meaning of options and applying closely held values to those options. Although some economists encourage thinking about decisions as though they are going to be made repeatedly, in reality, some decisions are, roughly speaking, singular: getting married, buying a house, and per the Allais paradox, having the opportunity to gain a $1 million. Like the story of Solomon, who suggested dividing a baby so two possible mothers could both have him (a bad idea), people do not marry half a person or buy half of a house. In other words, choosing the sure $1 million makes sense given the potential to gain nothing by choosing the gamble; people are wise to avoid catastrophic outcomes, such as having nothing for retirement or losing their home to a fire despite average outcomes turning out fine. However, when both options have a non-negligible potential to yield nothing (as in the second Allais problem), it now makes sense to shift to choosing the option with the higher outcome.

Applying a similar analysis of gist-based choices to gains and losses is justifiable if they are truly gains and losses: Reflection effects are exactly like framing effects except that the gain-loss versions are objectively different, not equivalent (e.g., 200 lives saved vs. 200 lives lost with no prior expectation of the number of people who will be killed). Framing effects are not justifiable because the net outcomes for both gains and losses are identical (e.g., 600 lives − 400 die = 200 saved), but they draw on the same gist-based intuitions as reflection effects. With reflection effects, it makes sense to like variability when the only other option is a sure loss or sure death (and to dislike variability when there is a sure gain vs. the possibility of no gain). Although framing effects per se are technically irrational, they are smart because they reflect a cognitively advanced way of thinking that is generally associated with good outcomes for individuals, as I discuss below. To be sure, the abilities to detect and to censor inconsistent framing responses are related to adaptive outcomes [51], but those tendencies are distinct from the intuitions that produce framing effects in the first place.

3.2. Prescribing Antibiotics

Applying FTT, categorical gist explains why patients who are in the emergency room (ER) want antibiotics even when they realize that their respiratory infection is probably viral (and hence, antibiotics are unlikely to help; [12]). So long as there are not harmful effects of taking antibiotics for the individual, the possibility of cure when a patient is sick enough to be in the ER (i.e., the status quo is a certain negative condition) is attractive. Indeed, this categorical gist of "why not take a risk" was endorsed by ER patients [12] and by physicians [52].

As the antibiotics example illustrates, the clinician's perspective centers on the individual patient, making categorical possibilities of cure or catastrophe salient. The public health perspective aggregates individuals, making population averages or expected values salient. Thus, there is a predictable difference in emphasis between clinicians and public health experts on the issue of antibiotic resistance. However, this gap between representing antibiotic decisions as categorical gist versus expected value can be bridged if the concerns of each perspective are taken into account.

For example, the consequences to an individual patient of the inevitable categorical absence of antibiotics to treat life-threatening infections can be stressed to clinicians, along with the fact that antibiotics have non-negligible side effects for individuals. Clearly, reducing the overprescribing of antibiotics involves more than factual knowledge that antibiotics should not be prescribed for viral illnesses because physicians in the study had that knowledge and still endorsed categorical gist [52]. From this perspective, clinicians need to be persuaded that a given respiratory infection has a nil chance of being bacterial (i.e., treatable with antibiotics), and that the possibility of side effects for an individual is not nil.

This analysis also suggests that prescribing antibiotics is not simply a motivational issue (e.g., pleasing patients), but, rather, is due to a plausible mental model of the decision options. The model is plausible in the sense that it is reasonable and strategic; why not take a risk (by prescribing antibiotics) if a patient is very ill, might get better, and there is little downside potential? Reframing the option of forgoing antibiotics as avoiding both needless side effects and inevitable harm to other patients (with no possibility of upside for individuals) would allow patients and physicians to better access core values about avoiding harm to others. Research on FTT indicates that gist representations of options act as cues to retrieve relevant values, which are stored in long-term memory as fuzzy gist principles (e.g., saving lives is good; [45,53]). Thus, because values re retrieved (and implemented) in a probabilistic way that depends on cues, reframing the gist of options can increase value-concordant choices (e.g., [54,55]).

3.3. Taking Unhealthy Risks

Adolescents face risky decisions in everyday life that also resemble choices in framing problems. For example, imagine a teenager choosing between hanging out with friends under adult supervision versus going to a party where there are more friends, but also alcohol and illegal drugs [19]. Both options offer socially rewarding outcomes. However, the second option involves larger rewards along with risks, such as getting in trouble with parents or with the law. FTT assumes that this decision is represented at multiple levels of precision, but younger people and adults who are developmentally delayed in their mental representations rely on more precise representations, as compared to mature adults [34,56–58]). Focusing on precise details emphasizes the higher social rewards for the party option when compared to the hanging-out option and the low probability of getting in trouble by going to the party. Like many risky behaviors in adolescence, risk-reward ratios favor the party option; similarly, the rewards of sex and crime typically exceed the status quo and the chances of contracting HIV or getting convicted of a crime are low. Thus, precise thinking often favors risk-taking for greater rewards. Of course, FTT suggests that thinking about HIV or about committing serious crimes as calculated risks is developmentally immature and perhaps a little crazy [42,43].

Conversely, under typical middle-class circumstances, mature thinking in terms of categorical gist favors risk aversion for rewards. Consistent with FTT, adolescents and adults who showed standard framing effects in problems such as the ones that I discussed were less likely to report taking unhealthy risks in everyday life (e.g., initiate sex early in life or have many sexual partners; [57]). Risk takers were both more likely to choose sure losses (because the sure losses are smaller than the uncertain losses) and risky gains (because the risky gains are larger than the sure gains). Adults who engage in developmentally inappropriate risk taking, including criminal risk taking, were also less likely to show typical adult framing effects, again, choosing sure losses and risky gains [58]. The amount of self-reported risk taking correlated inversely with the degree of framing biases.

In addition, other measures of categorical risk thinking, such as agreement with the cruder "No risk is better than some risk", as opposed to the more precise ordinal gist "Less risk is better than more risk" also predict real-world risk taking, with categorical thinking associated with lower risk taking (see [57]). That is, respondents were asked to check off all of the values that guided their decisions about sex. Endorsement of these two statements was correlated, but agreeing with the categorical but not ordinal gist halved the chances of initiating sex as a young adolescent, when compared to agreeing with the ordinal but not categorical gist: Percentages of initiation were 30% versus 61%, respectively, in one study and agreeing with both gist principles was intermediate [35]. Other studies examined categorical risk taking by assessing agreement with statements, such as, "It only takes once to get HIV", with similar results.

According to expected value, EUT, and PT, the amount of reward should mitigate the amount of risk—a decision maker should be willing to trade risk for reward. Categorical thinking is antithetical to this view. However, according to FTT, mature adults grow out of this technically rational thinking that focuses on trading off magnitudes of risk and reward. Adults who do not take unhealthy risks would view the teen's choices as something like "Have some fun with friends or take a chance and have some fun with friends but risk catastrophe" (and having fun is better than catastrophe, which is no fun at all). Differences in the magnitude of fun are glossed over in this simplest gist representation, but such differences are pivotal for risk takers.

The risk-promotion effect in adolescence is both cognitive (representational) and motivational (reward-related). Research shows that even when teens endorse rewards and values to a similar degree when compared to non-risk-taking adolescents or young adults, their behavior is less likely to be consistent with their own values (e.g., [59]). Thus, reward sensitivity is one of the causal factors that elevates teen risk taking, but their cognition also focuses on amounts of rewards, rather than the presence or absence of rewards, making them more vulnerable. A meta-analysis of controlled experiments on development of risk preferences confirmed this conclusion that preference for risks declined from childhood to adulthood for cognitive reasons [44], although motivation and impulsivity change during this period, too.

Moreover, reward sensitivity and impulsivity produce different kinds of risk-taking. When risk-taking is impulsive, it is frequently regretted afterwards (when outcomes are bad); it conflicts with teens' perception of risks and rewards upon reflection in the cold light of day [34]. However, in Reyna and Farley's review of the literature, almost all of the studies showed that teens' risky behaviors were predictable based on their reflective perceptions of risks and rewards. Teens were aware of potential bad outcomes and even overestimated the risks, but, on balance, felt that taking lethal risks was "worth it", as is consistent with rational choice theories. A randomized experiment targeting this "hyperrationality" in teens, teaching objective risks, but also how to perceive them in terms of categorical gist, was effective in reducing self-reported risk taking [45]. The intervention did not change adolescents' hormones and it encouraged non-reflective thinking (gist-based intuition), going beyond stereotypes about adolescence and advanced decision making.

3.4. Buying Insurance

A caution is in order before totally abandoning the idea of expected value or maximizing expected utility as benchmarks for rational decision making. FTT recognizes that expected value must be kept in mind and combined with gist. Expected utility may turn out to be epiphenomenal because it seems to be the result of combining linear expected value with gist representations, producing a nonlinear representation that does not, in itself, represent human information processing, at least for small stakes [60,61]. The coherence rules for combining ordinal preferences, however, remain useful as an ideal that humans endorse; people want to have consistent preferences and realign their choices if they notice that they are incoherent. Similar considerations apply to detecting egregious violations of expected value, as when the odds are stacked against players in casinos, when patients reject medications with very small risks despite almost-certain and irreversible loss of function, and when people pay exorbitant amounts for insurance, especially if the coverage has major gaps in protection.

As discussed, it is sometimes difficult for people to tolerate risk for good reasons. Although economists have argued that decisions should be thought of as repeated to avoid decision paradoxes, this "fix" fails to address many situations that characterize real life for people of middle or low incomes. Thinking back to our retirement example, although people are better off in the aggregate if they gamble for more money, the all-or-none disaster for an individual remains if he or she has nothing or loses substantial money in a variable stock market. Gist-based thinking explains why people buy insurance when the expected value goes against them. That is, insurance companies make money selling insurance because they pick premiums that provide a favorable expected value. Despite unfavorable odds, people buy insurance to protect against the categorical possibility of being left homeless (they rarely have the funds to replace their homes without insurance); they reject "probabilistic" insurance that offers a high likelihood (but not certainty) of coverage for the same reason: the possibility of total loss remains. By recognizing that the gist of insurance is categorical for consumers, but that payments often reflect highly unfavorable expected values calculated by actuaries, it should be possible to bring insurance choices into better alignment with consumers' values. Providing "safety-net" coverage that appeals to gist intuitions is more likely to be effective with consumers, rather than persuading individuals to ignore the potential for calamitous risk.

4. Overview and Implications for Resolving World Problems

It is presumptuous to claim that any of us has much to offer to resolve world problems. However, it is useful to note that even small progress is something. Much suffering and death that occurs in the world is linked to young people: For the most part, they commit the violent crimes, transmit sexual infections (e.g., HIV), have lethal accidents because of alcohol, start substance use that ends in addictions, and fight wars—although they are rarely the decision makers that initiate wars. A small number of criminals as adults commit disproportionate crime, and yet we know relatively little about their brains, and why they commit crimes and other seemingly similar adults do not. Ordinary adults also make bad decisions, such as drinking and driving, that produce preventable tragedies or that leave them in poverty, such as not saving for retirement or not buying insurance (or perhaps paying too much for insurance). Professionals also make far from ideal decisions, overprescribing antibiotics that could transform the miracle of curing infections into incurable worldwide epidemics. These decisions add up and challenge state and federal budgets, siphoning resources that could be used to resolve other arguably larger world problems.

Here, I have offered some surprising observations about good and bad decision making, how those are connected to social, economic, and health problems, and how to think about good and bad decision making in a new way. One of the radical aspects of FTT is that it holds that gist representations and associated processing are more advanced developmentally than verbatim processing, although gist produces systematic biases, such as the Allais paradox and framing effects. Gist is the simple, but not simple-minded, meaning of information about options, whether that information is gathered via verbal description or through experience. That simple gist is frequently categorical, which eschews the trading off of risk and reward that is the foundation of virtually all decision theories, but it facilitates taking action. To illustrate, prescribers can trade off the probabilities and consequences of arthritic-pain relief for the risk of opioid addiction, or, if Krebs et al.'s [15] results hold up, recognize that the choice is between options offering the same pain relief with or without opioids, but the opioid option carries a catastrophic risk of addiction.

This review cannot spell out the process models that justify how categorical gist, ordinal gist, and verbatim representations are extracted and combined (but see [6,7,42,61]). However, it should be pointed out that gist-based intuition is not the same as mental shortcuts or "heuristics", and that FTT explains why certainty and zero have unique effects, and in ways that contradict prior accounts, such as EUT and PT. Experiments and mathematical models have been used to test these predictions.

Consistent with FTT's predictions, gist-based biases grow from childhood to adulthood—and not because children's responses are random or disorganized. In fact, when clear instructions and props to support memory are used, children choose roughly according to expected value, discriminating levels of risk and reward. They also respond correctly in probability judgment problems and in other tasks of judgment and decision making that are subject to irrational biases in adulthood.

Beyond the developmental evidence, why is objective responding—as opposed to systematic subjective biases—not an ideal approach to decision making? After all, conventional conceptions of intelligence emphasize analytical ability (used to compute expected value) and the suppression of contextual cues. Consider autism. Some subtypes of autism have been analyzed as involving greater reliance on verbatim than gist processing [29,62,63]). Thus, as FTT predicts, individuals with autism are less likely to exhibit gist-based biases, such as framing effects (as well as false memories and conjunction effects that are also due to gist processing; [63,64]). As predicted by FTT, those with autism show more consistency in preferences in cases in which changes in context and meaning would otherwise drive inconsistencies (e.g., [65]). However, their information processing is also more literal, which presents problems in ordinary life. Gist takes context and meaning into account, which allows people to make more adaptive decisions in everyday life.

The simple meaningful distinctions that have been discussed explain risk preferences in the laboratory (e.g., in framing effects and the Allais paradox) and in life (e.g., in sexual risk taking, antibiotics decisions, and criminal behavior), and, contrary to conventional wisdom, choices in the laboratory and life are correlated once theoretically motivated measures are used. Gist thinkers engage in less unhealthy risk taking as adolescents and adults. Ironically, those who are less likely to exhibit the technically irrational biases of mature adults are more likely to take unhealthy risks, such as having unprotected sex or engaging in criminal behavior. Cognitive representations account for this risky behavior controlling for motivational and personality factors, such as reward sensitivity and impulsivity, that are also important in determining behavior.

The theoretical analysis presented here suggests that a good decision can be thought about from multiple perspectives: From a verbatim perspective, choosing the higher-expected-value options (B and D) is the smart choice in the Allais problems (and indifference is the designated preference for equal-expected-value framing problems). From an EUT perspective, choosing the risk-averse option for both Allais problems (A and C) is optimal, given a risk-averse preference; a risk-seeking preference is fine, too, so long as choices are consistent. However, I have argued that inconsistent choices can be smart if they systematically reflect getting the gist of options (i.e., getting the *correct* gist that captures the important and decision-relevant essence of the options). Crucially, if the choice is offered as a one-time prospect, rather than a repeated decision in which getting zero dollars becomes unlikely, FTT argues that choosing some money over the possibility of no money makes sense just as choosing more money over less money makes sense when the possibility of nothing cannot be avoided. People's ability to discriminate and combine numbers operates in the background modulating preferences, but healthy adults tend to rely on gist.

Relying on the gist of options provides better access to one's values because values are stored in memory in a gisty form. According to FTT, being in touch with values that promote health, morality, and the social good is not necessarily a question of reflective, so-called "higher order" cognition about details. Apparently, the average person negotiates life with a surprising lack of knowledge of details about even everyday objects, let alone climate change or international diplomacy [66]. I am not saying that reflection is bad, but only that it does not underlie a great deal of advanced cognition and it is a separate mental faculty. According to FTT, knowledge is a prerequisite to good decision making to the degree that it promotes understanding the gist of important decisions. Simply memorizing facts is unlikely to improve decisions without understanding the "why" behind the facts and being able to digest the facts so as to recognize what is of core importance [67]. Thus, FTT expands the conception of decision making beyond a conflict between values and consequences, reward and impulsivity, or heart and mind (i.e., between affect or emotion and reflection) to a view that encompasses insightful and contextual meaning.

Funding: Preparation of this article was supported in part by the National Institutes of Health (National Institute of Nursing Research R21NR016905) and the National Institute of Food and Agriculture (NYC-321407). Valerie F. Reyna received research support through grants from the Patient-Centered Outcomes Research Institute (PCORI) and the National Institutes of Health (R01NR014368).

Conflicts of Interest: The author declares no conflicts of interest.

References

1. Stanovich, K.E. Rational and irrational thought: The thinking that IQ tests miss. *Sci. Am. Mind Spec. Collect. Ed.* **2015**, *23*, 12–17. [CrossRef]
2. Ceci, S.J. *On Intelligence: A Bio-Ecological Treatise on Intellectual Development*; Harvard University Press: Cambridge, MA, USA, 1996.
3. Sternberg, R.J. Speculations on the role of successful intelligence in solving contemporary world problems. *J. Intell.* **2018**, *6*, 4. [CrossRef]
4. Kintsch, W.; Mangalath, P. The construction of meaning. *Top. Cogn. Sci.* **2011**, *3*, 346–370. [CrossRef] [PubMed]
5. Reyna, V.F.; Corbin, J.C.; Weldon, R.B.; Brainerd, C.J. How fuzzy-trace theory predicts true and false memories for words, sentences, and narratives. *J. Appl. Res. Mem. Cogn.* **2016**, *5*, 1–9. [CrossRef] [PubMed]
6. Broniatowski, D.A.; Reyna, V.F. A formal model of fuzzy-trace theory: Variations on framing effects and the Allais Paradox. *Decision* **2017**. [CrossRef]
7. Reyna, V.F. A new intuitionism: Meaning, memory, and development in fuzzy-trace theory. *Judgm. Decis. Mak.* **2012**, *7*, 332–359. [PubMed]

8. Nisbett, R.E.; Ross, L. *Human Inference: Strategies and Shortcomings of Social Judgment*; Prentice-Hall: Englewood Cliffs, NJ, USA, 1980.
9. Pinker, S. *The Better Angels of Our Nature: Why Violence Has Declined*; Viking: New York, NY, USA, 2011.
10. Coalition for Evidence-Based Policy. Available online: http://coalition4evidence.org/wp-content/uploads/2015/04/Coalition-Board-of-Advisors-Update-04-24-15.pdf (accessed on 30 May 2018).
11. Brewer, N.T.; Chapman, G.B.; Rothman, A.J.; Leask, J.; Kempe, A. Understanding and increasing vaccination behaviors: Putting psychology into action. *Psychol. Sci. Public Interest* **2018**, *18*, 149–207. [CrossRef] [PubMed]
12. Broniatowski, D.A.; Klein, E.Y.; Reyna, V.F. Germs are germs, and why not take a risk? Patients' expectations for prescribing antibiotics in an inner city emergency department. *Med. Decis. Mak.* **2015**, *35*, 60–67. [CrossRef] [PubMed]
13. Gilovich, T.; Griffin, D.W.; Kahneman, D. *Heuristics and Biases: The Psychology of Intuitive Judgment*; Cambridge University Press: New York, NY, USA, 2002.
14. Drug Overdose Death Data. Available online: https://www.cdc.gov/drugoverdose/data/statedeaths.html (accessed on 30 May 2018).
15. Krebs, E.E.; Gravely, A.; Nugent, S.; Jensen, A.C.; DeRonne, B.; Goldsmith, E.S.; Kroenke, K.; Bair, M.J.; Noorbaloochi, S. Effect of opioid vs nonopioid medications on pain-related function in patients with chronic back pain or hip or knee osteoarthritis pain: The SPACE randomized clinical trial. *JAMA* **2018**, *319*, 872–882. [CrossRef] [PubMed]
16. National Academies of Sciences, Engineering, and Medicine. *Pain Management and the Opioid Epidemic: Balancing Societal and Individual Benefits and Risks of Prescription Opioid Use*; The National Academies Press: Washington, DC, USA, 2017.
17. SAMHSA. *Results from the 2013 National Survey on Drug Use and Health: Summary of National Findings*; US Department of Health and Human Services: Washington, DC, USA, 2014. Available online: https://www.samhsa.gov/data/sites/default/files/NSDUHresultsPDFWHTML2013/Web/NSDUHresults2013.pdf (accessed on 30 May 2018).
18. Bickel, W.K.; Mellis, A.M.; Snider, S.E.; Athamneh, L.N.; Stein, J.S.; Pope, D.A. 21st century neurobehavioral theories of decision making in addiction: Review and evaluation. *Pharmacol. Biochem. Behav.* **2018**, *164*, 4–21. [CrossRef] [PubMed]
19. Reyna, V.F. Neurobiological models of risky decision-making and adolescent substance use. *Curr. Addict. Rep.* **2018**, *5*, 128–133. [CrossRef]
20. Ore, O. Pascal and the invention of probability theory. *Am. Math. Mon.* **1960**, *67*, 409–419. [CrossRef]
21. Von Neumann, J.; Morgenstern, O. *Theory of Games and Economic Behavior*; Princeton University Press: Princeton, NJ, USA, 1947.
22. Frank, R.H. *Microeconomics and Behavior*; McGraw-Hill Education: New York, NY, USA, 2015.
23. Sternberg, R.J. Successful Intelligence in Theory, Research, and Practice. In *The Nature of Human Intelligence*; Sternberg, R.J., Ed.; Cambridge University Press: New York, NY, USA, 2018; pp. 308–321.
24. Allais, M. Le comportement de l'homme rationnel devant le risque: Critique des postulats et axiomes de l'école Américaine. *Econometrica* **1953**, *21*, 503–546. [CrossRef]
25. Tversky, A.; Kahneman, D. Rational choice and the framing of decisions. *J. Bus.* **1986**, *59*, S251–S278. [CrossRef]
26. Kahneman, D. *Thinking, Fast and Slow*; Farrar, Straus and Giroux: New York, NY, USA, 2011.
27. Stanovich, K.E.; West, R.F. On the relative independence of thinking biases and cognitive ability. *J. Personal. Soc. Psychol.* **2008**, *94*, 672–695. [CrossRef] [PubMed]
28. Ashby, N.J.S.; Rakow, T.; Yechiam, E. 'Tis better to choose and lose than to never choose at all. *Judgm. Decis. Mak.* **2017**, *12*, 553–562.
29. Reyna, V.F.; Brainerd, C.J. Dual processes in decision making and developmental neuroscience: A fuzzy-trace model. *Dev. Rev.* **2011**, *31*, 180–206. [CrossRef]
30. Reyna, V.F.; Brust-Renck, P. When numerically superior people make numerically inferior choices (and rate them as attractive): The gist of numeracy. **2018**. Manuscript submitted for publication.
31. Weller, J.A.; Levin, I.P.; Shiv, B.; Bechara, A. Neural correlates of adaptive decision making in risky gains and losses. *Psychol. Sci.* **2007**, *18*, 958–964. [CrossRef] [PubMed]
32. Romer, D.; Reyna, V.F.; Satterthwaite, T.D. Beyond Stereotypes of Adolescent Risk Taking: Placing the Adolescent Brain in Developmental Context. *Dev. Cogn. Neurosci.* **2017**, *27*, 19–34. [CrossRef] [PubMed]

33. Morsanyi, K.; Chiesi, F.; Primi, C.; Szűcs, D. The illusion of replacement in research into the development of thinking biases: The case of the conjunction fallacy. *J. Cogn. Psychol.* **2017**, *29*, 240–257. [CrossRef]

34. Reyna, V.F.; Farley, F. Risk and rationality in adolescent decision-making: Implications for theory, practice, and public policy. *Psychol. Sci. Public Interest* **2006**, *7*, 1–44. [CrossRef] [PubMed]

35. Mills, B.A.; Reyna, V.F.; Estrada, S. Explaining contradictory relations between risk perception and risk taking. *Psychol. Sci.* **2008**, *19*, 429–434. [CrossRef] [PubMed]

36. Reyna, V.F.; Ellis, S.C. Fuzzy-Trace Theory and framing effects in children's risky decision making. *Psychol. Sci.* **1994**, *5*, 275–279. [CrossRef]

37. Schlottmann, A.; Wilkening, F. Judgment and decision making in young children. In *Judgment and Decision-Making as a Skill: Learning, Development, Evolution;* Dhami, M., Schlottmann, A., Waldmann, M., Eds.; Cambridge University Press: Cambridge, UK, 2011; pp. 55–83.

38. Morsanyi, K.; Handley, S.J.; Evans, J.S. Decontextualised minds: Adolescents with autism are less susceptible to the conjunction fallacy than typically developing adolescents. *J. Autism Dev. Disord.* **2010**, *40*, 1378–1388. [CrossRef] [PubMed]

39. Jacobs, J.; Klaczynski, P. (Eds.) *The Development of Children's and Adolescents' Judgment and Decision-Making;* Erlbaum: Mahwah, NJ, USA, 2005.

40. Kogut, T.; Slovic, P. The development of scope insensitivity in sharing behavior. *J. Exp. Psychol. Learn. Mem. Cognit.* **2016**, *42*, 1972–1981. [CrossRef] [PubMed]

41. Liberali, J.M.; Reyna, V.F.; Furlan, S.; Stein, L.M.; Pardo, S.T. Individual differences in numeracy and cognitive reflection, with implications for biases and fallacies in probability judgment. *J. Behav. Decis. Mak.* **2012**, *25*, 361–381. [CrossRef] [PubMed]

42. Reyna, V.F.; Brainerd, C.J. The origins of probability judgment: A review of data and theories. In *Subjective Probability;* Wright, G., Ayton, P., Eds.; Wiley: New York, NY, USA, 1994; pp. 239–272.

43. Blalock, S.J.; Reyna, V.F. Using fuzzy-trace theory to understand and improve health judgments, decisions, and behaviors: A literature review. *Health Psychol.* **2016**, *35*, 781–792. [CrossRef] [PubMed]

44. Defoe, I.N.; Dubas, J.S.; Figner, B.; Van Aken, M.A. A meta-analysis on age differences in risky decision making: Adolescents versus children and adults. *Psychol. Bull.* **2015**, *141*, 48–84. [CrossRef] [PubMed]

45. Reyna, V.F.; Mills, B.A. Theoretically motivated interventions for reducing sexual risk taking in adolescence: A randomized controlled experiment applying fuzzy-trace theory. *J. Exp. Psychol. Gen.* **2014**, *143*, 1627–1648. [CrossRef] [PubMed]

46. Peters, E. Educating good decisions. *Behav. Public Policy* **2017**, *1*, 162–176. [CrossRef]

47. Peters, E.; Västfjäll, D.; Slovic, P.; Mertz, C.; Mazzocco, K.; Dickert, S. Numeracy and decision-making. *Psychol. Sci.* **2006**, *17*, 407–413. [CrossRef] [PubMed]

48. Cokely, E.T.; Kelley, C.M. Cognitive abilities and superior decision making under risk: A protocol analysis and process model evaluation. *Judgm. Decis. Mak.* **2009**, *4*, 20–33.

49. Beyth-Marom, R.; Fischhoff, B.; Quadrel, M.J.; Furby, L. Teaching adolescents decision making. In *Teaching Decision Making to Adolescents;* Baron, J., Brown, R., Eds.; Routledge: London, UK, 1991; pp. 19–60.

50. Beroggi, G.E.G. An experimental investigation of preference elicitation methods in policy decision-making. *J. Multi Criteria Decis. Anal.* **2000**, *9*, 76–89. [CrossRef]

51. Parker, A.M.; Bruine de Bruin, W.; Fischhoff, B.; Weller, J. Robustness of decision-making competence: Evidence from two measures and an 11-year longitudinal study. *J. Behav. Decis. Mak.* **2017**. [CrossRef]

52. Klein, E.Y.; Martinez, E.M.; May, L.; Saheed, M.; Reyna, V.F.; Broniatowski, D.A. Categorical risk perception drives variability in antibiotic prescribing in the emergency department: A mixed methods observational study. *J. Gen. Int. Med.* **2017**, *32*, 1083–1089. [CrossRef] [PubMed]

53. Reyna, V.F. A theory of medical decision making and health: Fuzzy-trace theory. *Med. Decis. Mak.* **2008**, *28*, 850–865. [CrossRef] [PubMed]

54. Fraenkel, L.; Peters, E.; Charpentier, P.; Olsen, B.; Errante, L.; Schoen, R.; Reyna, V.F. A decision tool to improve the quality of care in Rheumatoid Arthritis. *Arthritis Care Res.* **2012**, *64*, 977–985. [CrossRef] [PubMed]

55. Fujita, K.; Han, H.A. Moving beyond deliberative control of impulses: The effect of construal levels on evaluative associations in self-control conflicts. *Psychol. Sci.* **2009**, *20*, 799–804. [CrossRef] [PubMed]

56. Kwak, Y.; Payne, J.W.; Cohen, A.L.; Huettel, S.A. The rational adolescent: Strategic information processing during decision making revealed by eye tracking. *Cogn. Dev.* **2015**, *36*, 20–30. [CrossRef] [PubMed]

57. Reyna, V.F.; Estrada, S.M.; DeMarinis, J.A.; Myers, R.M.; Stanisz, J.M.; Mills, B.A. Neurobiological and memory models of risky decision making in adolescents versus young adults. *J. Exp. Psychol. Learn. Mem. Cogn.* **2011**, *37*, 1125–1142. [CrossRef] [PubMed]

58. Reyna, V.F.; Helm, R.K.; Weldon, R.B.; Shah, P.D.; Turpin, A.G.; Govindgari, S. Brain activation covaries with reported criminal behaviors when making risky choices: A fuzzy-trace theory approach. *J. Exp. Psychol. Gen.* **2018**, in press.

59. Helm, R.K.; Reyna, V.F.; Franz, A.A.; Novick, R.Z. Too young to plead? Risk, rationality, and plea bargaining's innocence problem in adolescents. *Psychol. Public Policy Law* **2018**, *24*, 180–191. [CrossRef]

60. Koszegi, B.; Rabin, M. A model of reference-dependent preferences. *Q. J. Econ.* **2006**, *121*, 1133–1166.

61. Reyna, V.F.; Chick, C.F.; Corbin, J.C.; Hsia, A.N. Developmental reversals in risky decision-making: Intelligence agents show larger decision biases than college students. *Psychol. Sci.* **2014**, *25*, 76–84. [CrossRef] [PubMed]

62. Diehl, J.J.; Bennetto, L.; Young, E.C. Story recall and narrative coherence of high-functioning children with autism spectrum disorders. *J. Abnorm. Child Psychol.* **2006**, *34*, 83–98. [CrossRef] [PubMed]

63. Miller, H.L.; Odegard, T.N.; Allen, G. Evaluating information processing in autism spectrum disorder: The case for fuzzy trace theory. *Dev. Rev.* **2014**, *34*, 44–76. [CrossRef]

64. Wojcik, D.Z.; Díez, E.; Alonso, M.A.; Martín-Cilleros, M.V.; Guisuraga-Fernández, Z.; Fernández, M.; Matilla, L.; Magán-Maganto, M.; Díez-Álamo, A.M.; Canal-Bedia, R.; et al. Diminished false memory in adults with autism spectrum disorder: Evidence of identify-to-reject mechanism impairment. *Res. Autism Spectr. Disord.* **2018**, *45*, 51–57. [CrossRef]

65. De Martino, B.; Harrison, N.A.; Knafo, S.; Bird, G.; Dolan, R.J. Explaining enhanced logical consistency during decision making in autism. *J. Neurosci.* **2008**, *28*, 10746–10750. [CrossRef] [PubMed]

66. Sloman, S.; Fernbach, P. *The Knowledge Illusion: Why We Never Think Alone*; Riverhead Press: New York, NY, USA, 2017.

67. Rabinowitz, M.; Gertsel-Friedman, J. Orienting to see what's important: Learn to ignore the irrelevant. *Q. J. Exp. Psychol.* **2017**. [CrossRef] [PubMed]

Journal of
Intelligence

MDPI

Commentary

Intellectual Brilliance and Presidential Performance: Why Pure Intelligence (or Openness) Doesn't Suffice

Dean Keith Simonton

Department of Psychology, University of California, Davis, CA 95616, USA; dksimonton@ucdavis.edu

Received: 30 January 2018; Accepted: 7 March 2018; Published: 23 March 2018

Abstract: In recent years it has become popular on the internet to debate the IQ of the incumbent president of the United States. Yet, these controversies (and hoaxes) presume that IQ has some relevance to understanding the president's actual performance as the nation's leader. This assumption is examined by reviewing the empirical research on the intelligence–performance association in political leadership, with a special focus on U.S. presidents. The review starts by discussing at-a-distance assessment techniques, a method that has yielded reliable and valid measures of IQ, Intellectual Brilliance, and Openness to Experience; three correlated even if separable concepts. The discussion then turns to the reliable and valid measurement of presidential performance—or "greatness"—via successive surveys of hundreds of experts. These two lines of research then converged on the emergence of a six-predictor equation, in which Intellectual Brilliance plays a major role, to the exclusion of both IQ and Openness. The greatest presidents are those who feature wide interests, and who are artistic, inventive, curious, intelligent, sophisticated, complicated, insightful, wise, and idealistic (but who are far from being either dull or commonplace). These are the personal traits we should look for in the person who occupies the nation's highest office if we seek someone most likely to solve the urgent problems of today and tomorrow.

Keywords: presidential performance; Intellectual Brilliance; Openness to Experience; IQ

---

1. Introduction

This symposium of thought pieces is dedicated to the following question: "If intelligence is truly important to real-world adaptation, and IQs have risen 30+ points in the past century (Flynn effect), then why are there so many unresolved and dramatic problems in the world, and what can be done about it?" Needless to say, this issue has many possible responses. For instance, it just may be the case that while IQs have grown at, say, a roughly linear pace (even ignoring any asymptotic leveling off), the problems faced by the world have grown exponentially. Indeed, as evinced by the infamous "hockey stick graph" that Al Gore used in his 2006 documentary, "An Inconvenient Truth", to argue for human-caused global warming, problems could actually accelerate faster than exponentially, leaving the Flynn effect in the dust.

That said, I would like to treat a different answer here. Very often, scientists and other experts demonstrate the wherewithal to arrive at effective solutions to world problems, but they are powerless to implement those solutions because the power of implementation is confined to the highest levels of leadership, such as a president, prime minister, or even dictator. If intelligence is required for a leader to effectively understand and enact the appropriate measures, then perhaps the intelligence of the population (or voters) is not really relevant. What really matters is the intellect of the heads of state. In other words, the Flynn effect is not really relevant. What is critical is the particular kind of intellect found in the world's leaders. Here, I would like to concentrate on a specific manifestation: the relation between intelligence and performance in the United States presidency. In particular, I will review the relevant results from a research program addressing this question that began in 1986, and eventually came to include all U.S. presidents between George Washington and George W. Bush [1].[1]

As some readers may remember, during the 2016 presidential campaign, a major candidate, Donald Trump, explicitly boasted that he was extremely smart. Indeed, after his inauguration in early 2017, he made the more specific claim that he enjoyed a superlative IQ, and even challenged his own Secretary of State, Rex Tillerson, to take an IQ test. Moreover, the president eventually asserted that his intelligence was not just very high, but even attained the elevated level of genuine genius. Unfortunately, because I have been conducting empirical inquiries into presidential intelligence since the 1980s [2], I found myself dragged into the ensuing internet debate over Trump's actual IQ. Was it really true that he has an IQ of 156; well over three standard deviations above the population mean? Nor was this the first time I was put in the uncomfortable position of publically arbitrating the supposed IQs of U.S. chief executives. Back in 2001 a widely circulated internet hoax maintained that George W. Bush's intelligence was well below average, weighing in at a mere IQ of 91. When I published a far more reasonable IQ estimate five years later [3], I found myself under vicious attacks by those who argued that my estimate was way too high—or still way too low. Not understanding the statistical methods that I had used, the common assumption was that my endeavors were purely partisan. In any event, it seems that many people out there really care about the IQ scores of the White House incumbent. Just google "presidents IQ" for the evidence.

But why should it even matter in the first place? Presumably, the answer is that general intelligence, as assessed by IQ tests, bears a strong positive association with actual presidential performance. Presidents with higher IQs would supposedly do a better job solving the nation's problems as well as the problems confronting the world at large, whether those problems concern military conflicts, terrorism, immigration, poverty, crime, discrimination, or climate change. But what scientific evidence do we actually possess for such a relationship? After all, few if any U.S. presidents can claim a certified score on an IQ test, and the vast majority of presidents died before taking such a test was even possible. Furthermore, how is it conceivable to assess a president's overall leadership? Without such an assessment, the intelligence–performance question becomes moot anyway.

Here, I begin by addressing the assessment of intelligence and related constructs, and then turn to the measurement of leader performance. I conclude by discussing their correspondence. It will then become apparent that intelligence, as usually defined, is a far too narrow a construct to provide an optimal predictor of presidential leadership.

2. Intellect, IQ, Intellectual Brilliance, and Experiential Openness

The only way to assess intelligence in all of the U.S. presidents is to utilize some at-a-distance assessment technique [4,5]. An early prototype was Woods' [6] attempt to estimate Intellect in members of European royal families by means of the personality descriptors routinely supplied in biographical entries. Woods' method was subsequently applied by Cox [7], Thorndike [8,9], and later still, by Simonton [10], who focused on just those royals who assumed their nation's throne as a monarch (king, queen, or sultan). Simonton's study showed that Woods' ratings of Intellect were highly correlated with such biographical descriptors as Intelligent, Able, Shrewd, and Educated. One primary drawback of these calculations is that the evaluators were aware of the identity of those being rated, a deficiency that has a remedy, as will be seen shortly.

An alternative approach was introduced by Cox [7] as part of Terman's [11] classic longitudinal study of over 1500 high-IQ children (for background, see [12,13]). Employing the original definition of IQ as the literal quotient of mental age divided by chronological age multiplied by 100, Cox

---

[1] Technically speaking, the same labor-intensive methods could be extended to former president Barack Obama, once the requisite biographical data become available (cf. [2]). In contrast, these methods cannot be fully applied to the current incumbent until after he completes his term in office. Nonetheless, I leave it as an exercise for the reader to estimate how the current incumbent might rate on the descriptors defining the Intellectual Brilliance factor.

calculated estimates for 301 geniuses, including both creators and leaders. The IQ estimates were based on detailed chronologies of early intellectual development, using multiple independent raters to obtain reliable scores. In essence, the intelligence measure is a gauge of precocity in intellectual development during childhood, adolescence, and early adulthood (see also [14] for a slight variation on this technique). An especially impressive feature of her estimation strategy is that she provided four estimates rather than just one. She first calculated separate IQs for ages 0–16 and 17–26, and then provided both a raw estimate and an estimate corrected for data reliability (which was made possible by her using multiple independent raters). Unhappily, only 8 of the 301 had served as the U.S. chief executive, and all of these were active prior to the 20th century (viz. George Washington, John Adams, Thomas Jefferson, James Madison, J. Q. Adams, Andrew Jackson, Abraham Lincoln, and U. S. Grant). Not a large sample of presidents, to be sure.

Yet another method returns to biographical descriptors, this time applied to presidents of the United States, rather than European monarchs [2]. Moreover, important improvements were implemented over what was conducted by Woods [6], Thorndike [8,9], and Simonton [10]. To begin with, a research team extracted the descriptors from biographical materials with all identifying information removed. To avoid the introduction of potential political biases, these materials were carefully selected to represent the consensus of historical scholarship on the American presidency [15]. Next, a totally separate team of several independent raters used these anonymous extracts to check off the applicable descriptors using the Gough Adjective Check List (ACL) [16].[2] Because not all 300 adjectives could be reliably assessed, the descriptors were reduced to a subset of 110 assessments that had sufficiently high reliability coefficients. These reliable assessments were then subjected to a factor analysis that yielded 14 orthogonal dimensions. For our present purposes, just one of these factors is the most important; namely, the one labeled Intellectual Brilliance. This factor had salient positive loadings on Wide Interests (0.85), Artistic (0.84), Inventive (0.76), Curious (0.74), Intelligent (0.64), Sophisticated (0.62), Complicated (0.61), Insightful (0.54), Wise (0.46), and Idealistic (0.43), but negative loadings on Dull (-0.71) and Commonplace (-0.41). The reliability (coefficient alpha) for Intellectual Brilliance was 0.90, a highly respectable figure [2]. Better yet, scores on this measure were obtained for all 39 U.S. presidents between Washington and Ronald Reagan, inclusively. Notably, the factor scores were validated by calculating correlations with independent assessments of related constructs, such as IQ, creativity, charisma, idealism, book authorship, and birth order (all positive except the last; [2,17]; cf. [7,9,20–22]). Critically, Intellectual Brilliance does *not* correlate with the president's party affiliation, thus indicating a lack of bias in the biographical reference works [3].

Admittedly, exploratory factor analysis is sometimes more an art than a science. Although the rotated factors exhibited the desired simple structure, assigning labels to the extracted factors can always be subjected to second-guessing. That possibility certainly applies to the cluster of traits that were styled as Intellectual Brilliance. At that time, and in the numerous subsequent studies published since, that label was deliberately chosen to make intelligence an adjective rather than a noun. The configuration of descriptors were taken to indicate a certain pervasive brilliance of an intellectual kind. More specifically, Intellectual Brilliance can be defined as an inclusive cognitive propensity that spans broad and artistic interests, a pronounced curiosity and inventiveness, noticeable sophistication and insightfulness, plus more than average wisdom and idealism. This cognitive emphasis contrasted with the other factors, which more often concerned emotions, motivations, or attitudes (e.g., Forcefulness, which was defined by the descriptors of Energetic, Active, Determined, Demanding, and Restless).[3]

---

[2] The same biographical personality profiles have been used in later research to extract additional characteristics, such as creativity, charisma, narcissism, and proactivity [17–19].

[3] It should be evident that Intellectual Brilliance has little, if any, conceptual overlap with Emotional Intelligence, a popular construct that has often been associated with effective leadership [23,24]. Most notably, the former concerns cognition,

Just as importantly, Intellectual Brilliance obviously encompasses far more than mere intelligence. First of all, the descriptor Intelligent cannot be taken to define the factor, because its loading falls right in the middle of the pack rather than having the highest loading of all (viz. 0.21 below Interests Wide, but 0.21 above Idealistic). Moreover, most of the component descriptors concern creativity, and to a lesser extent, sophistication, wisdom, and idealism (cf. [25]). Furthermore, many adjectives seem to tap into facets of the Openness to Experience dimension of the Big Five Personality Model [26]. This factor includes the six facets of "Openness to Fantasy, Aesthetics, Feelings, Actions, Ideas, and Values" [27] (p. 223). In fact, the following ACL adjectives correlate positively with Openness scores in the general population: Wide Interests, Imaginative, Intelligent, Original, Insightful, Curious, Sophisticated, Artistic, Clever, Inventive, Sharp-Witted, Ingenious, and Wise (but with negative correlations for Commonplace, Narrow Interests, Simple, Shallow, and Unintelligent; [26]). The overlap with Intellectual Brilliance is obvious. This conspicuous overlap also suggests that Intellectual Brilliance might only be serving as a proxy for Openness to Experience. Such a connection is significant insofar as Openness has already been shown to have a strong association with both creativity and leadership [27,28]. So perhaps we should really speak of Openness rather than Intellectual Brilliance—and thus drop intellect or intelligence out of the discussion altogether.

Fortunately, this possibility can be directly addressed by using yet another at-a-distance method for assessing individual differences in historical figures [5]. Because eminent personalities usually attract the attention of biographers, their biographers become ready-made experts regarding the personal qualities of their subjects. As such, the biographers can respond to surveys using observer-based rather than self-report measures, including versions of Big Five personality questionnaires. This technique was actually applied to presidents of the United States, most of whom can claim multiple biographies [29,30]; for methodological critique, see [31]. The use of multiple biographers as survey respondents would thus help reduce the intrusion of partisan bias. The upshot of this was that 32 presidents eventually received assessments on all five factors, including Openness to Experience. Not surprisingly, these observer-based Openness scores correlate highly with the Intellectual Brilliance scores ($r = 0.69$; [3]). Yet, it is also the case that both of these scores correlate positively with Cox's [7] IQ estimates, predicated on a totally distinct method ($rs = 0.70-0.92$, depending on the specific Cox estimates chosen [3]). Perhaps these high correlations should come as no surprise given that "intelligence" and related traits are included in both assessments. But the real question is which of the three assessments most strongly correlates with actual presidential performance: IQ, Intellectual Brilliance, or Openness to Experience? Once one of the three is accounted for, do the remaining two become superfluous? To address this issue, we first must discuss how that performance is assessed.

3. Presidential Leadership, Performance, and Greatness

Experts on the U.S. presidents, largely historians of American political history, have been repeatedly surveyed to determine the performance of former presidents (ignoring incumbents who have not yet completed their terms). Indeed, the first such survey was published in 1948 [32]. Although the ratings will change somewhat from survey to survey (not even counting the addition of new former presidents), the shifts tend to be relatively modest, comparable to the shifts in relative individual rankings in test–retest reliabilities for IQ scores. As a direct consequence, research shows that the alternative assessments exhibit a substantial consensus [33]. Presidents like Lincoln, Washington, and Franklin Roosevelt are placed towards the top, while presidents like Andrew Johnson, Warren Harding, and Richard Nixon regularly fall towards the bottom. Plus, the more mediocre chief executives will compete in the middle two quartiles (or roughly ranks 10 to 30). So strong is the agreement that when a measure of presidential performance is defined based on a factor analysis,

the latter emotion. If each defining trait is scrutinized one by one, it is difficult to discern any connection with affect, as defined in Emotional Intelligence.

the resulting 12-item composite features a (coefficient alpha) reliability of 0.99, which is as good as it possibly gets [3]. This reliable composite has frequently been labeled a presidential "greatness" factor [33–36].

From time to time, survey respondents will be asked to provide more finely differentiated evaluations of presidential performance [21,37]. The ratings then allow us to pinpoint the more specific leadership qualities that are getting at least partially tapped by the global measure; much like the correlations between general intelligence (Spearman's g) and measures of separate cognitive abilities, whether verbal, visual, spatial, mathematical, of memory, etc. Thus, we find that the comprehensive greatness assessment agrees with Maranell's survey ([21]; of 571 experts) results for Accomplishments ($r = 0.97$), Strength ($r = 0.96$), Presidential Prestige ($r = 0.95$), and Activity ($r = 0.90$), and with Ridings and McIver's survey ([37]; of 719 experts) findings for Accomplishments ($r = 0.94$), Presidential Leadership ($r = 0.93$), Appointments ($r = 0.90$), and Political Skill ($r = 0.90$). It should be obvious from the high correlations that when these separate assessments are factor-analyzed along with the overall assessments, a single-factor solution is still obtained (see also [38]).

One might be tempted to ascribe the above agreement to some grand halo effect in the evaluation of presidential leadership. Yet, opposed to this attribution is the fact that some hypothesized performance criteria do not correspond strongly with the broad greatness factor. For example, Ridings and McIver [37] also had expert respondents gauge the presidents on Character and Integrity, but this measure did not correlate very highly with the other assessments [39]. It is sad to say, but these virtues do not seem to define core components of presidential greatness! Some great presidents are not great persons, just as some great persons do not make great presidents (e.g., Woodrow Wilson versus Jimmy Carter). Any composite indicator is better left without Character and Integrity included.

4. Intelligence–Performance Correspondence

Using a sample of 342 European monarchs, Simonton [10,40] conducted the first assessment of the association between intelligence and leader performance. Rated intelligence (an extension of Woods' [6] "Intellect" measure) exhibited statistically significant correlations with a monarch's Leadership ($r = 0.67$), achieved Eminence ($r = 0.32$), assessed Morality ($r = 0.23$, an extension of Woods' [6] "Virtue" measure), and objective Historical Activity ($r = 0.13$, a measure of the number of notable events that occurred during his or her reign). Although promising, these two inquiries suffered from the problem mentioned earlier: the measures were not generated by raters blind to the identity of the leaders being rated. In addition, because monarchs represent a rather outdated form of political leadership in the 20th century, it seemed desirable to look at a political position of unquestioned contemporary importance: the presidents of the United States.

Such was the impetus for the investigation mentioned earlier that obtained an Intellectual Brilliance assessment for the first 39 U.S. presidents [2]. For the primary performance criterion, Simonton used the most recent global assessment, a survey of 846 experts on the presidency [41], finding a sizable correlation ($r = 0.56$). In fact, Intellectual Brilliance was the only factor out of the 14 extracted dimensions—such as Moderation, Machiavellianism, Achievement Drive, Inflexibility, and Conservatism—that exhibited any association whatsoever with presidential greatness. This is not to say that these other traits are utterly irrelevant, but only that their repercussions tend to be confined to particular leader behaviors, and frequently their effects are moderated by situational variables [1,2]. For example, the magnitude of Inflexibility influences the president's use of the legislative veto power, but only in interaction with the size of the chief executive's electoral mandate and the degree to which his party controls Congress [42]. In a nutshell, Inflexibility only proves adaptive when the president has strong political support among voters and legislators.

As a further confirmation of its predictive power, Intellectual Brilliance was shown to correlate significantly with all prior survey results, essentially yielding a rare seven-fold replication. Finally, because several other variables have been shown to predict presidential performance besides Intellectual Brilliance ([22,33]; see also [1]), Simonton [2] examined whether this single dispositional factor would survive as a predictor when placed in a multiple regression equation that included total years in office, years as wartime commander-in-chief, assassination, status as a war hero, and administration scandals (a negative predictor). Intellectual Brilliance retained its predictive utility (standardized partial regression coefficient $\beta = 0.26$). The six-predictor equation accounted for 82% of the variance in assessed performance, a result that has been replicated several times as new former presidents are added to the sample and alternative predictors defined [17,39,43–45]. Indeed, so conspicuously successful have been these replications that the equation became known in the presidential studies literature as the "Simonton model" [43].[4]

However, the predictive relevance of Intellectual Brilliance was seriously challenged when Rubenzer and Faschingbauer devised their assessment of presidential Openness to Experience by surveying presidential biographers [29,30]. The researchers showed that Openness displayed significant correlations with presidential performance ($rs = 0.25$–0.32, [29]; using [37,41]). Although the zero-order correlations were lower than those found using Intellectual Brilliance, any direct comparison is somewhat misleading because the scores are not based on the same presidents. Where Intellectual Brilliance features scores for all 39 presidents up to Reagan, the Openness scores were missing for several presidents who were too obscure to attract a sufficient number of biographers (e.g., John Tyler, Zachary Taylor, Rutherford Hayes, Grover Cleveland, and William McKinley). Hence, a decision was made to attempt a head-to-head comparison that relied on imputation methods for estimating missing values. To provide more data for the imputed scores, Cox's [7] four IQ estimates were added as well. Given that no president was missing a value across all three measures—Intellectual Brilliance, Openness, and IQ—it was then possible to obtain scores for all presidents from Washington to George W. Bush. The results were reported by Simonton ([3], Table 1).

Because the focus of this article is the intelligence–performance relation, let us concentrate on the relative predictive utility of these three alternative indicators. In this case, presidential performance was assessed by a 12-item composite that incorporated the ratings from all major expert surveys (i.e., the measure with the 0.99 coefficient alpha mentioned earlier). Then the following two points must be emphasized [3]: First, Intellectual Brilliance claims a far higher correlation with presidential performance ($r = 0.56$) than does either Openness to Experience ($r = 0.34$) or any of the four Cox IQ estimates ($rs = 0.31$–0.34). Second, only Intellectual Brilliance makes a statistically significant contribution to the Simonton six-predictor model ($\beta = 0.29$, $p < 0.01$; which is actually slightly higher than the 0.26 as first found in [2]). In contrast, if Intellectual Brilliance is replaced by either Openness or any of the Cox IQ estimates, their predictive utility shrinks to a nonsignificant effect ($\beta = 0.19$, $p > 0.05$). In other words, without Intellectual Brilliance in our inventory of available predictors, we would be obliged to fall back on a five-predictor equation containing just the factors of years in office, war years, assassination, scandals, and war hero status (cf. [33]). The total amount of variance explained would be correspondingly reduced. To illustrate, omitting Intellectual Brilliance from the equation predicting the Murray and Blessing [41] ratings lowers the percentage of variance accounted for from 82% to 77% (cf. [3,33]). That lost increment of 5% is not trivial.[5]

If Intellectual Brilliance cannot be equated with either IQ or Openness, we might ask how it compares with Sternberg's [49] concept of Successful Intelligence, which he discusses in this special issue. Some congruence is apparent, but not enough to make the two concepts equivalent. In the first

---

4   These successive replications involved more than just applying the equation to an enlarged sample upon each new survey. The equation would also test whether other potential predictors should be added, or even replace the predictors in the original equation. Many individual and situational variables exhibit zero-order correlations with presidential performance measures, but without adding any increment to the explained variance once the other six variables are already in the equation. That means that the correlation represents some combination of indirect and/or spurious relationships (see [46] for further discussion).

5   Although some have suggested that leadership might be a curvilinear inverted-U function of intelligence, the relation between Intellectual Brilliance and presidential greatness is strictly positive linear (cf. [47,48]). Nonetheless, an adverse effect is found in another location: Intellectual Brilliance tends to be negatively correlated with a candidate's margin of victory in the popular vote ($r = -0.36$ [2]). The 2016 presidential election just might be an exception to this statistical relation.

place, analytical intelligence plays a much bigger and more explicit role in Successful Intelligence, whereas Intellectual Brilliance contains only the single generic descriptor of Intelligent, which might even be taken to encompass a broader intelligence, such as Gardner's [50] construct of interpersonal intelligence. Second, although both Intellectual Brilliance and Successful Intelligence include creativity as a component, creativity plays a much bigger role in the latter than in the former. Not only does Intellectual Brilliance omit most of the adjectives making up the ACL's Creative Personality Scale (e.g., Confident, Egotistical, Individualistic, Informal, Original, Resourceful, Sexy, and Snobbish; [51]), but Simonton [17] was also able to extract a measure of Creative Style that could be empirically differentiated from Intellectual Brilliance. Third, although Wise is included for both Intellectual Brilliance and Successful Intelligence, common sense is not; nor is practicality, even though Practical is included among the descriptors in the ACL [3]. Maranell's [21] survey measure of Practicality is even negatively correlated with Intellectual Brilliance [2]. Finally, Intellectual Brilliance contains traits that do not seem to have any counterpart in Successful Intelligence, such as Sophisticated and Idealistic. In short, however essential Successful Intelligence may be for success in general, Intellectual Brilliance is more specifically tailored to what it takes to attain presidential greatness.[6]

5. Final Inferences

It should be clear by now than all internet debates about the IQs of United States presidents are terribly misplaced. It doesn't really matter much whether George W. Bush has an IQ of 91, or Donald Trump an IQ of 156. What we all should be debating is the Intellectual Brilliance of the person occupying the White House. Although this factor includes intelligence among its components, that trait is only one among a dozen, and even then features a rather middling factor loading. We also have to ask such questions as: How much curiosity and breadth of interests does the person display? Is the leader sophisticated, even complicated, rather than dull or commonplace? How inventive, artistic, or insightful are they? And what about the leader's wisdom and idealism? Even if in varying degrees, these are evidently the qualities that are most strongly associated with exceptional presidential performance, an inclusive criterion that incorporates such specific leader assets as Strength, Prestige, Activity, Accomplishments, and Political Skill. This identifies the leadership that is most likely to solve the problems of today and anticipate the problems of tomorrow. Or, at least, these are the leaders who are most likely to be open to those who offer innovative solutions to those problems. We witness today the consequences of an American presidency that spurns the best that science has to offer with respect to the biggest problems of our time.

Such were the implications that should have been drawn from Simonton's [3] systematic comparison of presidential Intellectual Brilliance, Openness, and IQ. Yet, everyone who downloaded the article seems to have become fixated on the IQ scores, ignoring the far more crucial scores of Intellectual Brilliance. To provide a concrete example, many on the internet observed that J. Q. Adams ended up with the highest IQ estimate: somewhere between 165 and 175. In contrast, one of the few bona fide geniuses ever to serve as president, Thomas Jefferson, only scored somewhere between 145 and 160, and thus their IQ estimates didn't even overlap. If their respective records of early intellectual development are scrutinized as closely as Cox's [7] raters did, this disparity makes perfect sense. Adams was clearly the more cognitively precocious. Only when we view the column containing the Intellectual Brilliance scores do we spot a dramatic contrast. Where J. Q. Adams was only a little more than one standard deviation above the presidential mean, Jefferson was more than three standard deviations above that same mean! Indeed, Jefferson displayed more Intellectual Brilliance than any president who ever served in that office! Then, who was the greater president? Jefferson by far! Where

---

[6] Because Intellectual Brilliance may put more stress on personality in comparison with Successful Intelligence, it might be more analogous to the concept of the "intelligent personality" and academic performance, but with that cluster of dispositional traits focused on presidential leadership (cf. [52]). That is where this performance predictor has greater affinity with Openness as well.

J. Q. Adams is most often rated as an only slightly above-average chief executive, Jefferson is usually placed in the top four—right below the triumvirate of Washington, Lincoln, and Franklin Roosevelt. Indeed, Jefferson owns the visage right beside Washington on Mount Rushmore. The only misfortune in Jefferson's posthumous reputation was his placement on the ill-fated $2 bill! So, please, anyone who wants to make the presidency great again has to know what really to look for.

The obvious next question is whether the voters in presidential elections can be encouraged or trained to cast their ballots more wisely. The answer is far from easy because a host of extraneous factors impinge on the ideal "rational voter" (cf. [53,54]). For one thing, voters are often more strongly influenced by emotion rather than cognition, relying excessively on spontaneous emotional reactions that may even be governed by primitive processes that hark back to the early phases of human evolution [55]. Worse yet, voter behavior is heavily shaped by situational factors that have nothing to do with the specific candidates running for the nation's highest office [1]. For example, several such contextual factors would predict that the person inaugurated as U.S. president in 2017 would be affiliated with the Republican rather than Democratic Party, regardless of who the nominees happened to be. After all, the Democrats had occupied the White House for two consecutive terms, and had already lost control of both branches of Congress as well as most state governorships and legislatures. Warren G. Harding, who is often considered the worse chief executive ever, was elected under somewhat similar circumstances. Yet, he was the president whose Intellectual Brilliance fell two standard deviations below the mean. Absolutely nobody scored lower!

In any event, if Intellectual Brilliance rather than IQ or Openness to Experience represents the primary personal factor behind presidential performance, then can that distinctive configuration of traits generalize to other forms of political leadership, or even to leadership positions in general?

On the one hand, it could be that this specific factor is distinctive to the U.S. presidency, and that other positions, such as British Prime Minister or CEO of Fortune 500 companies, require a somewhat different mix of characteristics; albeit some subset may incorporate intelligence, creativity, openness, and perhaps wisdom or idealism. If so, such complications would render the solution to the world's urgent problems all the more difficult. In the absence of a one-size-fits-all profile for effective leadership, each political system must identify its idiosyncratic pattern of optimal traits—and then put somebody in office who exemplifies those traits.

On the other hand, it might hold that Intellectual Brilliance can serve as a much broader basis for predicting leader performance. Precisely the same contributing traits may be involved, but with only slight alterations in the weights they are assigned. It must be stressed that all traits defining this factor represent characteristics applicable to the general population. That inclusive applicability was guaranteed when the ACL was originally standardized. Because everybody can vary on these traits, everyone can vary in estimated Intellectual Brilliance as well. That variation might then predict performance in a wider range of domains besides leadership. In partial support of this conjecture are the results of Simonton's [25] secondary analysis of the at-a-distance assessments that Thorndike [9] posthumously published for 91 eminent creators and leaders. This analysis revealed a factor defined by sensitiveness; intelligence; and a liking for art, music, beauty, words, reading, and things. This trait configuration seems to roughly approximate Intellectual Brilliance. Indeed, Knapp [56] had earlier labelled this complex factor as an "intellectual sensitivity" rather than "intelligence" dimension. Yet, this very same factor emerged as the prime predictor of achieved eminence across all domains, from artists, scientists, and inventors to politicians, military figures, and entrepreneurs.

Without doubt, more research is required before the impact of Intellectual Brilliance can be fully evaluated. Yet one conclusion is safe to make right now: just picking heads of state according to hypothetical scores on an IQ test will not accomplish anything useful. That inference is powerful because the solutions to the world's problems very often must be implemented by its leaders. To offer a specific example, consider the following recent case: A virtually universal consensus exists among scientists that the earth is rapidly warming, and that human production of CO_2 is the main causal agent. So persuasive is the case that the majority of the world's nations were willing to sign the 2016

J. Intell. **2018**, *6*, 18

Paris Agreement dedicated to the reduction of greenhouse gases. Even so, it only took one leader, the president of the most powerful (but also most polluting) nation on the planet, to decide to withdraw his country from this epochal accord—under the utterly unjustified belief that climate change was a big hoax!

Conflicts of Interest: The authors declare no conflict of interest.

References

1. Simonton, D.K. Presidential leadership: Performance criteria and their predictors. In *The Oxford Handbook of Leadership*; Rumsey, M.G., Ed.; Oxford University Press: New York, NY, USA, 2012; pp. 327–342.
2. Simonton, D.K. Presidential personality: Biographical use of the Gough Adjective Check List. *J. Pers. Soc. Psychol.* **1986**, *51*, 149–160. [CrossRef]
3. Simonton, D.K. Presidential IQ, Openness, Intellectual Brilliance, and leadership: Estimates and correlations for 42 US chief executives. *Polit. Psychol.* **2006**, *27*, 511–639. [CrossRef]
4. Simonton, D.K. The "other IQ": Historiometric assessments of intelligence and related constructs. *Rev. Gen. Psychol.* **2009**, *13*, 315–326. [CrossRef]
5. Song, A.V.; Simonton, D.K. Personality assessment at a distance: Quantitative methods. In *Handbook of Research Methods in Personality Psychology*; Robins, R.W., Fraley, R.C., Krueger, R.F., Eds.; Guilford Press: New York, NY, USA, 2007; pp. 308–321.
6. Woods, F.A. *Mental and Moral Heredity in Royalty*; Holt: New York, NY, USA, 1906.
7. Cox, C. *The Early Mental Traits of Three Hundred Geniuses*; Stanford University Press: Stanford, CA, USA, 1926.
8. Thorndike, E.L. The relation between intellect and morality in rulers. *Am. J. Sociol.* **1936**, *42*, 321–334. [CrossRef]
9. Thorndike, E.L. Traits of personality and their intercorrelations as shown in biographies. *J. Educ. Psychol.* **1950**, *41*, 193–216. [CrossRef]
10. Simonton, D.K. Intergenerational transfer of individual differences in hereditary monarchs: Genetic, role-modeling, cohort, or sociocultural effects? *J. Pers. Soc. Psychol.* **1983**, *44*, 354–364. [CrossRef] [PubMed]
11. Terman, L.M. *Genetic Studies of Genius*; 5 volumes; Stanford University Press: Stanford, CA, USA, 1925–1959.
12. Robinson, A.; Simonton, D.K. Catharine Morris Cox Miles and the lives of others (1890–1984). In *A Century of Contributions to Gifted Education: Illuminating Lives*; Robinson, A., Jolly, J.L., Eds.; Routledge: London, UK, 2014; pp. 101–114.
13. Simonton, D.K. Reverse engineering genius: Historiometric studies of exceptional talent. *Ann. N. Y. Acad. Sci.* **2016**, *1377*, 3–9. [CrossRef] [PubMed]
14. Simonton, D.K. Childhood giftedness and adulthood genius: A historiometric analysis of 291 eminent African Americans. *Gift. Child Q.* **2008**, *52*, 243–255. [CrossRef]
15. Armbruster, M.E. *The Presidents of the United States and Their Administrations from Washington to Reagan*, 7th ed.; Horizon Press: New York, NY, USA, 1982.
16. Gough, H.G.; Heilbrun, A.B., Jr. *The Adjective Check List Manual*; Consulting Psychologists Press: Palo Alto, CA, USA, 1965.
17. Simonton, D.K. Presidential style: Personality, biography, and performance. *J. Pers. Soc. Psychol.* **1988**, *55*, 928–936. [CrossRef]
18. Deluga, R.J. Relationship among American presidential charismatic leadership, narcissism, and related performance. *Leadersh. Q.* **1997**, *8*, 51–65. [CrossRef]
19. Deluga, R.J. American presidential proactivity, charismatic leadership, and rated performance. *Leadersh. Q.* **1998**, *9*, 265–291. [CrossRef]
20. Emrich, C.G.; Brower, H.H.; Feldman, J.M.; Garland, H. Images in words: Presidential rhetoric, charisma, and greatness. *Adm. Sci. Q.* **2001**, *46*, 527–557. [CrossRef]
21. Maranell, G.M. The evaluation of presidents: An extension of the Schlesinger polls. *J. Am. Hist.* **1970**, *57*, 104–113. [CrossRef]
22. Simonton, D.K. Presidential greatness and performance: Can we predict leadership in the White House? *J. Pers.* **1981**, *49*, 306–323. [CrossRef]
23. Goldman, D. *Emotional Intelligence: Why It Can Matter More Than IQ*; Bantham: New York, NY, USA, 1995.

24. Salovey, P.; Mayer, J.D. Emotional intelligence. *Imagin. Cogn. Pers.* **1990**, *9*, 185–211. [CrossRef]
25. Simonton, D.K. Personality correlates of exceptional personal influence: A note on Thorndike's (1950) creators and leaders. *Creat. Res. J.* **1991**, *4*, 67–78. [CrossRef]
26. John, O.P. The "Big Five" factor taxonomy: Dimensions of personality in the natural language and in questionnaires. In *Handbook of Personality Theory and Research*; Pervin, L.A., Ed.; Guilford Press: New York, NY, USA, 1990; pp. 66–100.
27. McCrae, R.R.; Greenberg, D.M. Openness to experience. In *The Wiley Handbook of Genius*; Simonton, D.K., Ed.; Wiley: Oxford, UK, 2014; pp. 222–243.
28. Ilies, R.; Gerhardt, M.W.; Le, H. Individual differences in leadership emergence: Integrating meta-analytic findings and behavioral genetics estimates. *Int. J. Sel. Assess.* **2004**, *12*, 207–219. [CrossRef]
29. Rubenzer, S.J.; Faschingbauer, T.R.; Ones, D.S. Assessing the U.S. presidents using the revised NEO Personality Inventory. *Assessment* **2000**, *7*, 403–420. [CrossRef] [PubMed]
30. Rubenzer, S.J.; Faschingbauer, T.R. *Personality, Character, & Leadership in the White House: Psychologists Assess the Presidents*; Brassey's: Washington, DC, USA, 2004.
31. Simonton, D.K. Does character count in the Oval Office? *PsycCRITIQUES* **2004**, *49*. [CrossRef]
32. Schlesinger, A.M., Sr. Historians rate the U.S. presidents. *Life* **1948**, *68*, 73–74.
33. Simonton, D.K. Presidential greatness: The historical consensus and its psychological significance. *Polit. Psychol.* **1986**, *7*, 259–283. [CrossRef]
34. Balz, J. Ready to lead on day one: Predicting presidential greatness from political experience. *PS Polit. Sci. Polit.* **2010**, *43*, 487–492. [CrossRef]
35. Curry, J.L.; Morris, I.L. Explaining presidential greatness: The roles of peace and prosperity? *Pres. Stud. Q.* **2010**, *40*, 515–530. [CrossRef]
36. Wendt, H.W.; Light, P.C. Measuring "greatness" in American presidents: Model case for international research on political leadership? *Eur. J. Soc. Psychol.* **1976**, *6*, 105–109. [CrossRef]
37. Ridings, W.J., Jr.; McIver, S.B. *Rating the Presidents: A Ranking of U.S. Leaders, from the Great and Honorable to the Dishonest and Incompetent*; Citadel Press: Secaucus, NJ, USA, 1997.
38. Simonton, D.K. Latent-variable models of posthumous reputation: A quest for Galton's G. *J. Pers. Soc. Psychol.* **1991**, *60*, 607–619. [CrossRef]
39. Simonton, D.K. Predicting presidential greatness: Equation replication on recent survey results. *J. Soc. Psychol.* **2001**, *141*, 293–307. [CrossRef] [PubMed]
40. Simonton, D.K. Leaders as eponyms: Individual and situational determinants of monarchal eminence. *J. Pers.* **1984**, *52*, 1–21. [CrossRef]
41. Murray, R.K.; Blessing, T.H. The presidential performance study: A progress report. *J. Am. Hist.* **1983**, *70*, 535–555. [CrossRef]
42. Simonton, D.K. Presidential inflexibility and veto behavior: Two individual-situational interactions. *J. Pers.* **1987**, *55*, 1–18. [CrossRef]
43. Cohen, J.E. The polls: Presidential greatness as seen in the mass public: An extension and application of the Simonton model. *Pres. Stud. Q.* **2003**, *33*, 913–924. [CrossRef]
44. Simonton, D.K. Predicting presidential greatness: An alternative to the Kenney and Rice Contextual Index. *Pres. Stud. Q.* **1991**, *21*, 301–305.
45. Simonton, D.K. Intelligence and presidential greatness: Equation replication using updated IQ estimates. *Advant. Psychol. Res.* **2002**, *13*, 143–153.
46. Simonton, D.K. Presidential greatness and its socio-psychological significance: Individual or situation? Performance or attribution? In *Leadership at the Crossroads: Psychology and Leadership*; Hoyt, C., Goethals, G.R., Forsyth, D., Eds.; Praeger: Westport, CT, USA, 2008; Volume 1, pp. 132–148.
47. Antonakis, J.; House, R.J.; Simonton, D.K. Can super smart leaders suffer too much from a good thing? The curvilinear effect of intelligence on perceived leadership behavior. *J. Appl. Psychol.* **2017**, *102*, 1003–1021. [CrossRef] [PubMed]
48. Simonton, D.K. Intelligence and personal influence in groups: Four nonlinear models. *Psychol. Rev.* **1985**, *92*, 532–547. [CrossRef]
49. Sternberg, R.J. Speculations on the role of successful intelligence in solving contemporary world problems. *J. Intell.* **2018**, *6*, 4. [CrossRef]
50. Gardner, H. *Frames of Mind: A Theory of Multiple Intelligences*; Basic Books: New York, NY, USA, 1983.

51. Gough, H.G. A Creative Personality Scale for the Adjective Check List. *J. Pers. Soc. Psychol.* **1979**, *37*, 1398–1405. [CrossRef]

52. Chamorro-Premuzic, T.; Furnham, A. Intellectual competence and intelligent personality: A third way in differential psychology. *Rev. Gen. Psychol.* **2006**, *10*, 251–267. [CrossRef]

53. Simonton, D.K. Further Details on VOTER HELPER™ 1.0: A response to the editor's comments. *Polit. Psychol.* **1993**, *14*, 555–558. [CrossRef]

54. Simonton, D.K. Putting the best leaders in the White House: Personality, policy, and performance. *Polit. Psychol.* **1993**, *14*, 539–550. [CrossRef]

55. Shenkman, R. *Political Animals: How Our Stone-Age Brain Gets in the Way of Smart Politics*; Basic Books: New York, NY, USA, 2016.

56. Knapp, R.H. A factor analysis of Thorndike's ratings of eminent men. *J. Soc. Psychol.* **1962**, *56*, 67–71. [CrossRef]

Journal of
Intelligence

MDPI

Commentary
How to Think Rationally about World Problems

Keith E. Stanovich

Department of Applied Psychology and Human Development, University of Toronto, 252 Bloor St. West, Toronto, ON M5S 1V6, Canada; keith.stanovich@utoronto.ca

Received: 27 February 2018; Accepted: 18 April 2018; Published: 25 April 2018

Abstract: I agree with the target essay that psychology has something to offer in helping to address societal problems. Intelligence has helped meliorate some social problems throughout history, including the period of time that is covered by the Flynn effect, but I agree with Sternberg that other psychological characteristics may be contributing as well, particularly increases in rationality. I also believe that increasing human rationality could have a variety of positive societal affects at levels somewhat smaller in grain size than the societal problems that Sternberg focuses on. Some of the societal problems that Sternberg lists, however, I do not think would be remedied by increases in rationality, intelligence, or wisdom, because remedy might be the wrong word in the context of these issues. Issues such as how much inequality of income to tolerate, how much pollution to tolerate, and how much we should sacrifice economic growth for potential future changes in global temperature represent issues of clashing values, not the inability to process information, nor the lack of information, nor the failure to show wisdom.

Keywords: rationality; intelligence; world problems; meliorism

1. Introduction

The topic of this symposium is:

If intelligence is truly important to real-world adaptation, and IQs have risen 30+ points in the past century (Flynn effect), then why are there so many unresolved and dramatic problems in the world, and what can psychology do about them?

The topic elicits three reactions from this commentator. I will elaborate on each, but, taken singly, my initial reactions were these:

1. Many world problems have, in fact, lessened over the years of the Flynn effect (world-wide starvation and hunger for example). Perhaps the problems that remain, or that have not lessened significantly, are those that are really difficult to solve, and thus, are most intractable.
2. Intelligence is important, but may not be enough to solve some of the problems. The many real problems that society still faces may be due to deficits of rationality rather than intelligence.
3. Many of the remaining world problems involve complex value conflicts—where people differ in their judgments about the optimal solution. These problems are often framed with a myside bias. On both sides of the political spectrum, many of us see a social issue in which our side has not totally won and define it as a "problem", when in fact, what we are seeing is not a problem per se, but a social compromise in which neither side has totally won the day.

Most of my commentary will focus on reactions #2 and #3, but for completeness, I will begin with a brief nod to #1.

2. Maybe Things Really Aren't So Bad After All

The framing of Sternberg's essay sometimes makes it seem as if we are supposed to adopt the default view that the world is getting worse. Although significant problems do remain, there is a good case to be made that we have been increasingly solving social problems throughout the past 100 years and more. In other words, significant progress in solving the world's problems has occurred.

Steven Pinker's book *The Better Angels of Our Nature* ([1], see also [2]) shows that a variety of large-scale negative social phenomena have, in fact, been decreasing throughout history—and that the decrease encompasses the period of the Flynn effect (however, see [3]). So, for example, Pinker shows that murder and violence have been decreasing throughout history. Likewise, various types of prejudice have been decreasing throughout history and throughout the period of the Flynn effect. The rights of vulnerable groups, such as children and women, have been increasing throughout history. Domestic violence has decreased, as has crime in general and child abuse in particular. Hate crimes have been decreasing throughout history, as have hunger and poverty. (Pointing this out is not to endorse a cavalier attitude toward the problems that are caused by modernity, an attitude that Gopnik [4] sees in Pinker's work).

All of these positive developments are the result of cumulative cultural ratcheting [5] enabling change to be biased in a positive direction. These cultural changes may have, in part, resulted from Flynn-like changes in abstract thinking. Indeed, Pinker [1] argues just that. But interestingly, Pinker follows Flynn [6] in arguing that the increase in abstract thinking is the result of the spread of scientific thinking making hypothetical thought more habitual. Such a view is consistent with my argument [7,8] that modernity, in the form of schooling and scientific reasoning has increased decontextualizing thinking styles among the population—and that this increases algorithmic-level functioning by making cognitive decoupling less capacity demanding and unnatural.

From my standpoint, as a researcher studying rational thinking, a causal model that operates in this manner—with rational/scientific culture as a causal influence on abstract reasoning (and hence IQ) becomes especially interesting. Rationality is a cultural achievement. Rational beliefs and actions are supported by strategies and knowledge that were not part of our biological endowment, but were cultural discoveries. The development of probability theory, logic, concepts of empiricism, and scientific inference throughout the centuries have provided humans with conceptual tools to aid in the formation and revision of belief and in their reasoning about action. As a culture, we have been engaging in a progressive cultural critique of the cognitive tools we use to act and think more rationally [7,9]. Although rationality is a cultural product, it has individual effects as well. My research group has long argued that one can measure individual differences in rational thinking [10,11].

This is my preferred place to look for the answers to the problem that Sternberg has set for us in his essay—why, despite the Flynn effect, are there are still so many unresolved and dramatic problems in the world. For Sternberg is certainly right in his target article that there are some big problems facing us and it certainly seems like the 30 extra IQ points that we have gotten from the Flynn effect have not totally solved these problems.

3. Rationality and Its Practical Effects

As a cognitive scientist, I am a so-called Meliorist [7,12]—which is someone who believes that there are defects in our thinking and that these defects can be remedied. As a Meliorist, I am concerned about the real-life effects of bad thinking. A Meliorist worries about things: parents who fail to vaccinate their children; the billions of dollars that are wasted on quack medical remedies; the many retirements that are ruined through failures to think through foreseeable financial implications of actions earlier in life; the pyramid sales schemes that sweep through middle-class neighborhoods; the children with reading disabilities who are treated with pseudoscientific methods involving balance beams and tinted lenses when other proven treatments exist; the many people who fail to process the implications of credit card debt; that information about probabilities is misused in legal proceedings (thereby freeing the guilty and convicting the innocent); that clinical psychologists persist in using psychodiagnostic instruments with no proven efficacy; and, that otherwise intelligent prosecutors pursue innocent people because of a theory that was developed too early on the basis of too little evidence.

What we have in many of these examples are cases of smart people acting foolishly—a phenomenon that both Sternberg [13] and I [14,15] have written about previously. People tend to find this phenomenon perplexing, but they really should not. Foolish behavior results when people make poorly considered judgments and take injudicious actions. As I have argued in previous publications, the skills of judgment and decision making are not assessed on IQ tests, so it should not be surprising that a person could have a high measured IQ but have modest or low judgment and decision making skills. There is no paradox in the "smart but acting foolish" phenomenon, because the intelligence construct that the tests actually measure (general mental "brightness") is not the same as the tendency to make judicious decisions—what most cognitive scientists would call rational thinking. If we were clear about the fact that the two concepts (intelligence and rationality) are different, the sense of paradox or surprise at the "smart but acting foolish" phenomenon would vanish. What perpetuates the surprise is that we tend to think of the two traits as one.

The confusion is fostered because psychology has a measurement device for one (intelligence) but not the other (rationality). Psychology has a long and storied history (of over one hundred years) of measuring the intelligence trait. Although there has been psychological work on rational thinking, this research started much later and was not focused on individual differences. Our research group has tried to remedy this situation by creating a beta version of what a test of rationality would look like—our Comprehensive Assessment of Rational Thinking, the CART [16].

A novice psychology student might be a bit confused at this point—thinking that somewhere along the line, they have heard definitions of intelligence that included rationality. Such a student would be right. Many theoretical definitions of intelligence incorporate the rationality concept by alluding to judgment and decision making in the definition. Other definitions emphasize behavioral adaptiveness, and thus also fold rationality into intelligence. The problem here is that none of these components of rationality—adaptive responding, good judgment, and decision-making—are assessed on commonly used tests of intelligence. In terms of the old psychometric distinction between the measures of typical performance and measures of maximum performance, rational thinking assessments lean more toward the typical performance end of the continuum than do intelligence tests. Many rational thinking task items suggest a compelling intuitive response that happens to be wrong. In these tasks, unlike the case for intelligence tests, the subject must detect the inadequacy of the intuitive response that is automatically triggered. They must then suppress this response while selecting a better alternative. Intelligence tests also tend to present problems that are unambiguously framed by their instructions. Rational thinking tasks, in contrast, often require the subject to choose a particular construal. In fact, it is this design feature that makes the task diagnostic. In a probabilistic reasoning task, the entire point is to see how dominant or nondominant the statistical interpretation is over the narrative interpretation.

The "smart but acting foolish" syndrome that is mentioned above suggests that one of the answers to the topic theme of this symposium ("why are there so many unresolved and dramatic problems in the world, given the Flynn effect") might be that what society really needs is more rationality in addition to intelligence. I perhaps can embellish this conjecture by expanding upon a thought experiment from one of Baron's earliest books [17]. Baron (p. 5) asks us to imagine what would happen if we were able to give everyone a harmless drug that increased their algorithmic-level cognitive capacities (discrimination speed, STM capacity, etc.)—in short, that increased their intelligence. Imagine that everyone in North America took a pill before retiring and then woke up the next morning with one more slot in their working memories. Both Baron and I believe that there is little likelihood that much would change the next day in terms of human happiness. It is very unlikely that people would be better able to fulfill their wishes and desires the day after taking the pill. In fact, it is quite likely that people would simply go about their usual business—only more efficiently. If given more short-term memory capacity, people would, I believe: carry on using the same ineffective medical treatments, keep making the same poor financial decisions, keep misjudging risks, and to continue making other suboptimal decisions. The only difference would be that they would be able to do all of these things much more quickly due to their enhanced algorithmic-level computational abilities! I think that Baron is right that, in contrast to the working memory pill, increasing rational thinking skills—processes of accurate belief formation, belief consistency assessment, and behavioral regulation—might really improve our own lives and those of others.

In another book, I have described making the choice between more intelligence or more rationality as asking the question: Would you rather get what you want slowly or get what you don't want much faster? I agree with some of the thrust of Sternberg's essay in thinking that society's focus on intelligence at the expense of rationality has meant that what we have been fostering is the tendency to get what we do not want much faster!

With my "get what you want" phrasing, I am referring here to one of two types of rationality identified by philosophers—instrumental rationality. Most colloquially, instrumental rationality amounts to behaving in the world so that you get exactly what you most want, given the resources (physical and mental) available to you. Somewhat more technically, instrumental rationality can be characterized as the optimization of the individual's goal fulfillment. Economists and cognitive scientists have refined the notion of optimization of goal fulfillment into the technical notion of expected utility.

The other aspect of rationality that is studied by cognitive scientists is termed epistemic rationality. This aspect of rationality concerns how well beliefs map onto the actual structure of the world. The two types of rationality are related. In order to take actions that fulfill our goals, we need to base those actions on beliefs that are properly calibrated to the world.

When properly defined, virtually no person wishes to eschew epistemic rationality and instrumental rationality. Most people want their beliefs to be in some correspondence with reality, and they also want to act in ways to maximize the achievement of their goals. Manktelow [18] has emphasized the practicality of both types of rationality by noting that they concern two critical things: What is true and what to do. Epistemic rationality is about what is true and instrumental rationality is about what to do. For our beliefs to be rational they must correspond to the way the world is—they must be true. For our actions to be rational, they must be the best means toward our goals—they must be the best things to do. Nothing could be more practical or useful for a person's life than the thinking processes that help them to find out what is true and what is best to do.

In our comprehensive assessment of rational thinking, the CART [16], we assess aspects of instrumental rationality and irrationality, such as: the ability to display disjunctive reasoning in decision making; the tendency to show inconsistent preferences because of framing effects; the tendency to substitute affect for difficult evaluations; the tendency to over-weight short-term rewards at the expense of long-term well-being; the tendency to have choices affected by vivid stimuli; and, the tendency for decisions to be affected by irrelevant context. Aspects of epistemic rationality that are assessed include: the tendency to show incoherent probability assessments; the tendency toward overconfidence in knowledge judgments; the tendency to ignore base rates; the tendency not to seek falsification of hypotheses; the tendency to try to explain chance events; the tendency to evaluate evidence with a myside bias; and, the tendency to ignore the alternative hypothesis.

Although measures of individual differences in these rational thinking components are correlated with individual differences in intelligence, the relationship is not high enough to warrant the idea that an IQ test provides a measure of rational thinking. The magnitude of the observed correlation leaves plenty of room for dissociations between intelligence and rationality.

One way to illustrate the potential for dissociation is to consider some examples from the literature showing that professionals—all of whom must be well above average in intelligence, have been shown to make dozens of the rational thinking errors that are assessed on the CART. For example, practicing physicians have shown framing effects in real-life medical problems [19]; ignoring the base-rate likelihood has been demonstrated in studies of medical personnel, lawyers, stockbrokers, sportswriters, economists, and meteorologists [20,21]; stock market investors mistakenly think that they can "beat the market" because they fail to appreciate the role of chance [22]; clinical psychologists have been shown to rely too heavily on single-case evidence of low diagnosticity [23,24]; lawyers have been found to be more likely to settle a case out of court when it was described, or framed, in terms of gains rather than equivalent losses [25]; overconfidence has been shown to reduce the earnings of professional traders [26–28]; and, physicians and clinical psychologists often fail to engage in diagnostic hypothesis testing [24,29–31].

These aspects of rational thinking have been linked to practical real-world behaviors in many different studies. Table 15.1 of Stanovich et al. [16] contains many such examples. The selection of examples mentioned here clearly show that there are many practical ways that the world would be a better place if everyone became more rational. For example, increased rationality would mean that people would deal better with certain risks. More people would wear seatbelts and fewer would text while driving, thus reducing casualties from traffic accidents. Thaler and Sunstein [32] were rightly lauded for showing how environmental changes (nudges) could lead to many similar incremental improvements.

Perhaps some of these improvements might be considered small-bore when compared to the large-scale problems that Sternberg enumerates in the target essay (climate change, poverty, pollution, violence, terrorism, opioid poisoning, income disparities, a divided society). But society seems to appreciate most of these small-bore improvements because many of them are nonzero-sum—a gain in outcome for one participant in an interchange does not entail a loss for another. Perhaps the reason that some of the large-scale problems that Sternberg mentions remain unsolved is because they have more of a zero-sum quality to them.

4. Value Conflicts Versus Optimizable Solutions

The speculation at the end of the last section suggests that perhaps we need to form a taxonomy of the different social problems that Sternberg mentions (climate change, poverty, pollution, violence, terrorism, opioid poisoning, income disparities, and a divided society) because they are in different categories. Two problems on Sternberg's list (poverty, violence) are in the category I discussed in my first section above—things that Pinker [1] shows actually have improved greatly throughout history, including during the period of the Flynn effect (Pinker would include terrorism in this category too, but I will treat it as a more controversial case). Perhaps the improvement was due to some combination of increasing intelligence and increasing rationality (or, additionally, wisdom). These problems have not been reduced to zero of course, but startling improvements have been made in both.

Other issues in Sternberg's list—such as climate change, pollution, and income disparities—may be of a different type. Perhaps, in some of these cases, what we are looking at are not problems but rather cases of conflicting values in a society with diverse worldviews. Pollution reduction and curbing global warming often require measures that have as a side effect restrained economic growth. The taxes and regulatory restraints necessary to markedly reduce pollution and global warming often fall disproportionately on the poor. For example, raising the cost of operating an automobile through congestion zones, raised parking costs, and increased vehicle and gas taxes restrains the driving of poorer people more than that of the affluent. I have lived in several environmentally progressive cities where the measures invoked to make driving expensive have indeed driven poorer people on to buses, but they have not affected my behavior. I am free to ride mass transit to make an environmental statement, but I am not forced on to it for monetary reasons, like my less affluent fellow citizens.

There is no way to minimize global warming and maximize economic output (and hence, jobs and prosperity) at the same time. People differ on where they put their "parameter settings" for trading off environmental protection versus economic growth. Differing parameter settings on issues such as this are not necessarily due to lack of knowledge [33,34]. They are the result of differing values or differing worldviews.

The point is that such large-scale problems as climate change and pollution control involve tradeoffs, and it is not surprising that the differing values that people hold may result in a societal compromise that pleases neither of the groups on the extremes. But, it is displaying a myside bias to think that if everyone were more intelligent, or more rational, or wiser that they would put the societal setting just where our own setting currently is. There is, in fact, empirical evidence showing that more knowledge or intelligence or reflectiveness does not resolve zero-sum value disagreements such as these [33,35–38].

The case of income disparities is complex, but it illustrates the same thing—that there is no one point that is the optimal level of income disparity. Disputes about it are value conflicts, and are not conflicts between the intelligent/rational/moral versus the unintelligent/irrational/immoral. Nor are they conflicts between the knowledgeable and unknowledgeable. Certainly it is not hard to look at cross-national statistics on the Gini index and per-capita GDP and conclude that the income inequality in the United States seems to be less than optimal. But, beyond that gross conclusion, there is little that can be said. There is no optimal level of the Gini index for a given country (the Gini index is the most commonly used measure of inequality in economics—where a higher Gini index indicates more inequality).

So, talking about "the problem" of income inequality seems to be somewhat a misnomer when no one knows what the optimal Gini coefficient is. Gini coefficients have been rising throughout the developed world in the last 30 years [39]. We might grant that the coefficient for the United States is too high. But does Australia have an income inequality problem? Does Sweden? How do we know when we have solved this problem? It is unlike poverty, which we want to reduce to zero.

Australia has the same Gini coefficient now that the United States had in 1985. So, however much inequality was a problem in the United States in 1985 (and there was plenty of talk about it being a problem in the Reagan era) then it is to that degree a problem in Australia now. Sweden—which is often lauded for its level of equality—has had the largest increase of all the OECD countries since 1985. Has that country been making massive economic mistakes? Or under some conditions, can a rising Gini index be a good thing? One only has to look at the full set of time changes across all of the OECD countries to see the impossibility of knowing what the optimal Gini coefficient is. If a certain country was exemplary in year X, another country was exemplary in year X + K, because most (but not all) countries have varying indices. Was Denmark the best country in 2010 because it has the lowest coefficient? Are Turkey and Greece the two OECD countries that are most on track because they are the rare countries in which Gini coefficients are decreasing? We might be able to make ordinal statements about income inequality at times—like my stipulation above that it certainly seems like the US index is higher than optimal—but it is not the kind of "problem" that has a maximizable solution, like poverty.

The concept of income inequality involves some particularly tricky trade-offs between values. The present settings of the inequality parameter at any grain size of social organization (world, country, state, county, city) reflect a social compromise resulting from conflicting values, where these values all reflect a particular public good—just like the values of increasing economic prosperity and decreasing global warming both foster public goods, but in a trade-off relationship. Take, for example, the fact that, although income inequality has been increasing in the past couple of decades in most industrialized, first-world countries, worldwide indices of income inequality have been decreasing during the same period [40]. These two trends may well be related—through the effects of trade and immigration [41]. Any such linkage creates value conflicts from the standpoint of, say, a particular citizen in the United States who is concerned about income inequality in their own country. That same person might support aspects of globalization (maximizing free trade and immigration, for example), because they are supporters of decreasing world poverty and world inequality. But, the very same mechanisms that are supporting decreases in world inequality may well be supporting increases in inequality within the United States—which the same person might also deplore. For example, globalization has enabled the shift in manufacturing to poorer countries, which often eliminates the middle layers of the economy of wealthier countries.

A complementary citizen of the United States might maximally prioritize decreasing inequality within the United States, and hence be a supporter of reduced trade and reduced immigration. But such a person might not like the concomitant effect of increasing worldwide inequality. The structure of the world economy might actually prevent maximizing the values of increasing immigration, decreasing income inequality within the United States, and decreasing inequality throughout the world at the same time. These three goals might not all be statistically achievable simultaneously [41,42]. The varying settings of the inequality parameter among countries—and disagreements among people and ideologies—reflect the natural variability of people's values. Disagreements about the level of the inequality parameter would not disappear if we were to maximize the rationality of the population, or its knowledge—neither would they disappear were we to make everyone wiser.

To take one last example of the paradoxes and complex trade-offs that surround the issue of income inequality (again compared to the much simpler issues of poverty reduction or hunger reduction), consider the following facts about income equality in the United States in the last 30 years: the top 10% of the population in income and wealth has pulled away from the middle of the population more than the middle has detached from the poor [39]. So, when trying to reduce overall inequality—in the manner that would affect an omnibus statistic like the Gini index—we need to make a value judgment about which of these gaps we want to concentrate on more. The obvious answer here for any equality advocate—that we want to work on both gaps—simply will not do. Some of the policies focused on closing one of these gaps may well operate to increase the other gap [43].

When we say that we are against inequality we really have to make a value judgment about which of these kinds of gaps mean more to us. Note that a focus on poverty does not have this trade-off. A focus on poverty tries to raise up the bottom strata of the population regardless of what it does to other levels. Capitalism and industrialization have precisely the effect that I am suggesting here. As countries go from destitute to industrialized, their poverty decreases, but in the earliest stages of this development their income inequality most often increases [40]. Finally, there is the issue of economic mobility—which is different from income inequality. It is possible for mobility to be high even when income equality is low. Indeed, in the United States economic mobility has not changed throughout the period when the Gini index has been rising [44].

In short, some of the social problems that appear in Sternberg's list do not have a univariate solution. They have multivariate states of stability that are based on citizens of different political persuasions trading off values in different ways (income inequality, climate, pollution). One other problem that Sternberg mentions, terrorism, would seem to be more like one of the simpler cases. One would think that terrorism would be like poverty and violence—a situation where everyone could agree that the optimal setting would be zero. But even in a case like this, there can be value conflicts. Both John Kerry [45] and Barack Obama [46] have argued that we should acclimate to some nonzero level of terrorism in the United States as a part of our accommodation to other values like globalization. Needless to say, not all Americans agree with the Kerry/Obama position that the optimal parameter setting for terrorism is above zero. Thus, even in the case of terrorism, we have value trade-offs that will not disappear once everyone is educated, intelligent, rational, and wise.

In the conclusion section of the target essay, Sternberg adds "a divided society" to the list of large-scale social issues already mentioned (climate change, income disparities, etc.). This, as an issue, is a quintessential illustration of the kind of problem that is going to be most opaque to solution via an appeal to mental faculties, such as intelligence, rationality, knowledge, or wisdom. Political divisiveness in society is by definition due to value conflict. Thinking that political divisiveness can be resolved by increasing any valued cognitive characteristic would seem to be the epitome of myside bias [47]. To put it a bit more colloquially, for a conservative to think that if we were all highly intelligent, highly rational, extremely knowledgeable, and very wise, all divisiveness would disappear because we would then all be Republicans would seem to be the height of myside thinking. Likewise, for a liberal to think that if we were all highly intelligent, highly rational, extremely knowledgeable, and very wise that all divisiveness would disappear because we would all then be Democrats would seem again to epitomize myside thinking [37,48–51].

A bit of a similar problem crops up when I wrestle with Sternberg's conceptualization of wisdom. It involves basically two dimensions. One is balancing the common good against one's own interests where the common good extends to one's family, one's community, one's nation, and the world. The second dimension involves balancing that common good over the long term as well as the short term. Call these two dimensions the social group parameter and the time parameter, respectively. With two different parameters, both on very wide continua, this definition seems to leave plenty of room for value conflicts. Along the time dimension, how long is long and how short is short? Are long and short defined in the same way across all domains? Beyond pure selfishness, the distribution of the social group concern leaves many degrees of freedom. To put it in an oversimplified way, how much less than 100% moral concern to the self do I have to allocate (and where) before I am deemed a wise person? Am I deemed wise if I allocate 50% to myself and 50% to others? And if so, does it matter where I put the 50% allocated to others?

There just seems to be too many degrees of freedom here for this characteristic to be usefully definable, first of all. Second of all, the causal link between a particular allocation of concern for others and how these large-scale problems are supposed to be solved is very unclear. With the social parameter, do I have to use all of the categories of others (family, community, nation, world)? Or is it okay if I put 50% on myself and 50% on my family? And if the latter allocation is deemed unwise, is it worse than putting 80% on myself, 10% on my nation, and 10% on the world? And if that allocation is insufficient, where do I find the godlike judge who tells me what the distribution should be?

Just like the example of the United States and the Gini coefficient, I think that the appeal to wisdom is only going to be helpful in a weak ordinal sense. I mentioned before that I was quite willing to stipulate that the Gini coefficient in the United States seems inordinately high (but then recall that it was very easy to complicate this judgment by appeals to linkages to decreases in the world Gini coefficient). Similarly, studies of temporal discounting in cognitive science would seem to support Sternberg's assumption that most people are too short-term in their thinking [52–55]. I can imagine the time parameter doing some work at least in a weak ordinal sense. But the social group parameter is much more problematic. How would we ever know what is a wise allocation of moral concern over self, family, community, nation, and world? This parameter, for example, must be radically contextually dependent. So, what an increase in wisdom would even mean with regard to this parameter I am unsure of, unless again it is just a weak ordinal suggestion that less should be allocated to oneself and more to the other four groups.

I do not wish to present an overly pessimistic view of our present intellectual landscape, however. Work has been done on the possibility of the rational adjudication of conflicting values [56–60]. I myself devoted a chapter of a 2004 book (chapter 8) to the possibility of rationally critiquing goal formation. But, this work has not advanced to a level that we would call prescriptive for the size of the world problems that are the focus of Sternberg's target article. It is possible, though, that alternative conceptions of wisdom, going beyond those articulated in the target article (see [61–63]), might be able to do some prescriptive work. What makes me skeptical that alternative conceptions can actually do that work, however, is the nature of some of the social problems on Sternberg's list.

At the heart of most concepts of wisdom is an emphasis on balancing values and interests. But, the claim that wisdom can help with an ongoing social issue, like inequality or pollution prevention, is not just the claim that we need more people balancing interests/values. It is the additional (implied) claim that the interests/values on either side of the issue are not already balanced in the optimal way. It is a meta-claim about the proper balance of interests. No conception of wisdom that I know of prescribes exactly where the quantitative balance should be struck regarding an ongoing issue that has already been the subject of much debate (like income inequality).

Wisdom can help bring unrecognized social problems to our attention. But, for problems where people already are consciously aware of the conflicting values and interests, then wisdom is of limited help, unless the conception of wisdom becomes itself a bit like a political position. In such situations, proponents of wisdom as a solution would seem to be presuming that wisdom is more on their side of the issue than the other side. This position (implicitly the position that wisdom is defined as "going more in the direction of my political party on an issue where interests compete") seems to define wisdom as having a particular social/political content. Defining wisdom as having socio-political content seems to conflict with most definitions of wisdom of which I am aware.

5. Conclusions

I agree with the target essay that psychology might have something to offer in helping us to address societal problems. I do believe that intelligence has helped meliorate some social problems throughout history, including the period of time that is covered by the Flynn effect. I agree with Pinker [1] that increases in intelligence may well have helped us deal with some large-scale social problems like violence, poverty, and hunger. I would go further than Pinker though, and agree with Sternberg that other psychological characteristics may be contributing as well. I think that the positive developmental trends for violence and poverty that Pinker attributes to intelligence could be equally attributed to societal increases in rationality during the same period. As I have argued above, rationality is a cultural achievement and its benefits cumulate because of cultural ratcheting. We are more rational than we were 100 years ago, although of course, 100 years ago, we did not have the parallel test of rationality to prove it!

I also think that increasing human rationality could have a variety of positive societal effects at levels somewhat smaller in grain size than the societal problems that Sternberg focuses on. These are areas that are not trivial in their effects on human happiness. People have their lives ruined and families disintegrate because of irrational thinking about financial matters, short-term thinking about their lives, and the innumeracy of various types that we measure on our rational thinking assessment, the CART [16]. For example, risks are evaluated in various suboptimal ways [64] that result in thousands of deaths due to texting and electronics-distracted driving [65]. Irrational thinking sustains pathological gambling and other behavioral problems [66]. Irrational thinking is what has sustained the dangerous anti-vaccine movement [67]. Some of these real-world problems can be remedied by increasing rational thinking. Similarly, financial decisions, medical decisions, legal decisions, and educational decisions might be improved by teaching more people the tools of rational thinking.

Some of the societal problems that Sternberg lists, however, I do not think would be remedied by increases in rationality or intelligence. I do not think that they would be remedied by knowledge or wisdom either, primarily because remedy might be the wrong word in the context of these issues. Issues like how much inequality of income to tolerate, how much pollution to tolerate, and how much we should sacrifice economic growth for potential future changes in global temperature represent issues of clashing values, not the inability to process information, or the lack of information, or the failure to show wisdom. They are fundamental differences in worldview and on such a large-scale basis are not driven by psychological characteristics that can be normatively evaluated.

Of course, by value conflicts I do not mean the absurdly myside ways these are framed in our current debased political culture ("our values differ because the opposing political party is evil and mine is virtuous"). I mean value conflicts in terms of deep philosophical tradeoffs—tradeoffs between things like: equality and liberty; union wages versus health care costs; and, pollution and economic growth. As Isaiah Berlin said upon receiving an honorary degree at the University of Toronto in a ceremony that I attended, "if these ultimate human values by which we live are to be pursued, then compromises, trade-offs, arrangements have to be made if the worst is not to happen. So, much liberty for so much equality, so much individual self-expression for so much security, so much justice for so much compassion. My point is that some values clash: the ends pursued by human beings are all generated by our common nature, but their pursuit has to be to some degree controlled—liberty and the pursuit of happiness, I repeat, may not be fully compatible with each other, nor are liberty, equality, and fraternity" [68].

Nonetheless, there are plenty of problems for psychologists to work on at a smaller grain-size. It is not unimportant to save for retirement, wear a seatbelt, refrain from electronics while driving,

J. Intell. **2018**, *6*, 25

consider baserates in decision making, and understand the cost-benefit tradeoffs when taking actions in the world. These are the type of rational thinking outcomes that can improve the world.

Conflicts of Interest: The author declares no conflict of interest.

References

1. Pinker, S. *The Better Angels of Our Nature*; Viking: New York, NY, USA, 2011.
2. Pinker, S. *Enlightenment Now: The Case for Reason, Science, Humanism and Progress*; Viking: New York, NY, USA, 2018.
3. Cirillo, P.; Taleb, N.N. On the statistical properties and tail risk of violent conflicts. *Phys. Stat. Mech. Appl.* **2016**, *452*, 29–45. [CrossRef]
4. Gopnik, A. A cure for contempt. *Atlantic* **2018**, *321*, 39–41.
5. Tomasello, M. *The Cultural Origins of Human Cognition*; Harvard University Press: Cambridge, MA, USA, 1999.
6. Flynn, J.R. *What is Intelligence?* Cambridge University Press: Cambridge, MA, USA, 2007.
7. Stanovich, K.E. *The Robot's Rebellion: Finding Meaning in the Age of Darwin*; University of Chicago Press: Chicago, IL, USA, 2004.
8. Stanovich, K.E. *Rationality and the Reflective Mind*; Oxford University Press: New York, NY, USA, 2011.
9. Stanovich, K.E. *Decision Making and Rationality in the Modern World*; Oxford University Press: New York, NY, USA, 2010.
10. Stanovich, K.E.; West, R.F. Individual differences in rational thought. *J. Exp. Psychol. Gen.* **1998**, *127*, 161–188. [CrossRef]
11. Stanovich, K.E.; West, R.F. Individual differences in reasoning: Implications for the rationality debate? *Behav. Brain Sci.* **2000**, *23*, 645–726. [CrossRef] [PubMed]
12. Stanovich, K.E. *Who is Rational? Studies of Individual Differences in Reasoning*; Erlbaum: Mahwah, NJ, USA, 1999.
13. Sternberg, R.J. (Ed.) *Why Smart People Can Be So Stupid*; Yale University Press: New Haven, CT, USA, 2002.
14. Stanovich, K.E. Dysrationalia: A new specific learning disability. *J. Learn. Disabil.* **1993**, *26*, 501–515. [CrossRef] [PubMed]
15. Stanovich, K.E. *What Intelligence Tests Miss: The Psychology of Rational Thought*; Yale University Press: New Haven, CT, USA, 2009.
16. Stanovich, K.E.; West, R.F.; Toplak, M.E. *The Rationality Quotient: Toward a Test of Rational Thinking*; MIT Press: Cambridge, MA, USA, 2016.
17. Baron, J. *Rationality and Intelligence*; Cambridge University Press: Cambridge, MA, USA, 1985.
18. Manktelow, K.I. Reasoning and rationality: The pure and the practical. In *Psychology of Reasoning: Theoretical and Historical Perspectives*; Manktelow, K.I., Chung, M.C., Eds.; Psychology Press: Hove, UK, 2004; pp. 157–177.
19. McNeil, B.; Pauker, S.; Sox, H.; Tversky, A. On the elicitation of preferences for alternative therapies. *N. Engl. J. Med.* **1982**, *306*, 1259–1262. [CrossRef] [PubMed]
20. Garcia-Retamero, R.; Hoffrage, U. Visual representation of statistical information improves diagnostic inferences in doctors and their patients. *Soc. Sci. Med.* **2013**, *83*, 27–33. [CrossRef] [PubMed]
21. Koehler, D.J.; Brenner, L.; Griffin, D. The calibration of expert judgment: Heuristics and biases beyond the laboratory. In *Heuristics and Biases: The Psychology of Intuitive Judgment*; Gilovich, T., Griffin, D., Kahneman, D., Eds.; Cambridge University Press: New York, NY, USA, 2002; pp. 686–715.
22. Malkiel, B.G. *A Random Walk Down Wall Street*; Norton: New York, NY, USA, 2016.
23. Baker, T.B.; McFall, R.M.; Shoham, V. Current status and future prospects of clinical psychology: Toward a scientifically principled approach to mental and behavioral health care. *Psychol. Sci. Public Interest* **2009**, *9*, 67–103. [CrossRef] [PubMed]
24. Lilienfeld, S.O. Psychological treatments that cause harm. *Perspect. Psychol. Sci.* **2007**, *2*, 53–70. [CrossRef] [PubMed]
25. Belton, I.K.; Thomson, M.; Dhami, M.K. Lawyer and nonlawyer susceptibility to framing effects in out-of-court civil litigation settlement. *J. Empir. Leg. Stud.* **2014**, *11*, 578–600. [CrossRef]

26. Hilton, D.J. Psychology and the financial markets: Applications to understanding and remedying irrational decision-making. In *The Psychology of Economic Decisions (Vol. 1): Rationality and Well-Bein*; Brocas, I., Carrillo, J.D., Eds.; Oxford University Press: Oxford, UK, 2003; pp. 273–297.
27. Odean, T. Volume, volatility, price, and profit when all traders are above average. *J. Financ.* **1998**, *53*, 1887–1934. [CrossRef]
28. Statman, M.; Thorley, S.; Vorkink, K. Investor overconfidence and trading volume. *Rev. Financ. Stud.* **2006**, *19*, 1531–1565. [CrossRef]
29. Croskerry, P. A universal model of diagnostic reasoning. *Acad. Med.* **2009**, *84*, 22–1028. [CrossRef] [PubMed]
30. Croskerry, P. Context is everything or how could I have been that stupid? *Healthc. Q.* **2009**, *12*, 167–173. [CrossRef]
31. Groopman, J. *How Doctors Think*; Houghton Mifflin: Boston, MA, USA, 2007.
32. Thaler, R.H.; Sunstein, C.R. *Nudge: Improving Decisions about Health, Wealth, and Happiness*; Yale University Press: New Haven, CT, USA, 2008.
33. Henry, P.J.; Napier, J.L. Education is related to greater ideological prejudice. *Public Opin. Q.* **2017**, *81*, 930–942. [CrossRef]
34. Kahan, D.M. Climate-science communication and the measurement problem. *Political Psychol.* **2015**, *36*, 1–43. [CrossRef]
35. Kahan, D.M. Ideology, motivated reasoning, and cognitive reflection. *Judgm. Decis. Mak.* **2013**, *8*, 407–424.
36. Kahan, D.M.; Jenkins-Smith, H.; Braman, D. Cultural cognition of scientific consensus. *J. Risk Res.* **2011**, *14*, 147–174. [CrossRef]
37. Kahan, D.; Peters, E.; Dawson, E.; Slovic, P. Motivated numeracy and enlightened self-government. *Behav. Public Policy* **2017**, *1*, 54–86. [CrossRef]
38. Kahan, D.; Peters, E.; Wittlin, M.; Slovic, P.; Ouellette, L.; Braman, D.; Mandel, D. The polarizing impact of science literacy and numeracy on perceived climate change risks. *Nat. Clim. Chang.* **2012**, *2*, 732–735. [CrossRef]
39. OECD. *An Overview of Growing Income Inequalities in OECD Countries: Main Findings*; Organisation for Economic Co-operation and Development: Paris, France, 2011. Available online: http://www.oecd.org/els/soc/dividedwestandwhyinequalitykeepsrising.htm (accessed on 15 February 2018).
40. Roser, M. Global Economic Inequality. 2017. Available online: https://ourworldindata.org/global-economic-inequality (accessed on 15 February 2018).
41. Borjas, G.J. *We Wanted Workers: Unraveling the Immigration Narrative*; Norton: New York, NY, USA, 2016.
42. Lakner, C.; Milanovic, B. *Global Income Distribution: From the Fall of the Berlin Wall to the Great Recession*; Policy Research Working Paper 6719; World Bank: Washington, DC, USA, 2016.
43. Reeves, R.V. *Dream Hoarders*; Brookings Institution Press: Washington, DC, USA, 2017.
44. Chetty, R.; Hendren, N.; Kline, P.; Saez, E.; Turner, N. Is the United States still a land of opportunity? Recent trends in intergenerational mobility. *Am. Econ. Rev.* **2014**, *104*, 141–147. [CrossRef]
45. Bai, M. Kerry's undeclared war. *New York Times*. Available online: http://www.nytimes.com/2004/10/10/magazine/kerrys-undeclared-war.html (accessed on 15 February 2018).
46. Goldberg, J. The Obama Doctrine. *The Atlantic*. Available online: https://www.theatlantic.com/magazine/archive/2016/04/the-obama-doctrine/471525/ (accessed on 15 February 2018).
47. Stanovich, K.E.; West, R.F.; Toplak, M.E. Myside bias, rational thinking, and intelligence. *Curr. Dir. Psychol. Sci.* **2013**, *22*, 259–264. [CrossRef]
48. Chambers, J.R.; Schlenker, B.R.; Collisson, B. Ideology and prejudice: The role of value conflicts. *Psychol. Sci.* **2013**, *24*, 140–149. [CrossRef] [PubMed]
49. Crawford, J.T.; Brandt, M.J.; Inbar, Y.; Chambers, J.; Motyl, M. Social and economic ideologies differentially predict prejudice across the political spectrum, but social issues are most divisive. *J. Personal. Soc. Psychol.* **2017**, *112*, 383–412. [CrossRef] [PubMed]
50. Ditto, P.H.; Liu, B.; Clark, C.A.C.; Wojcik, S.; Chen, E.; Grady, R.; Celniker, J.; Zinger, J. At least bias is bipartisan: A meta-analytic comparison of partisan bias in liberals and conservatives. *Perspect. Psychol. Sci.* **2018**, *13*, 297–333. [CrossRef]
51. Tetlock, P.E. Rational versus irrational prejudices: How problematic is the ideological lopsidedness of social psychology? *Perspect. Psychol. Sci.* **2012**, *7*, 519–521. [CrossRef] [PubMed]
52. Ainslie, G. *Breakdown of Will*; Cambridge University Press: Cambridge, MA, USA, 2001.

53. Loewenstein, G.F.; Read, D.; Baumeister, R. (Eds.) *Time and Decision: Economic and Psychological Perspectives on Intertemporal Choice*; Russell Sage: New York, NY, USA, 2003.
54. Mischel, W.; Ayduk, O.N.; Berman, M.; Casey, B.J.; Jonides, J.; Kross, E.; Shoda, Y. "Willpower" over the life span: Decomposing impulse control. *Soc. Cognit. Affect. Neurosci.* **2011**, *6*, 252–256. [CrossRef] [PubMed]
55. Rachlin, H. *The Science of Self-Control*; Harvard University Press: Cambridge, MA, USA, 2000.
56. Baron, J. Norm-endorsement utilitarianism and the nature of utility. *Econ. Philos.* **1996**, *12*, 165–182. [CrossRef]
57. Baron, J. Parochialism as a result of cognitive biases. In *Understanding Social Action, Promoting Human Rights*; Goodman, R., Jinks, D., Woods, A., Eds.; Oxford University Press: New York, NY, USA, 2012; pp. 203–238.
58. Gewirth, A. *Self-Fulfillment*; Princeton University Press: Princeton, NJ, USA, 1998.
59. Harris, S. *The Moral Landscape*; Free Press: New York, NY, USA, 2010.
60. Nozick, R. *The Nature of Rationality*; Princeton University Press: Princeton, NJ, USA, 1993.
61. Grossmann, I. Wisdom in context. *Perspect. Psychol. Sci.* **2017**, *12*, 233–257. [CrossRef] [PubMed]
62. Grossmann, I.; Na, J.; Varnum, M.E.; Kitayama, S.; Nisbett, R.E. A route to well-being: Intelligence versus wise reasoning. *J. Exp. Psychol. Gen.* **2013**, *142*, 944–953. [CrossRef] [PubMed]
63. Staudinger, U.M.; Gluck, J. Psychological wisdom research: Commonalities and differences in a growing field. *Annu. Rev. Psychol.* **2011**, *62*, 215–241. [CrossRef] [PubMed]
64. Fischhoff, B.; Kadvany, J. *Risk: A Very Short Introduction*; Oxford University Press: New York, NY, USA, 2011.
65. Strayer, D.L.; Cooper, J.C.; Turrill, J.; Coleman, J.; Hopman, R. Talking to your car can drive you to distraction. *Cognit. Res. Princ. Implic.* **2016**, *1*, 1–16. [CrossRef] [PubMed]
66. Toplak, M.E.; Liu, E.; Macpherson, R.; Toneatto, T.; Stanovich, K.E. The reasoning skills and thinking dispositions of problem gamblers: A dual-process taxonomy. *J. Behav. Decis. Mak.* **2007**, *20*, 103–124. [CrossRef]
67. Offit, P.A. *Deadly Choices: How the Anti-Vaccine Movement Threatens Us All*; Basic Books: New York, NY, USA, 2011.
68. Berlin, I. A Message to the 21st Century. In *The New York Review of Books*; University of Toronto Convocation: Toronto, ON, Canada, 2014.

Journal of
Intelligence

MDPI

Commentary

Speculations on the Role of Successful Intelligence in Solving Contemporary World Problems [†]

Robert J. Sternberg

Department of Human Development, College of Human Ecology, Cornell University, B44 MVR, Ithaca, NY 14853, USA; rjs487@cornell.edu

† This article is based in part on my William James Fellow Award address to the Association for Psychological Science, May 2017, Boston, MA, USA.

Received: 7 December 2017; Accepted: 19 January 2018; Published: 23 January 2018

Abstract: In this article, I argue that conventional views of intelligence and its measurement have contributed toward at least some of the societal problems of today. I suggest that to escape from a degenerative process, society needs to consider the importance not only of intelligence, as conventionally defined but also of successful intelligence, involving in addition to conventional analytical intelligence, common sense, creativity, and wisdom.

Keywords: intelligence; creativity; wisdom

1. Introduction to the Symposium on the Application of Theory and Research on Intellectual Abilities to the Solution of Vexing World Problems

This article is the first in a symposium of thought pieces on the following topic: "If intelligence is truly important to real-world adaptation and IQs have risen 30+ points in the past century (Flynn effect), then why are there so many unresolved and dramatic problems in the world and what can be done about it?"

The goal of the symposium is to have articles representing a number of different points of view with regard to constructs that might be relevant to solving serious problems facing the world today. These articles (including the present one) are speculative. We really do not have validated scientific data on how, say, analytical intelligence, creativity, common sense, or wisdom can be applied effectively to problems of climate change, poverty, or pollution. But if psychological scientists shy away from these problems, they may leave all of the speculation to individuals who bring no scientific perspective at all to these issues. Authors in the symposium are not expected to provide solutions but rather to point the way for how various constructs might help policy-makers and others address world problems.

My motivation in organizing this symposium is that I believe that psychology and related disciplines have a great deal to contribute to the solution of world problems but have been sidelined in favor of other fields, such as economics and the law. In this symposium, we examine in particular the role of theory and research on intellectual abilities. Examples of some of the constructs to be considered are intelligence (as conventionally defined), rational thinking, creativity, reasoning (biased and unbiased) and wisdom. These are all components of successful intelligence.

In particular, I have chosen invitees whom I view as experts on constructs particularly relevant to the solution of world problems and who I believe have an interest in the solution of such problems. Again, the articles will provide no final answers or detailed solutions but rather, directions for theory, research and policy analysis, as appropriate. Obviously, articles for this symposium involve some dose of personal opinion and speculation but all are to be grounded in psychological theory and research.

So, here is the first article, on successful intelligence. Successful intelligence is one's ability to formulate, execute, evaluate and then, as needed, reformulate one's plans for one's life [1,2]. It encompasses creative, analytical, practical and wise thinking. That is, one needs creative thinking to generate ideas, analytical thinking to decide whether the ideas are good ideas, practical thinking to implement the ideas and persuade others of their value and wise thinking to ensure that the ideas help to achieve a common good, in the long- as well as the short-term.

2. A Mesopotamian Tale

There is a Mesopotamian tale, retold by W. Somerset Maugham, about a servant who, seeing Death staring at him in a strange way in Baghdad, flees to Samarra to escape Death. When the merchant for whom the servant works sees Death in Baghdad, he asks Death why he gave the man such a strange stare. Death explains that the stare was only because he was surprised to see the servant in Baghdad, when in fact Death had an appointment with the servant the next day in Samarra.

Are we, in the world, creating a race to Samarra? I suggest that viewing intelligence in a conventional way (see essays in [3,4]) metaphorically may be leading us toward, rather than away from, catastrophe in Samarra. Rather, we need to view intelligence in terms of "successful intelligence," or the ability to formulate, execute, and evaluate plans for the conduct of a life that is personally meaningful and fulfilling [5]. Particularly important in this formulation, as described below, is wisdom.

3. Conventional Intelligence Is Not Enough to Solve World Problems

What, exactly, is intelligence (see essays in [4])? Intelligence often is seen in terms of ability to learn and reason and in terms of adaptation to the environment [6–9]. Traditionally, it has been operationalized in terms of what IQ tests or tests of abstract thinking measure and of the processes underlying such tests (see [6,10]).

I have suggested that the processes of intelligence can be understood in terms of three kinds of components of intelligence [11,12]. *Metacomponents* are higher order executive processes that plan what to do, monitor it while it is being done, and evaluate it after it is done. The main metacomponents are:

- Recognizing the existence of a problem (e.g., that intelligence tests may favor students from some cultural backgrounds over students from other cultural backgrounds);
- Defining the nature of the problem (e.g., that the students who are disfavored may actually be quite intelligent in their natural environmental contexts, even if not in the context of traditional intelligence tests);
- Constructing a mental representation of the problem (e.g., learning what kinds of tasks are representative of adaptive and hence intelligent performance in various cultural settings);
- Formulating a strategy to solve the problem (e.g., planning to devise tests relevant to various cultural milieus);
- Monitoring problem solving while it is in process (e.g., empirically determining whether the tests that have been created indeed are relevant to the various milieus);
- Evaluating problem solving after it is completed (e.g., determining whether the new tests have construct validity in the environments for which they are intended) (see [13,14] for related ideas regarding creativity).

Performance components actually solve the problems. And knowledge-acquisition components learn how to solve the problems in the first place [11]. Other scholars' theories have similar problem-solving processes (see, e.g., [15]).

There are broader views of abilities (e.g., [5,16]) but society has yet to adopt them. Even with respect to traditional views, intelligence has proven to be somewhat problematical in terms of its role in society (see, e.g., [17]).

Professor James Flynn of the University of Otago has found that during the 20th century, IQs rose worldwide about 3 points per decade, or roughly 30 points [18]. Even better, in the United States, IQs are continuing to rise [19]. A difference of 30 points is huge: It is the difference between a gifted IQ and an average one and between an average IQ and one at the borderline of labeling someone "intellectually challenged." Average IQs remain 100 because test publishers periodically re-standardize tests to make the average 100. Without doubt, increased levels of intelligence in a traditional sense have brought societies in the world many blessings, such as advances in science and technology.

Unfortunately, the steep rise in IQ has bought us, as a society, much less than anyone had any right to hope for. People are probably better at figuring out complex cell phones and other technological innovations than they would have been at the turn of the twentieth century. But in terms of our behavior as a society, are you impressed with what 30 points has brought us? Higher IQs have not brought with them generally satisfying solutions to some of the world's or the country's major problems—rising income disparities, climate change, pollution, organized violence, terrorism, deaths by opioid poisoning, among others. Today many children are being poorly educated and many still do not learn to read well [20]. Depending on one's opinions, one may see many other serious problems as well but it is not clear how many, if any of those have been solved.

What all these problems have in common is that the use of conventional intelligence to maximize gains for one group or another can result in a reduction of the common good. Conventional intelligence easily can be used to maximize the gains of an individual or a group at the expense of other individuals or groups. Policies that benefit particular groups in the short term but that hurt the common good in the long term also then end up hurting in the long term the groups the received the short-term benefits. For example, if climate change continues, eventually everyone will suffer, regardless of short-term benefits to particular groups.

Most of the academic tests used in schools—in the United States, SATs, ACTs, GREs and so on; in other countries, similar tests with different names—are basically IQ proxies. They are not the same as IQ tests but scores on them are moderately to highly correlated with IQ [21–23]. Our society, in placing so much emphasis on scores on standardized tests, is making a serious and possibly irreversible mistake [11,12,24–26]. In my view, we are creating an educational race that rewards people who score highly on skills that will help their own life chances to a small to moderate extent [25–28]. But the race does little to choose winners who will create a positive, meaningful, and enduring difference to our future [29,30]. We have created a race to Samarra. The skills our schools emphasize matter somewhat for school and life success but they are the beginning, not the end of the story of what matters [31,32].

We need to be developing virtues such as good character, compassion, active citizenship and ethical leadership, and other important skills such as creativity, common sense and wisdom—using one's knowledge and skills for a common good, by understanding other people's points of view and by ethically balancing one's own interests with other people's and larger interests of society and the world [31,33,34]. Judging by international trends, we seem to be doing much the opposite. "Other people's interests" seem to extend largely to people we imagine to be like us but not much to those in our self-constructed outgroups. Much of the current (2018) political leadership around the world nicely illustrates this idea of favoring people perceived to be like the leaders (e.g., people of a certain economic group, religion, socially-defined race, ethnicity, or political persuasion).

Conventional intelligence is insufficient for creating a better world. Moreover, it has a dark side [33–35]. The dark side is rather obvious: Intelligence can be used for good ends (e.g., Nelson Mandela, Martin Luther King) but it equally well can be used for bad ends (e.g., Adolph Hitler, Josef Stalin, and those, like the fictional Lord Voldemort, who must not be named). Intelligence is a measure of adaptive skills [36–38]. But those skills are for oneself, not for society or the world as a whole. People can adapt just fine but sometimes, at the expense of others. Many problems in the world show how some people are learning to adapt just fine and are just as fine with leaving others behind.

Intelligence is thus important but provides no guarantee of a better world. Intelligence was used to develop nuclear weapons, poisonous gases, and the fossil fuels in part behind climate change: Intelligence can make the world much better but it also can destroy the world, at least as we know it.

4. Creativity Is Not Enough to Solve World Problems

Creativity is partly an attitude toward life, not merely an ability [39,40]. Moreover, it always takes place within a system [41–47]. Creativity can provide part of the answer to creating a better world [48,49]. The creative attitude is one of buying low and selling high—taking good ideas that others are reluctant to accept, persuading others of their value, and then moving on to the next unpopular idea [48]. Most people fail to be creative not because they cannot be but rather because they are afraid to be. Creativity involves three kinds of "defiance" [50]:

- **Defying the crowd:** Creative people are willing to stand up to the resistance that creativity almost inevitably sparks in others (the crowd). Often people, including scientists, value creativity except when it threatens them personally—they prefer ideas that do not require them to challenge their fundamental ways of thinking.
- **Defying oneself:** Creative people are willing to stand up to their own prior ideas and conceptions and to move on as they change, the world changes and their potential contribution to the world changes. Often people are willing to stand up to others but not to themselves, with the result that their "new" ideas are minor re-workings of their old ideas—"old wine in new bottles."
- **Defying the Zeitgeist:** Creative people are willing to stand up to the often preconscious presuppositions under which they and the crowd have operated. An example has been significance testing: For a long time, the use of significance testing has been simply part of the Zeitgeist, whereas now Bayesian researchers more and more are challenging it. Often people do not want to challenge the presuppositions with which they have become comfortable and that define their personal and professional lives. Creative people do so.

Creativity includes insightful thinking [51,52] and other kinds of innovative thought. There are multiple kinds of creativity [45,49], ranging from baby steps (what Kaufman & Beghetto refer to as "little c") forward to giant steps that change the face of the world (what Kaufman & Beghetto refer to as "Big C"). Creativity can be measured and developed, at least to some extent, in any part of the world [14]. The computer on which this article is being written and most of the conveniences of modern life, are possible only because of creativity, or the creation of new ideas and products that are both novel and somehow useful [53]. But creativity also has a dark side [54,55]. People can use creativity for good purposes (e.g., formulation of medicines to cure diseases, composition of symphonies, writing of classic novels) or for bad purposes (e.g., designing devastating bombs, formulating and executing terrorist attacks, designing novel means for committing genocide and perhaps for covering up the acts). The world needs more than just creativity, just as it needs more than just intelligence.

5. Common Sense

Practical intelligence, or "common sense," is involved when skills are utilized, implemented, applied, or put into practice in real-world contexts. It involves individuals applying their abilities to the kinds of problems they confront in daily life, such as on the job or in the home. Practical intelligence involves applying the components of intelligence to experience so as to (a) adapt to, (b) shape, and (c) select environments. Adaptation is involved when one changes oneself to suit the environment. Shaping is involved when one changes the environment to suit oneself. And selection is involved when one decides to seek out another environment that is a better match to one's needs, abilities, and desires. People differ in their balance of adaptation, shaping, and selection and in the competence with which they balance among these three possible courses of action. One would hope that world leaders would apply these skills with facility. They often do not.

Underlying practical intelligence is tacit knowledge [56]. The concept of tacit knowledge reflects the idea that much of the knowledge relevant to real-world performance is acquired through everyday experiences without conscious intent. Tacit knowledge guides action without being easily articulated. It is knowledge needed in order to work effectively in an environment that one is not explicitly taught and that often is not even verbalized [25,27]. My colleagues and I represent tacit knowledge in the form of production systems, or sequences of "if-then" statements that describe procedures one follows in various kinds of everyday situations [27].

We have studied tacit knowledge in domains as diverse as bank management, sales, academic psychology, primary education, clerical work, social interaction and military leadership [27,57]. The measurement of tacit knowledge derives from an assessment of how individuals rate responses to practical problems. The format on tacit-knowledge tests is akin to that on situational-judgment tests. Individuals are presented with a brief problem description and are asked to evaluate the quality of potential solutions to the problem. For example, in a hypothetical situation presented to a business manager, a subordinate whom the manager does not know well has come to him for advice on how to succeed in business. The manager is asked to rate each of several responses (usually on a 1 = low to 9 = high scale) according to its importance for succeeding in the company. Examples of responses might include (a) setting priorities that reflect the importance of each task; (b) trying always to work on what you are in the mood to do; and (c) doing routine tasks early in the day to make sure you get them done. Tacit-knowledge (TK) tests typically consist of several problem situations. Responses are scored by comparing an individual's ratings on all the alternatives to a standard based on expert or consensus judgment.

The score an individual receives on a TK test is viewed as an indicator of his or her practical ability. Previous research has examined the relationship of TK scores to domain-specific experience, general cognitive ability and various indicators of performance. Generally, individuals with greater experience in a domain (e.g., business managers versus business students) receive higher TK scores. Tacit-knowledge scores also correlate fairly consistently with performance across a variety of domains. Individuals with higher TK scores have been found to have higher salaries, better performance ratings, more productivity and to work in more prestigious institutions [58].

Finally, TK tests appear to tap abilities that are distinct from those measured by traditional intelligence or ability tests. The correlations between scores on TK tests and scores on traditional intelligence tests have ranged from negative to moderately positive [27]. More importantly, TK scores have been found to explain performance above and beyond that accounted for by tests of general cognitive ability [27]. Thus, TK tests offer a promising approach for assessing an individual's practical abilities.

Given that TK tests show minimal correlations with IQ, it might make sense to use such tests for selecting individuals who will be in a position to affect policy, at whatever level. Our current system of selection is such that someone with a high IQ but minimal common sense easily could end up in such a position. Come to think of it, we almost certainly have in the world myriad such people—people affecting important world decisions who were chosen for their academic intelligence but not for their common sense (see also [59]).

6. We Also Need Wisdom to Solve World Problems

Wisdom in conjunction with creativity, common sense, and conventional intelligence, can help to create a better world [60–62]. I believe wisdom should be seen as an integral part of successful intelligence, to the extent that intelligence encompasses the idea not only of success for the individual but also for society and the world. There are many definitions of wisdom but almost all of them point to wisdom as a key to creating a better world. In my own definition [61], wisdom involves using both one's analytical and practical intelligence and one's creativity, as well as one's knowledge base, for a common good over the long as well as the short term. So, at least by definition, wisdom cannot be used toward dark ends. One achieves the common good by balancing one's own interests with the interests of others and larger interests (such as of one's family, one's community, one's nation, or the world), over the long as well as the short term, through the infusion of positive ethical values. However one defines wisdom, it is clearly a key to solving world problems.

6.1. Kinds of Wisdom

Wisdom can be seen as being of different kinds, depending on two dimensions, domain generality and depth (see Table 1).

Table 1. Kinds of Wisdom.

Domain Generality/Depth of Wisdom	Deep	Shallow
Domain General	Domain-General/Deep Deeply insightful advice across domains	Domain-GeneralShallow Modestly insightful advice across domains
Domain Specific	Domain-Specific/Deep Deeply insightful advice in a single domain	Domain-Specific/Shallow Modestly insightful advice in a single domain

Domain-general deep wisdom is the kind of wisdom we often think of when we think about wisdom. It refers to people who reflect deeply on complex problems across a wide variety of domains and then reach wise solutions. The thinking of great thinkers such as Socrates or Aristotle would fall into this category but so would the thinking of great recent leaders such as Martin Luther King or Nelson Mandela.

Domain-general shallow wisdom is the kind of wisdom we may think of when we watch a Hollywood movie in which a person, usually an elderly person, gives wise advice, especially to a younger person. The person is wise enough for a movie or a TV show but the level of advice is at the level of the old TV show, "Father Knows Best." The individual exhibits wisdom, perhaps across a number of domains but for simple everyday problems that perhaps younger people (and some older ones) just have not yet learned how to solve. This is the kind of wisdom we often impart to our children in the face of the everyday problems they face at school.

Domain-specific deep wisdom applies to deep thinking about complex problems but within a relatively narrow domain. Someone, for example, may be wise in giving career advice but terrible in giving personal advice, or vice versa. Some of us have had wise mentors, for example, who gave us sound professional advice but who made a mess of their personal lives and perhaps the personal lives of others as well.

Domain-specific shallow wisdom is superficial wisdom that applies simply in a single domain. There is a lot of that around in the political sphere.

6.2. Non-Wisdom

Regrettably, much more common in the world than wisdom is non-wisdom, or the lack of wisdom (see Table 2).

Table 2. Kinds of Non-wisdom.

Kinds of Non-Wisdom	Manifestation
Quasi-wisdom	Near wisdom—incomplete reflection or insight
Veneer of wisdom	False appearance of wisdom as a result of position of power or authority
Pseudo-wisdom	False appearance of wisdom motivated by self-interest
Dark pseudo-wisdom	False appearance of wisdom motivated by evil intentions

Quasi-wisdom is near-wisdom, or advice that comes with incomplete reflection or insight. A person may give advice that cosmetically seems wise but that misses important factors that should have been taken into consideration.

The *veneer of wisdom* occurs when someone, perhaps someone in a position of leadership or authority, is thought to be wise by virtue of his or her position, or perhaps by virtue of other kinds of skills, such as intelligence or creativity, or by virtue of a vast store of knowledge. It is a mere appearance of wisdom, or perhaps wisdom that is a "micron thick." The person may be smart or creative or knowledgeable but be unable or unwilling to use his or her skills or knowledge wisely—toward a common good.

Pseudo-wisdom is the deliberate attempt to appear wise by someone who is anything but, for example, a leader who uses his or her position of authority to serve his or her personal wants and desires or the wants and desires of his or her family or perceived allies, while trying to convey the impression of seeking a common good.

Dark pseudo-wisdom is like pseudo-wisdom, except that it is the appearance of wisdom in the service of evil ends, such as abusing children or encouraging people to become suicide bombers. False religious leaders may take advantage of their position to harm others rather than to help them.

6.3. Foolishness

Whereas non-wisdom is the lack or nullity of wisdom, the opposite of wisdom is foolishness [63,64] (Table 3). If lack of wisdom is like a "zero," foolishness is like a "negative number." People can be highly intelligent or even creative and yet foolish. Indeed, high intelligence can be a risk factor for foolishness, precisely because people who are highly intelligent may believe they are immune to foolishness. Foolishness is exhibited through a series of six cognitive fallacies [64]. First, the *unrealistic-optimism fallacy* occurs when people think they are so smart and effective that they can do whatever they want. Second, the *egocentrism fallacy* occurs when people start to think that they are the only ones that matter, not the people who rely on them. Third, the *omniscience fallacy* occurs when people think that they know everything and lose sight of the limitations of their own knowledge. Fourth, the *omnipotence fallacy* occurs when people think they are all-powerful and can do whatever they want. Fifth, the *invulnerability fallacy* occurs when people think they can get away with anything, because they are too clever to be caught; and they figure that even if they are caught they can get away with what they have done because of who they imagine themselves to be. And finally, sixth, the *ethical disengagement* fallacy occurs when people think that ethics are important—for others but not for themselves. They see themselves as above ethical concerns.

Table 3. Kinds of Foolishness.

Fallacy	Manifestation
Unrealistic optimism	"If it's my idea, it must be good"
Egocentrism	"It's all about me"
False omniscience	"I know everything I need to know"
False omnipotence	"I am all-powerful"
False invulnerability	"No one can get back at me"
Ethical Disengagement	"Ethics are important for other people"

7. Conclusions

The world is facing huge, pressing, and even frightening problems—terrorism, climate change, increasing income disparities, drug abuse, a divided society, and feelings of many of hopelessness, especially, in some cases, after people see the leaders their fellow citizens choose or tolerate. Successful intelligence, integrating creative, practical, and analytical aspects of intelligence as well as wisdom, provides the potential for solutions to serious world problems. Successful intelligence viewed broadly draws on creativity, conventional (analytical) intelligence, common sense, and wisdom because it often requires people to come up with novel solutions, to analyze whether the solutions are indeed good ones, to implement the solutions and persuade other people of their value and most of all, to ensure that the solutions help to achieve a common good. The world today needs more creativity and wisdom and less foolishness. Our schools need to teach for wisdom [65] and develop broadly adaptive, creative, street-smart, wise and ethical leaders, not just traditionally smart and politically savvy ones [66]. Many of our societies in the world today have created for their members a race but unfortunately, a race to Samarra. Successful intelligence, broadly defined to include wisdom, is a key to finding a different and better race for the societies of the world to run.

Conflicts of Interest: The author declares no conflict of interest.

References

1. Sternberg, R.J. What does it mean to be smart? *Educ. Leadersh.* **1997**, *54*, 20–24.
2. Sternberg, R.J. Implications of a triangular theory of creativity for understanding creative giftedness. *Roeper Rev..* in press.
3. Sternberg, R.J. (Ed.) *Cambridge Handbook of Intelligence*; Cambridge University Press: New York, NY, USA, in press.
4. Sternberg, R.J.; Grigorenko, E.L. (Eds.) *The General Factor of Intelligence: How General Is It?* Lawrence Erlbaum Associates: Mahwah, NJ, USA, 2002.
5. Sternberg, R.J. *Wisdom, Intelligence, and Creativity Synthesized*; Cambridge University Press: New York, NY, USA, 2003.
6. Sternberg, R.J. (Ed.) *Human Abilities: An Information—Processing Approach*; Freeman: San Francisco, CA, USA, 1985.
7. Sternberg, R.J. Human intelligence: The model is the message. *Science* **1985**, *230*, 1111–1118. [CrossRef] [PubMed]
8. Sternberg, R.J. Inside intelligence. *Am. Sci.* **1986**, *74*, 137–143.
9. Sternberg, R.J.; Detterman, D.K. (Eds.) *What Is Intelligence?* Ablex: Norwood, NJ, USA, 1986.
10. Sternberg, R.J. *Advances in the Psychology of Human Intelligence*; Lawrence Erlbaum Associates: Hillsdale, NJ, USA, 1988; Volume 4.
11. Sternberg, R.J. *Beyond IQ: A Triarchic Theory of Human Intelligence*; Cambridge University Press: New York, NY, USA, 1985.
12. Sternberg, R.J. *The Triarchic Mind: A New Theory of Intelligence*; Viking: New York, NY, USA, 1988.
13. Sternberg, R.J.; Grigorenko, E.L.; Singler, J.L. (Eds.) *Creativity: The Psychology of Creative Potential and Realization*; American Psychological Association: Washington, DC, USA, 2004.
14. Niu, W.; Sternberg, R.J. Societal and school influences on student creativity: The case of China. *Psychol. Sch.* **2003**, *40*, 103–114. [CrossRef]
15. Davidson, J.E.; Sternberg, R.J. (Eds.) *The Psychology of Problem Solving*; Cambridge University Press: New York, NY, USA, 2003.
16. Gardner, H. *Frames of Mind: The Theory of Multiple Intelligences*; Basic: New York, NY, USA, 2011.
17. Herrnstein, R.; Murray, C. *The Bell Curve*; Basic: New York, NY, USA, 1994.
18. Flynn, J.R. Massive IQ gains in 14 nations: What IQ tests really measure. *Psychol. Bull.* **1978**, *101*, 171–191. [CrossRef]
19. Flynn, J.R. *Does Your Family Make You Smarter? Nature, Nurture, and Human Autonomy*; Cambridge University Press: New York, NY, USA, 2016.
20. Spear-Swerling, L.; Sternberg, R.J. The road not taken: An integrative theoretical model of reading disability. *J. Learn. Disabil.* **1994**, *27*, 91–103. [CrossRef] [PubMed]
21. Frey, M.C.; Detterman, D.K. Scholastic assessment or g? The relationship between the Scholastic Assessment Test and general cognitive ability. *Psychol. Sci.* **2004**, *15*, 373–378. [CrossRef] [PubMed]
22. Koenig, K.A.; Frey, M.C.; Detterman, D.K. ACT and general cognitive ability. *Intelligence* **2008**, *36*, 153–160. [CrossRef]
23. Sackett, P.R.; Shewach, O.R.; Dahlke, J.A. The predictive value of general intelligence. In *Human Intelligence: An Introduction*; Sternberg, R.J., Ed.; Cambridge University Press: New York, NY, USA, in press.
24. Sternberg, R.J. What should intelligence tests test? Implications of a triarchic theory of intelligence for intelligence testing. *Educ. Res.* **1984**, *13*, 5–15. [CrossRef]
25. Sternberg, R.J. Teaching critical thinking, Part 1: Are we making critical mistakes? *Phi Delta Kappan* **1985**, *67*, 194–198.
26. Sternberg, R.J. Managerial intelligence: Why IQ isn't enough. *J. Manag.* **1997**, *23*, 475–493. [CrossRef]

27. Sternberg, R.J.; Forsythe, G.B.; Hedlund, J.; Horvath, J.; Snook, S.; Williams, W.M.; Wagner, R.K.; Grigorenko, E.L. *Practical Intelligence in Everyday Life*; Cambridge University Press: New York, NY, USA, 2000.
28. Sternberg, R.J.; Hedlund, J. Practical intelligence, g, and work psychology. *Hum. Perform.* **1985**, *15*, 143–160. [CrossRef]
29. Sternberg, R.J. (Ed.) The theory of successful intelligence. In *Cambridge Handbook of Intelligence*, 2nd ed.; Cambridge University Press: New York, NY, USA, in press.
30. Sternberg, R.J. *College Admissions for the 21st Century*; Harvard University Press: Cambridge, MA, USA, 2010.
31. Sternberg, R.J. *What Universities Can Be*; Cornell University Press: Ithaca, NY, USA, 2016.
32. Sternberg, R.J. The Rainbow Project Collaborators; University of Michigan Business School Project Collaborators. Theory based university admissions testing for a new millennium. *Educ. Psychol.* **2004**, *39*, 185–198. [CrossRef]
33. Sternberg, R.J. ACCEL: A new model for identifying the gifted. *Roeper Rev.* **2017**, *39*, 152–169. [CrossRef]
34. Sternberg, R.J. Developing the next generation of responsible professionals: Wisdom and ethics trump knowledge and IQ. *Psychol. Teach. Rev.* **2017**, *23*, 51–59.
35. Ambrose, D. *Expanding Visions of Creative Intelligence: An Interdisciplinary Exploration*; Hampton Press: Cresskill, NJ, USA, 2009.
36. Ambrose, D. The optimal moral development of the gifted: Interdisciplinary insights about ethical identity formation. In *Handbook for Counselors Serving Students with Gifts and Talents*; Cross, T.L., Cross, J.R., Eds.; Prufrock Press: Waco, TX, USA, 2012; pp. 351–367.
37. Ambrose, D. Twenty-first century contextual influences on the life trajectories of creative young people. In *Creative Intelligence in the 21st Century: Grappling with Enormous Problems and Huge Opportunities*; Ambrose, D., Sternberg, R.J., Eds.; Springer: Rotterdam, The Netherlands, 2016; pp. 21–48.
38. Ambrose, D. Giftedness and wisdom. In *Cambridge Handbook of Wisdom*; Sternberg, R.J., Glueck, J., Eds.; Cambridge University Press: New York, NY, USA, 2005.
39. Schank, R.; Childers, P. *The Creative Attitude: Learning to Ask and Answer the Right Questions*; Macmillan: New York, NY, USA, 1988.
40. Sternberg, R.J. Teaching psychology students about creativity as a decision. *Psychol. Teach. Rev.* **2000**, *9*, 111–118.
41. Csikszentmihalyi, M. Implications of a systems perspective for the study of creativity. In *Handbook of Creativity*; Sternberg, R.J., Ed.; Cambridge University Press: Cambridge, UK, 1999; pp. 313–335.
42. Gardner, H. *Creating Minds*; Basic Books: New York, NY, USA, 2011.
43. Kaufman, J.C. *Creativity 101*, 2nd ed.; Springer: New York, NY, USA, 2016.
44. Kaufman, J.C.; Baer, J. The Amusement Park Theoretical (APT) Model of creativity. *Korean J. Think. Probl. Solving* **2004**, *14*, 15–25.
45. Kaufman, J.C.; Beghetto, R.A. Beyond big and little: The Four C Model of Creativity. *Rev. Gen. Psychol.* **2009**, *13*, 1–12. [CrossRef]
46. Reis, S.; Renzulli, J.S. *The Schoolwide Enrichment Model*, 3rd ed.; Prufrock Press: Waco, TX, USA, 2014.
47. Renzulli, J.S. Reexamining the role of gifted education and talent development for the 21st century: A four-part theoretical approach. *Gifted Child Q.* **2012**, *56*, 150–159. [CrossRef]
48. Sternberg, R.J.; Lubart, T.I. *Defying the Crowd: Cultivating Creativity in a Culture of Conformity*; Free Press: New York, NY, USA, 1995.
49. Sternberg, R.J. Creativity or creativities? *Int. J. Comput. Stud.* **2005**, *63*, 370–382. [CrossRef]
50. Sternberg, R.J. Creative giftedness is not just what creativity tests test. *Roeper Rev.* in press.
51. Sternberg, R.J.; Davidson, J.E. The mind of the puzzler. *Psychol. Today* **1982**, *16*, 37–44.
52. Sternberg, R.J.; Davidson, J.E. Insight in the gifted. *Educ. Psychol.* **1983**, *18*, 51–57. [CrossRef]
53. Sternberg, R.J.; Kaufman, J.C. (Eds.) *The Nature of Human Creativity*; Cambridge University Press: New York, NY, USA, 2018.
54. Cropley, D.H.; Cropley, A.J.; Kaufman, J.C.; Runco, M.A. (Eds.) *The Dark Side of Creativity*; Cambridge University Press: New York, NY, USA, 2010.
55. Sternberg, R.J. The dark side of creativity and how to combat it. In *The Dark Side of Creativity*; Cropley, D.H., Cropley, A.J., Kaufman, J.C., Runco, M.A., Eds.; Cambridge University Press: New York, NY, USA, 2010.
56. Polanyi, M.; Sen, A. *The Tacit Dimension*; University of Chicago Press: Chicago, IL, USA, 2009.

57. Sternberg, R.J.; Smith, C. Social intelligence and decoding skills in nonverbal communication. *Soc. Cogn.* **1985**, *2*, 168–192. [CrossRef]

58. Horvath, J.A.; Forsythe, G.B.; Bullis, R.C.; Sweeney, P.J.; Williams, W.M.; McNally, J.A.; Wattendorf, J.A.; Sternberg, R.J. Experience, knowledge, and military leadership. In *Tacit Knowledge in Professional Practice*; Sternberg, R.J., Horvath, J.A., Eds.; Lawrence Erlbaum Associates: Mahwah, NJ, USA, 1999; pp. 39–71.

59. Halberstram, D. *The Best and The Brightest*; Ballantine: New York, NY, USA, 1993.

60. Sternberg, R.J. Wisdom and education. *Perspect. Educ.* **2011**, *19*, 1–16. [CrossRef]

61. Sternberg, R.J. What is wisdom and how can we develop it? *Ann. Am. Acad. Political Soc. Sci.* **2004**, *591*, 164–174. [CrossRef]

62. Sternberg, R.J.; Glueck, J. (Eds.) *Cambridge Handbook of Wisdom*; Cambridge University Press: New York, NY, USA, in press.

63. Sternberg, R.J. Smart people are not stupid, but they sure can be foolish: The imbalance theory of foolishness. In *Why Smart People Can Be So Stupid*; Sternberg, R.J., Ed.; Yale University Press: New Haven, CT, USA, 2002; pp. 232–242.

64. Sternberg, R.J. Foolishness. In *Handbook of Wisdom: Psychological Perspectives*; Sternberg, R.J., Jordan, J., Eds.; Cambridge University Press: New York, NY, USA, 2005; pp. 331–352.

65. Sternberg, R.J.; Reznitskaya, A.; Jarvin, L. Teaching for wisdom: What matters is not just what students know, but how they use it. *Lond. Rev. Educ.* **2007**, *5*, 143–158. [CrossRef]

66. Sternberg, R.J. The development of adaptive competence. *Dev. Rev.* **2014**, *34*, 208–224. [CrossRef]

MDPI

St. Alban-Anlage 66

4052 Basel

Switzerland

Tel. +41 61 683 77 34

Fax +41 61 302 89 18

www.mdpi.com

Journal of Intelligence Editorial Office

E-mail: jintelligence@mdpi.com

www.mdpi.com/journal/jintelligence

www.ingramcontent.com/pod-product-compliance
Lightning Source LLC
Chambersburg PA
CBHW051316020426
42333CB00028B/3364